Jimmy and Rosalynn Carter: A Canadian Tribute

Arthur Milnes, Editor
Inaugural Fellow in Political History
Queen's University Archives

Volume VI in the Queen's University Archives
Library of Political Leadership
School of Policy Studies, Queen's University
McGill-Queen's University Press
Montreal & Kingston · London · Ithaca

EDITOR'S DEDICATION: To Tom Axworthy and Senator Hugh Segal, public servants and mentors. And in memory of the late Constance Milnes of Scarborough, a fan of Jimmy Carter, who told her son many times that America's 39th president was a "good and decent man."

© 2011 School of Policy Studies, Queen's University at Kingston, Canada

SCHOOL OF
Policy Studies

Publications Unit
Robert Sutherland Hall
138 Union Street
Kingston, ON, Canada
K7L 3N6
www.queensu.ca/sps/

All rights reserved. The use of any part of this publication for reproduction, transmission in any form, or by any means (electronic, mechanical, photocopying, recording or otherwise), or storage in a retrieval system without the prior written consent of the publisher—or, in case of photocopying or other reprographic copying, a license from the Canadian Copyright Licensing Agency—is an infringement of the copyright law. Enquiries concerning reproduction should be sent to the School of Policy Studies at the address above.

Library and Archives Canada Cataloguing in Publication

Jimmy and Rosalynn Carter : a Canadian tribute / foreword by
Jimmy Carter ; prologue by Joe Clark ; edited by Arthur Milnes.

(Library of political leadership occasional series ; VI)
Published for the School of Policy Studies, Queen's University.
Includes bibliographical references.
ISBN 978-1-55339-301-6 (bound).--ISBN 978-1-55339-300-9 (pbk.)

1. Carter, Jimmy, 1924-. 2. United States--Politics and government--1977-1981. 3. Presidents--United States--Messages. 4. Canada--Foreign relations--United States. 5. United States--Foreign relations--Canada. 6. Presidents--United States--Biography. 7. Carter, Rosalynn. I. Milnes, Arthur, 1966- II. Queen's University (Kingston, Ont.). School of Policy Studies III. Series: Library of political leadership series ; v6

E873.J54 2011   973.926092   C2011-900224-8

Table of Contents

Acknowledgements	v
Foreword By President Jimmy Carter	xi
Preface: A Pretty Good Canadian By the Right Honourable Joe Clark	xv
Introduction By Arthur Milnes	xix

Part I · White House Years, 1977 to 1981

Memorandum · 15-Minute Interview at 5:15 p.m.	1
Memorandum · Talking Points for President's Interview on Canada AM	2
Text of President Carter's Interview with Bruce Phillips of CTV's *Canada AM*	3
Welcoming Ceremony for Prime Minister Pierre Trudeau	5

Visit of Prime Minister Trudeau
    Toasts of the President and the Prime Minister at a Dinner
    Honouring the Prime Minister
	8

Prime Minister Pierre Trudeau Address to the US Congress	12

United States–Canada Agreement on a Natural Gas Pipeline
    Remarks of the President and Prime Minister Trudeau
    Announcing the Agreement
	18

Meeting with Prime Minister Pierre Elliott Trudeau of Canada Remarks on the Departure of the Prime Minister	21
Meeting with Prime Minister Trudeau of Canada Joint Communiqué	25
President Jimmy Carter on the Return of Six Americans From Iran Telephone Discussion with Prime Minister Joe Clark of Canada	27
Prime Minister Joe Clark to Reporters While on the Campaign Trail	29
Declassified US Intelligence Report	29

Our Nation's Past and Future: Address Accepting the Presidential
    Nomination at the Democratic National Convention
    in New York City
	35

Inaugural Address	43
United Nations Address Before the General Assembly (17 March 1977)	46
University of Notre Dame Address at Commencement Exercises at the University	52
United Nations Address Before the General Assembly (4 October 1977)	59
United States Naval Academy Address at the Commencement Exercises	66

Remarks of the President, President Anwar al-Sadat of Egypt, and Prime Minister Menachem Begin of Israel	73
Camp David Meeting on the Middle East Address Before a Joint Session of the Congress	77
Cairo, Egypt · Address Before the People's Assembly	83
Jerusalem, Israel · Address Before the Knesset	87
Address Delivered Before a Joint Session of the Congress on the Vienna Summit Meeting	93
Address to the Nation on Energy and National Goals: "The Malaise Speech"	100
Farewell Address to the Nation	110

Part II · The Man From Plains — 115

Plains High School	117
Ex-president still a Plains man; Jimmy Carter is right at home in the small Georgia town where he was raised	121
Jimmy Carter, The Teacher · By Steve Paikin	124
Special Evening with the Carters in Plains, Ga.	125
President Carter and Habitat for Humanity · By Murray Chown	129
Rosalynn Carter: A Tribute · By Thomas S. Harrison	131
Jimmy Carter's Greatest Speech · By David Lockhart	133
Trudeau, Clark remembered fondly by Carter in *White House Diary:* review	135
Walter Mondale remembers	138
An idealist in an age of hollow men Jimmy Carter's a giant of our time	142
Afghan mission worth cost to Canada	143
When Jimmy Carter faced radioactivity head-on	145
US President Carter was "visionary leader," despite 1979 "Malaise speech"	148

Part III · After the White House

Queen Charlotte Steelheads	151
The Promise and Peril of Democracy	161
Remarks by Jimmy Carter at the conference Human Rights Defenders on the Frontlines of Freedom	167
Camp David Accords · Jimmy Carter Reflects 25 Years Later	171
2002 Nobel Peace Prize Lecture	178
The United States and Cuba: A Vision for the 21st Century	183
President Carter's Cuba Trip Report	187
Remarks at Korea University A Nuclear North Korea and Peace in the Korean Peninsula?	194

Acknowledgements

I owe special thanks to President Carter and Rosalynn Carter who both took a great interest in this project. Besides the Foreword that President Carter so generously wrote, he and Mrs. Carter have been a constant source of encouragement and enthusiasm with notes and emails sent my way over the past year as this book came together. Their loyal and friendly assistants—Peggy Carson in Plains and Lauren Gilstrap at the Carter Center in Atlanta—went above and beyond the call of duty in providing assistance and encouragement. All the hard-working volunteers and staff at the Plains Better Hometown Committee also deserve recognition, particularly my friends Mill Simmons and Jan Williams.

Here in Ontario, Senator Hugh Segal and Mrs. Donna Segal—whose daughter Jacqueline is making all Kingston proud through her work at the Carter Center—have provided support for this project and all my work in recent years. I will never be able to fully repay them. Former Ontario Premier Bob Rae, now the Official Opposition's foreign affairs critic in the House of Commons, gave to this project the one thing people in public life have little of: his time. Last summer, Mr. Rae came to Kingston at my invitation and personally led a Sir John A. Macdonald-themed walking tour of Kingston on a beautiful July evening. About forty people came out and the funds generated through tickets sales allowed me to order photographs for this book and more. Canada's 16th prime minister, The Right Honourable Joe Clark, contributed the prologue to this volume and I am very grateful to him for doing so. As always, Senior Strategic Advisor, Colin Robertson, McKenna, Long and Aldridge LLP who is also Vice President and Fellow, Canadian Defence and Foreign Affairs Institute, provided advice and counsel I found truly beneficial.

At CTV in Scarborough, Anton Koschany, a close friend and executive producer of *W-5*, ensured we had permission to reprint the interview President Carter did with Bruce Phillips of *CTV News* in 1977. In Kitchener-Waterloo, JoAnn Lewis, partner family coordinator/executive assistant, Habitat for Humanity Waterloo Region, arranged for me to learn about the Carters' work there in 1993 as did her colleague, Professor Mark E. Havitz, chair of the Department of Recreation and Leisure Studies at the University of Waterloo.

At Queen's University Archives, University Archivist Paul Banfield has been a constant source of support and friendship. His word is his bond and he stands up for his friends and colleagues. I owe him a great deal. His staff, particularly Susan Office, also helped in countless ways. At the Canadian Press, I salute the assistance of Ottawa Bureau Chief Rob Russo and Andrea Gordon in Toronto in donating and arranging photographs for this book. At the Toronto Star, Martin Reg Cohn and my long-time friend and journalism mentor Fred Edwards (along with his wife, Donna Maloney, one of the finest editors I have ever been privileged to work with) assisted in countless ways. From the Carter Center and Jimmy Carter Library in Atlanta, I owe special thanks to Deanna Congileo, Albert Nason, Polly Nodine, David Stanhope and James Yancey for their friendly and timely assistance. Actor, and proud Canadian, Dan Aykroyd took time out of his busy schedule to share with me memories from his work on *Saturday Night Live* where he played the role of President Carter in sketches that have stood the test of time.

At Queen's, professors Kathy Brock and Jonathan Rose have provided continuous encouragement for all my endeavours. I owe a special thanks to Professor John Meisel, one of the most distinguished professors of politics to ever grace Queen's over its long history. I cannot thank him enough for both his advice and his support of myself and this volume. At the School of Policy Studies, publications coordinator Mark Howes and Valerie Jarus performed their usual magic. Copy editor and designer Anne Holley-Hime deserves special recognition. Donna Bainchet of Kingston Business Services does as well. I would like to thank the Director of the School of Policy Studies, Dr. Peter Harrison, for his support and enthusiasm, as well as that demonstrated by his predecessor, Dr. Arthur Sweetman, for the Library of Political Leadership series.

Frederick T. Courtright, president of the Permissions Company, the rights agency for the University of Arkansas Press, was a pleasure to deal with and quickly granted permission for us to republish President Carter's 1988 essay Queen Charlotte Steelheads from *An Outdoor Journal* at no charge.

Two groups merit recognition. In September of 2008 my wife and I travelled to Plains in the company of our close friends Beth and Murray Chown and Peter and Frances O'Malley to attend a luncheon with the Carters. In 2010, I again visited Plains, this time in the company of Tom Harrison, my old friend from Scarborough, and two other special friends, David Lockhart and Steve Paikin. On this trip we were privileged to have dinner with the Carters at the Plains Historic Inn. While any mistakes in this volume are mine, readers should know that this book is as much a result of their labours and enthusiasm as it is mine.

When I finished my work as research assistant to the Right Honourable Brian Mulroney on his *Memoirs*, Tom Axworthy was heading the Centre for the Study of Democracy at Queen's University. He took me under his wing at the CSD. Patiently, he demonstrated to me how to apply the privileged access to our nation's history that Mr. Mulroney had granted me in this new—for me—academic context. To discuss Canadian history and politics with Tom Axworthy is something I consider one of the great privileges of my career. In both respect and friendship, I wish to dedicate this volume to Tom, an inspirational mentor and friend.

Senator Hugh Segal also took me under his wing in 2008. Like Tom, he had served as the chief assistant to a prime minister of Canada. And again, like his friend, Senator Segal chose continued public service to Canada afterwards. The senator has provided financial support for my work, given constant advice, been a sounding-board and so much more—all while serving as one of the most activist senators in modern Canadian history. Senator Hugh Segal enriches community life here in Kingston and through his continued service in the Red Chamber, is helping make our nation a better place. In respect and friendship, I would also like to dedicate my work on this volume to him. His often lonely quest over many years now to battle poverty in Canada and his advocacy of a guaranteed annual income is one that I suspect the Carters would admire as much as I do.

Finally, I would be remiss if I did not mention my late mother, Connie Milnes, of Scarborough. While she has been gone for fifteen years, I remember as if yesterday the many times she told me of her admiration for Jimmy and Rosalynn Carter. A proud member of the United Church of Canada and active at Church of the Master in Scarborough, she often lamented my lack of attendance at church as I grew older. She would smile at the thought that it was Jimmy Carter who attracted me to my first church services in years during my inaugural visit to Plains. I definitely felt her presence that Sunday in rural Georgia as the Baptist pastor delivered his rousing sermon explaining the history of the hymn *Amazing Grace*. It was my mother's favourite hymn and I can still hear her singing it quietly to herself to this day. I also dedicate this volume to her memory. Jimmy Carter was her kind of president. She would have been very proud of this book, but not as proud as I am to be her son.

Arthur Milnes
Kingston and Scarborough
October 2010

The generous support of this volume by the following people is gratefully acknowledged:

The Right Honourable Joe Clark, 16th Prime Minister of Canada
The Right Honourable John Napier Turner, 17th Prime Minister of Canada
The Right Honourable Brian Mulroney, 18th Prime Minister of Canada
The Right Honourable Paul Martin, 20th Prime Minister of Canada

Bruce and Andrea Alexander
BMO Bank of Montreal, Kingston
Dr. Deborah Berry and Robert P. Tchegus
Nigel and Mary Bogle
Hon. James Bradley
Consul General Stephen Brereton
James Brown
Dr. John Chenier and Nancy Miller Chenier
Beth and Murray Chown
Catherine Christie and Philip Ambury
Hector Clouthier
Lauren Conway
Gavin Cosgrove
Jim Creskey
Michael Davies and the Davies Charitable Foundation
Julie Daxon
Stephen Dyck and Sandra Leffler
Susan and Jim Garrard
Bittu George
Margaret Gibson
Anita Granger and Rick Beazley
Ambassador Gordon and Patti Giffin
David and Ying Gilbert
Richard Gwyn
Leonard Harden
Thomas and Andrea Harrison
Joel and Patricia Heard
The Hon. Paul Hellyer
Her Worship Cathy Hickling
Anne Holley-Hime and Claude Scilley
Devon A. Jones

Lesley and Brad Kendall
Dr. Richard and Wendy Johnston
David and Diane Lockhart
Lawrence Martin
Greg McArthur and Hayley Mick
Paula and Daryl McClellan
J. Bruce McNaughton
Dill and Patrick McQuillan
Jay MacWilliam and Catherine Bogle
Professor John Meisel
Arthur Milnes and Alison Bogle
Margaret Milnes and Matthew Stuart
Sean Moore and Anne Caryle
Peter and Frances O'Malley
Orillia Museum of Art and History
Steve Paikin and Francesca Grosso
Marion Penrose
The Honourable David Peterson
The Honourable Bob Rae
Peter Radley
John Rainford
Jeffery and Sandra Richardson
Colin Robertson
Professor Jonathan Rose and Leslie E. Rose
A. Britton Smith
Unella Thomson
The Honourable Senator Hugh Segal and Donna Segal
Dr. Hans and Marion Westenberg
Willem Westenberg and Anne Duprat
Professor Peter Woolstencroft

Foreword

By President Jimmy Carter

Speaking at Queen's University in Kingston, Ontario, Canada in August of 1938, President Franklin Delano Roosevelt observed of Canada and the United States: "We as good neighbours are true friends, because we maintain our own rights with frankness, because we refuse to accept the twists of secret diplomacy, because we settle our disputes by consultation, and because we discuss our common problems in the spirit of the common good."

Almost 75 years after President Roosevelt delivered these words in his famous address at this Canadian university, I am pleased to contribute this foreword to this volume that pays tribute to my strong link with Canada that I have enjoyed before, during and after my service in the White House.

Growing up at our family farm in Archery, located a few miles outside Plains, Georgia, my first memories of Canada came from broadcasts on our radio. During the Great Depression, I heard about the birth of the Dionne Quintuplets in northern Ontario. To this day Rosalynn remembers the stories told in her family after a relative visited Niagara Falls while on their honeymoon. She decided that someday she and I would ourselves see the Horseshoe Falls. Years later we were able to travel there on our 50th wedding anniversary and met, quite by accident, our old friend Prime Minister Pierre Trudeau. He had chosen that very day to take his young daughter to see the falls, and we shared some time with this special man and his child.

It wasn't until the early 1950s, when I was serving as a young US Navy officer under Admiral Hyman Rickover that I first came to Canada. I was based in upstate New York, assisting our navy develop one of its first nuclear submarines, the *Seawolf*, at the very dawn of the nuclear age. When a nuclear accident occurred at a Canadian reactor facility near Chalk River, Ontario, I was sent there to lead the American team helping with the clean-up. As you'll see from the article written by Arthur after an interview with me, my experiences in Chalk River had a great impact on my thinking surrounding nuclear issues.

When I entered the White House in January 1977, Prime Minister Trudeau was the ranking leader in the G7. Rosalynn, I, and Vice President Walter Mondale, he from the border state of Minnesota, got along well with the prime minister immediately. The State Dinner we hosted for the Trudeaus in February 1977 still is one of our finest memories of our life at 1600 Pennsylvania Avenue.

"Pierre, your experience and naturally frank discussion were very helpful to me as a new president," I wrote to my new friend in Ottawa at the conclusion of his first visit with us. "I feel that our countries are being drawn even closer together. Margaret, you brought a delightful breath of fresh air and charm to Washington. Thank you. Your friend, Jimmy."

On matters of arms control, the environment, and international development, among others, Pierre and I shared similar views and worked very well together. Later, when Canada's government changed in 1979, it was my pleasure to begin working with Canada's 16th Prime Minister, Joe Clark. Sworn in at age 39, becoming the youngest prime minister in Canadian history, Joe was also a staunch ally and friend. This became clear to all in the late fall of 1979 and early winter of 1980 after Iranian militants occupied and kidnapped American hostages from our embassy in Tehran.

Six Americans were able to escape the clutches of the militants and found safe haven with Canada's ambassador to Iran, Ken Taylor, and his staff. This group of Canadians put their own lives in danger to give shelter to my countrymen. Joe and I worked with our officials in secrecy to determine how best to smuggle these Americans, along with their Canadian hosts, to safety.

Like all Americans, Rosalynn and I rejoiced when this small group of hostages was successfully freed. It was my happy task as president to call Prime Minister Clark and thank him for all Canada had done to accomplish this. I don't believe there has ever been a greater moment in the long history of Canadian-American relations. When the members of Team Canada marched into the opening ceremonies of the 1980 Winter Olympic Games at Lake Placid, New York, the American audience spontaneously got to their feet in sustained applause and gave tribute to Canada.

Upon leaving the White House in 1981, Rosalynn and I founded the Carter Center in Atlanta. I'm proud to say that prime ministers Clark and Trudeau played leading roles over the years in our activities. When Prime Minister Trudeau died in 2000, President Bill Clinton asked me to head the American delegation to the former prime minister's funeral in Montreal. While a sad occasion for the Trudeau family and me personally, my feelings were tempered by the honour I felt at being made an honourary pallbearer, along with President Fidel Castro of Cuba, Canadian poet Leonard Cohen, and others. It was at the funeral that Castro and I discussed plans for me to become the first American president to visit Cuba since that nation's revolution.

Rosalynn and I first met Arthur Milnes, a serious student of Canadian-

American relations, in 2005 when he visited Plains. Since then, I have been interviewed by him for various articles about my presidency on several occasions, and I hope you enjoy the resulting articles in this volume. He and his wife, Alison Bogle, have also become strong supporters of the Plains Better Hometown Program and attended our community auctions and other activities, often bringing great groups with them.

I recommend *Jimmy and Rosalynn Carter: A Canadian Tribute* to readers in Canada and the United States and to present and future students of Canadian-American relations. Congratulations to Arthur and all those who have worked so hard at Queen's University to bring this project to fruition in conjunction with the many people who graciously donated funds to the university to defray publication costs of this not-for-profit volume.

As in so many parts of his distinguished career as president, Franklin Roosevelt got it right during his famous speech at Queen's University in 1938. Canadians and Americans are more than good neighbours, we are true friends, and this book is testament to this fact.

Preface: A Pretty Good Canadian

By the Right Honourable Joe Clark
16th Prime Minister of Canada

My first encounter with President Jimmy Carter was indirect, but prophetic. I was Leader of Her Majesty's Loyal Opposition in the Canadian Parliament, and was in Chicago in 1976, in the aftermath of Watergate, to meet Americans interested in Canada, and address the Chicago Council on Foreign Relations. One of the hosts of my visit was a leading figure in the Democratic Party of Illinois, who told me he would have to miss my speech because of a prior commitment to meet "my candidate for the Democratic nomination for the Presidency, Governor Carter."

The Canadian: "I can certainly understand that priority, and I'm interested in Governor Carter. Could you tell me about him?"

The Democrat: "I've never met him."

The Canadian: "Why are you, a prominent Democrat, supporting a candidate you've never met?"

The Democrat: "Governor Carter is not implicated."

That was because Jimmy Carter had not been part of the Washington of Watergate—the scandals and distrusts of that period in American politics did not splash over to the Governor of Georgia. Indeed, his style and temperament and reputation seemed to represent a clear departure from—almost a repudiation of—the politics of that era. Jimmy Carter was not part of that Washington milieu. He was an "outsider" in a system of "insiders." Many commentators believe that caused, or complicated, some of his challenges as president, and I'll leave that argument to Americans, and to historians.

What is more striking is that virtually every observer agrees that those qualities as an outsider contributed significantly to his later, stellar, success as the most significant former president in American history. His roots are unquestionably deep in his country—both in the "ideal" of America as a society of freedom and equality and opportunity, but embedded also in the practical attributes of American accomplishment—ambition, ability, faith, luck—and "can do" optimism, the profound belief that obstacles can be overcome.

But he strikes a higher chord than mere ambition and accomplishment—a chord of purpose, empathy and obligation. Typically, in his Habitat for Humanity initiatives, Jimmy Carter doesn't just arrange for houses to be built, he helps actually build them. So the "outsider" status which may have hindered him in dealing with the power bases in his own superpower, have made him sympathetic to, and influential among, people, countries and groups who were themselves suspicious of, or were considered marginal by, those very power bases. Jimmy Carter's interest in human rights and development was not simply an aspect of his presidency—it was at the core of his personality, and was seen to be genuine enough to be trustworthy.

Now, what does that have to do with Canada, and the relations between his presidency and our country? I see two impacts.

One is systemic—however important our mutual trade, however broad and deep our human relations, however compelling our North American geography, Canada is not a major preoccupation of the "power-bases" of the United States of America. That is true of American business, American workers, America's culture industries and, in the case in question, certainly America's government and politics. In terms of actual "face time"—actual detailed attention by the leaders at the heart of any US administration, we rank well below California, or New York, or Texas—or Cuba, or Russia, or Mexico or China. That may not be a ranking by importance, but it is a ranking by attention.

Of course, in a real crisis, virtually any Canadian government can get the quick attention of Washington—but quick is different from sympathetic. And usually, on issues which are genuinely serious to Canada, our complex and multiple connections can make our voices heard—again, heard is different from heeded. We might be rich, and reasonable, and right next door, but we are rarely top-of-mind. That's why Canadian governments have to work so hard at ensuring our vital interests are understood in Washington. In Jimmy Carter, we had two advantages.

One was that he had actually worked here, with Canadians as partners, during a crucial and early period of his development and in an area of vital interest to him when he was later president. In the late fall of 1953, when he was only 29 years old, Jimmy Carter was stationed with the US Navy in upper New York State. When Canada's reactor at Chalk River, Ontario went into crisis in December of that year, we sought assistance from our American neighbours. Lt. Jimmy Carter led a team that worked hand-in-hand with Canadians in cleaning up that damaged reactor. It was the very dawn of the nuclear age. President Carter's later biographer, and colleague, Dr. Peter Bourne, has written about the profound impact these weeks in Canada had on Jimmy Carter.

Beyond that, he was interested in Canadian health care. Committed to providing a more comprehensive system of health care for his country, Jimmy Carter had examined our system and found much to admire in it. As much as any American president understands Canada, President Carter did. That was reflected in his working relationship with both Pierre Trudeau and myself and, of course, was reflected in some of the testing last days of his presidency.

Jimmy Carter was president in one of those unusual periods when the USA genuinely needed help, in extricating six American hostages from Iran, and Canada provided that help, quickly, effectively, in conditions of high risk, and without bargaining or posturing. The drama of how that happened—the courage and ingenuity of Ken and Pat Taylor and their colleagues in Tehran and Ottawa, the leadership of Flora MacDonald, the decisiveness of our cabinet, the tensions in Parliament—are a separate story, but one result was that Canada was firmly and positively fixed in the mind of the American administration and public.

Canada's other advantage with Jimmy Carter was in the way he saw the world, which was broadly similar to the international goals which most Canadians supported, for at least sixty years after the end of the Second World War. That consonance of view was true generally during his presidency, but became even clearer in his conduct and priorities as a ground-breaking former president. His Carter Center could have been merely another important library, cataloguing and reflecting upon a presidency in turbulent times. He, and Rosalynn Carter, instead, transformed it into an unprecedented international "bully pulpit," able to both enunciate high principles, and then pursue them concretely. They are a beacon of the international values which most Canadians like to think we represent. In terms of what Jimmy Carter says and does in the world, he's a pretty good Canadian.

Introduction

By Arthur Milnes

On 22 February, 1977, Prime Minister Pierre Trudeau became the first Canadian prime minister to address the US Congress. His speech came after a day of talks he held with the new president of the United States, Jimmy Carter of Georgia. In concluding that powerful address, Trudeau quoted Thomas Paine:

"My country is the world, and my religion is to do good."

In many ways those words of Paine's can be used to describe Jimmy Carter and his wife Rosalynn and their joint approach to their duties over the decades. President from 1977 to 1981, Carter has continued to champion the causes he brought to the American Oval Office—human rights, peace among nations, lifting the mushroom cloud's dark shadow, a cleaner environment and more—as a former president. In 1998, historian Douglas Brinkley noted the following:

> Carter spent the years after he left the White House tackling intractable problems in the world's most volatile trouble spots: observing nascent democratic elections, mediating potentially murderous conflicts, listening to those whose cries would otherwise go unheard, bringing aid to the afflicted, peace to the beleaguered, and hope to the despairing. He led efforts to eradicate medieval-sounding diseases such as guinea worm and river blindness and to make sure the world's children were immunized against polio and measles. He directed programs to make harvests more bountiful in countries facing agricultural ruin; he preached around the globe about the importance of religious tolerance; and he launched an imaginative urban rehabilitation program in Atlanta ... Along with his steadfast wife, Rosalynn, Carter has become a true citizen of the world, working to build societies in which the human spirit can prevail and where freedom and democracy can flourish."[1]

Brinkley's portrait of Carter is important because he makes the strong point that little in the values the Carters first brought to the White House more than thirty years ago have changed since they left high office.

> It was an insult to call Jimmy Carter a great "ex-president"—that if he had not promoted human rights from the White House, he would not have been embraced everywhere he went in South America in 1983. If he had not denounced apartheid in South Africa, pushed for the creation of Zimbabwe, or visited Nigeria and Liberia while president, he would not have been invited to set up Carter Center programs throughout Africa. If he had not overseen the Camp David accords that made peace possible between Israel and Egypt, he would not later have won the attention of the

---

[1] Douglas Brinkley, *The Unfinished Presidency*. (New York). Penguin Books. 1998. p. xv.

PLO's Yasir Arafat, Syria's Hafez-al-Assad, or Jordan's King Hussein. If he had not invited Nicaraguan president Daniel Ortega and his Sandinista cabinet to the White House in September 1979 and told them: "If you don't hold me responsible for everything that occurred under my predecessors, I will not hold you responsible for everything that occurred under your predecessors," his voice would have gone unheard during the 1990 Nicaraguan election. ... Some observers have suggested that Carter used the White House as a stepping-stone to the status of elder statesman. It is more accurate to say that instead of abandoning his agenda when he lost badly to Ronald Reagan in 1980, he choose to continue working towards programs and policies he believed in, in office or out of it. That he has tried to complete his unfinished agenda with such vigor and such success is a testament to his stubborn will and tenacious refusal ever to throw in the towel. Jimmy Carter may be many things, but quitter is not one of them—so this book, like his presidency, will remain unfinished as long as he's alive."[2]

Another writer, Frye Gaillard, provides this portrait of Carter in action as a warrior for peace and justice. Here was the 39th president during an election monitoring mission in Panama in 1989. "On the day after the election, with stories of vote fraud sweeping through the country, Carter went down to the National Counting Center, where the election results were being tallied, and witnessed the massive ballot-stuffing for himself. After mounting a platform in the middle of the room, he shouted at the election workers in Spanish, 'Are you honest or are you thieves?'"[3]

These and countless other stories involving the Carters were at the centre of a conversation in September 2008 involving six Canadians. Myself and my wife Alison Bogle, Beth and Murray Chown and Peter and Frances O'Malley had just spent an afternoon in Plains, Georgia that included a luncheon with the former president and first lady and a discussion with Jimmy Carter at the boyhood farm where he had grown up in the 1930s.

Over dinner at a Warm Springs restaurant the idea for this book was born. As a group we discussed who it was in the world that brought impeccable character and honour to global hot spots in times of crisis? Who was the world's most respected citizen? Who, in our lifetime, has single-handedly done more to make our world a better place through personal and often lonely efforts? Over and over again we came back to the same name: Jimmy Carter.

Two years later, another small group of Canadians, this time Thomas S. Harrison, David Lockhart, myself and Steve Paikin found ourselves having a similar discussion. Again, we had it in Georgia, this time in Plains. This talk

---

2 Ibid. p. xix.
3 Frye Gaillard, *Prophet from Plains: Jimmy Carter and His Legacy*. (Athens). University of Georgia Press. p. 60.

came after Jimmy and Rosalynn Carter returned to their home after spending three hours with us over dinner discussing their activities and memories of Canada and the Canadians they had worked with over the years.

Again, the group decided to collectively do its best to pay tribute to the special couple. This volume is the result of those discussions.

While the Carter presidency lacked a signature item in the area of Canadian-American relations—examples like the Auto Pact signed by President Lyndon Johnson and Prime Minister Lester Pearson, the Free Trade Agreement signed by Prime Minister Brian Mulroney and President Ronald Reagan, or the Canada–United States Acid Rain Treaty signed by Mulroney and President George H. W. Bush, are not present—what is striking is the respect Canada's leaders, both at the time and afterward, held and continue to hold for the 39th president. Both prime ministers Carter worked with in office—Joe Clark and Pierre Trudeau, leaders of different Canadian political parties—became enthusiastic participants in the activities of the Carter Center in Atlanta after leaving politics. As we shall see, Trudeau's writings are very laudatory when it came to his colleague from Plains. Brian Mulroney, who became prime minister after Carter had already left the White House, calls the peace treaty achieved at Camp David under Carter between Egypt and Israel one of the "greatest achievements of American diplomacy since the Second World War."[4] Another prime minister, John Turner, cited his admiration for Carter in generously donating to this tribute volume (as did Mulroney). From Joe Clark, readers will find an essay he personally wrote for this book.

Mr. Clark's concluding sentences in his essay bear repeating here. "[Jimmy and Rosalynn Carter] are a beacon of the international values which most Canadians like to think we represent. In terms of what Jimmy Carter says and does in the world, he's a pretty good Canadian."

It is difficult to imagine another American president in our lifetime generating so much respect from across the Canadian political spectrum. Leading Canadian journalist and commentator Lawrence Martin, author of the seminal volume in the study of Canadian-American relations, *The Presidents and the Prime Ministers*, says Canadians at large also held this positive view of Carter when the president held office. This continued, he argues, even as Carter faced political difficulties at home.[5]

> Serving as Washington Correspondent for the *Globe and Mail* in this period and tracking US–Canadian developments closely, it was striking to note the degree of goodwill Canadians maintained toward Jimmy

---

4 Personal communication with the editor.
5 Lawrence Martin. *The Presidents and the Prime Ministers Washington and Ottawa Face to Face: The Myth of Bilateral Bliss 1867-1982*. (Toronto). Doubleday Canada. 1982.

Carter. They saw him as a fair-minded man with a fair-minded view of the world. They sensed he shared Canadian values, much more so than the Republican Ronald Reagan who they viewed with suspicion.[6]

This is not to suggest that the Carter presidency was a perfect time in Canada–US relations. Canadian officials and cabinet ministers were very frustrated at the inability of the Carter White House to secure support for an East Coast fisheries treaty. While a treaty was signed, it was destined to fail in the United States Senate.[7]

Carter first visited Canada in the early 1950s at the time of the nuclear accident at our nation's facility at Chalk River, Ontario. He was a young US Navy officer and working with the legendary Admiral Hyman Rickover at the very dawn of the nuclear submarine era. The future president led a team called into the area to assist with the cleanup of the overheated Canadian reactor. Along with other service personnel, Carter was actually lowered into the reactor itself and exposed to levels of radiation that would be unthinkable today.

Carter biographer Dr. Peter Bourne, a former assistant secretary general of the United Nations who worked in the Carter White House, believes the Chalk River experience had a lasting impact on the man from Georgia, influencing him when he had to confront nuclear issues as the leader of the western alliance from 1977 to 1981.

"My sense is that up until that point in his career, [Carter] had approached nuclear energy and nuclear physics in a very scientific and dispassionate way," Bourne said in a 2008 interview. "The Chalk River experience made him realize the awesome and potentially very destructive power he was dealing with. It gave him a true respect for both the benefits but also the devastatingly destructive effect nuclear energy could have. I believe this emotional recognition of the true nature of the power mankind had unleashed informed his decisions as president, not just in terms of having his finger on the nuclear button, but in his decision not to pursue the development of the neutron bomb as a weapon."[8]

In Plains in 2008, Carter eagerly consented to sit for an interview about his early experiences in Canada and said he agreed with Bourne's assessment. Carter's pre-White House experiences in this area were noted with respect by his fellow world leaders after he became president in 1977. Writ-

---

6   Interview with the editor, 1 November, 2010.
7   See Lawrence Martin. *The Presidents and the Prime Ministers Washington and Ottawa Face to Face: The Myth of Bilateral Bliss 1867-1982*. (Toronto). Doubleday Canada. 1982. pp 269-273.
8   Arthur Milnes. When Jimmy Carter faced radioactivity head on. *Ottawa Citizen*. 28 January, 2009.

ing in political retirement, Trudeau (and co-author Ivan Head) highlighted the "impetus that Carter gave to non-proliferation measures."

They continued:

> At [international meetings in 1977] London ... a number of states, including Canada and—significantly—the Soviet Union, had agreed upon a detailed "trigger" list of components necessary for the construction of nuclear explosive devices, and agreed that an embargo should be placed upon their sale. This demonstration of practical cooperation, one which led to close and continuing consultations over the years, was a significant advance in this esoteric and perilous sector. Carter's interest was shaped by his experience as a former US naval officer who had served as an engineer aboard nuclear powered and armed submarines. He was the first nuclear-age NATO leader with a firsthand technical awareness of these awesome weapons.[9]

Trudeau found many areas in which he was to be impressed by the 39th president. Carter was of course the fourth American chief executive he had done business with on Canada's behalf.

"Jimmy Carter, the Democrat who succeeded Ford in 1977, was very cerebral, very well briefed, and highly principled," Trudeau wrote in his *Memoirs*. "He was well known for promoting human rights and—even rarer for an American president—he had a genuine interest in the Third World. His real claim to greatness resides in the fact that he was a man of peace and was instrumental in bringing together Anwar Sadat and Menachem Begin at Camp David to negotiate the Israeli-Egypt peace treaty."[10]

Trudeau's close associate, Tom Axworthy, who served as the 15th prime minister's principal secretary from 1981 to 1984, also raises Carter's work in the US Navy's nuclear program to partly explain the intellectual attraction between his boss and the president.

"Don't forget Carter was a nuclear engineer and deeply analytical," Axworthy said in an interview. "He loved facts. So did Trudeau. They approached issues in the same way. Trudeau was more surprised by Ronald Reagan who approached issues through story-telling, leaving the facts to others."[11]

Axworthy, a member of the Interaction Council of Former Heads of State and Government, also raises another area of commonality between Trudeau and Carter, one that might surprise many Canadians.

> At the Interaction Council Mr. Trudeau was part of a group of former leaders headed by Helmut Schmidt that oversaw the Declaration on

---

9   Ivan Head and Pierre Trudeau. *The Canadian Way: Shaping Canada's Foreign Policy, 1968-1984*. (Toronto). McClelland & Stewart, 1995. p. 205.
10 Pierre Trudeau, *Memoirs*, (Toronto). McClelland & Stewart. 1993. p. 219.
11 Email, Tom Axworthy to the editor, 2 November, 2010.

Human Responsibility that theologian Hans Kung and myself drafted. Carter was a great admirer of Kung and joined Schmidt and Trudeau and the other former leaders in Holland at a conference to discuss the declaration organized by the Interaction Council. I remember Kung, Carter and Trudeau having a fine time discussing theology. President Carter of course knows his Bible and though Mr. Trudeau never advertised it, he too had a deep faith. This religious bond between the two North Americans was not much in evidence with the other leaders who were more secular.[12]

One event during his presidency has forever bound Carter to Canada and Canadians: the successful rescue of six American hostages from revolutionary Iran in early 1980. After militants stormed the United States Embassy in the fall of 1979, these six Americans evaded capture and found safe haven in Canada's own embassy in Tehran. Canadian diplomats, led by Ambassador Ken Taylor, were able to assist in smuggling the Americans—with the assistance of the CIA—safely out of Iran. The Canadians also were able to escape.

"We worked very closely [Canada and the United States] to get our six hostages out," Carter said with great emotion earlier this year. "That was one of the most glorious days of my presidency." [13]

The aim of this volume, as with previous volumes in the Library of Political Leadership series, is to provide present and future students of Canadian political history with mainly primary-based accounts of significant periods in our history and the words of those leaders —both foreign and domestic— that impacted these times.

This book has three sections. Part I contains public statements by President Carter and Canadian prime ministers Trudeau and Clark made during the Carter presidency. They are taken from the *Public Papers of the Presidents* series published by the United States government itself. These volumes preserve all public statements of a US chief executive during their term(s) in office. Canadian government officials would do well to consider establishing similar present-day and historical collections of the addresses and statements of Canada's prime ministers. It also includes a number of important addresses delivered by Carter as president that illustrate the values he represented as president and the causes he championed—human rights, nuclear arms control and peace—that were of particular interest to the Canadian governments in office at the same time and to Canadians at large. For younger readers, I have included his acceptance speech at the 1976 Democratic Convention and his Inaugural and Farewell addresses

---

12 Ibid.
13 Arthur Milnes Fonds, Queen's University Archives, video of a conversation with Jimmy and Rosalynn Carter, 13 March, 2010.

to further round out the portrait of an American president from an earlier time. Finally, the section also includes archival records I was able to gather thanks to the staff of the Jimmy Carter Library in Atlanta.

Part II features an edited version of a conversation between the Carters and a small group of Canadians that took place in 2008. It provides, in Carter's own words, a description of his early years in rural Georgia and the society from which he came. In addition, a variety of newspaper articles and essays written by the editor and other participants in this discussion and another the Carters had with a group of Canadians in 2010 is also provided. All students of the life and times of Jimmy and Rosalynn Carter will agree that one must examine his roots in rural southwest Georgia to gain a proper understanding of his later career on the American and world stage.

Part III consists of major addresses—including Carter's Nobel Peace Prize Lecture—and articles written by President Carter in his post-presidential life. For the reader at university or college today, and in the future, it is hoped the inclusion of these additional addresses will shed further light on the profound and positive impacts Jimmy and Rosalynn Carter have had on the world.

In conclusion, it is important to return to where this essay began: Prime Minister Trudeau's 1977 address to the United States Congress. If there is one single quest that has driven Carter throughout his life, it has been the search for racial equality. A child of the deep American south who experienced life in a segregated society and then the Civil Rights revolution in his region and country, Carter has never shrunk from confronting this issue head on in both his personal and political life.

Canadians often assume a superior attitude when considering this aspect of America's development and history, despite our nation's own record of discrimination. My own university, Queen's, as just one example, officially ignored, until very recently, the African-Canadian graduate, Robert Sutherland, whose bequest in the nineteenth century single-handedly saved this institution during its early days.[14]

One Canadian who did not stand in triumph before Americans in this area was Pierre Trudeau. During Trudeau's address to Congress he paid the following tribute to our neighbours and friends in the United States.

> You have chosen to declare your beliefs in the protection of minorities, in the richness of diversity, in the necessity of accommodation. You have

---

14 The Queen's Policy Studies building was named Robert Sutherland Hall in his honour in 2009—more than a century after Mr. Sutherland's bequest saved the university from financial ruin.

contributed new fibre to that seamless fabric we call the history of mankind: that stumbling, incoherent quest by individuals and by nations for freedom and dignity. Liberty and the pursuit of happiness have not been theoretical concepts for Americans nor have they been regarded as elusive goals. You have sought each with vigour, and shared with all mankind the joy and the creativity, which are the products of freedom. You have illustrated throughout your history the resilience, the dedication and the inherent decency of American society. The United States achievement in recent years of conducting a great social revolution, in overcoming difficulties of immense complication and obdurateness, and doing so through the democratic process, is surely a model for all nations devoted to the dignity of the human condition. Freedom loving men and women everywhere are the beneficiaries of your example. Not the least among them are Canadians, for whom the United States has long since been the single most important external influence ... We in Canada, facing internal tensions with roots extending back to the seventeenth century, have much to gain from the wisdom and discipline and patience with you, in this country, in this generation have brought to bear to reduce racial tensions, to broaden legal rights, and to provide opportunity to all.

Jimmy and Rosalynn Carter are important American architects in the continuing quest for human dignity and freedom that our prime minister spoke of that day so long ago in Washington.

Part I

White House Years, 1977 to 1981

Memorandum
19 February 1977

To: The President
From: Patricia Bario
Re: 15-Minute Interview at 5:15 p.m.
             Monday with *Canada AM*[1]
             Meeting: 3/21/77 at 5:15 p.m.

Purpose of the meeting

To give you a chance to reaffirm directly to the Canadian people the friendship between our countries. And, to give them a feel for the kind of man the now US President is.

Background

Canada AM is a national network morning show, much like the *Today Show*.

Interviewing will be Bruce Phillips, their senior correspondent from Ottawa. Also present will be Andrew Cochran, producer, and Gail Thompson, story editor.

Questions should be philosophical—such as "How do you see your presidency?" But attached is a talking point memo from the National Security Council.

---

[1] Almost twenty years ago, while I was studying journalism at Ryerson Polytechnic University in Toronto, my radio broadcast instructor, Marjorie Nichol, an enthusiastic and inspirational teacher, shared a story about this interview that has remained with me over the years. Then on staff with *Canada AM*, she remembers well how White House staff, after originally consenting to the interview on President Carter's behalf, tried to withdraw this acceptance. Eventually, the matter ended up in the Oval Office. When President Carter heard that the Canadians had been told they could have an interview, he interceded and allowed it to go ahead, telling his staff that he was a man of his word. So it was that a Canadian broadcaster claimed the first-ever televised interview granted by the new president of the United States.

Memorandum

To: Pat Bario

From: Bob Hunter

Subject: Talking Points for President's Interview on *Canada AM*

I am particularly pleased that the first two leaders to visit the United States after my inauguration are from our closest neighbours—Mexico last week, and Prime Minister Trudeau from Canada now. This clearly symbolizes the importance we attach to relations with close friends—and my desire to strengthen the bonds of friendship.

This visit will give me a chance to meet with the prime minister, who is one of the world's great statesmen, and with whom later this spring I will be meeting other Western leaders at the summit.

There is deep admiration and respect for Canada in the United States. A sense of shared commitment to democratic institutions, and the best qualities of the human spirit. Commitment to peace, human justice, and human rights.

We seek to work with Canada in developing our own economics—completing recovery, avoiding inflation, and seeking to provide benefits for all our people. The two economies are intimately linked; and we share responsibilities for all our people.

We are particularly grateful to Canada for its help during the recent cold wave, in making additional energy supplies available.

Note: There are only three contentious issues that have to be handled delicately:

- Energy cooperation: the Canadians are very sensitive about having full control over their resources.
- Fish: it is possible that the maritime negotiations will not be completed by Monday afternoon. If asked, you should simply say that we hope to be able to reach agreement, in the interests of both countries, and are proceeding.
- Quebec: it is important not to get involved in any discussion of Quebec politics, on the grounds that "I don't think I should comment on what is happening in your country, particularly on an issue where people feel so deeply." However, carefully put, you can indicate how much we here admire the "strong, vigorous Canadian confederation"—which gets the idea across, without stumbling on the buzz word "unity."

Text of President Carter's Interview with Bruce Phillips of CTV's *Canada AM*

PHILLIPS: Mr. President, I would think that you are the first president in modern times for whom the subject of your northern neighbour could in any way be construed as a problem, the political stability of your neighbouring state; are you concerned about what's happening in Canada?

CARTER: Well, I think the Canadians are well able to take care of their own internal political problems. We have some of our own in our own country. But the stability, Canada as a friend, and as a reliable neighbour, is an integral part of our lives. And I'm not concerned about it at all.

PHILLIPS: Do you consider the future of the Canadian Confederation a matter affecting the vital interests of the United States?

CARTER: Well obviously it is. The stability there, in Canada, is of crucial importance to us. And the Confederation, itself, is obviously of importance to us. I don't have any way to predict what might happen in the future, but as I say, I'm not concerned about it at all.

PHILLIPS: Well, I take it that you would prefer to see Canada as a united country then?

CARTER: Well, if I were the one to make a decision, the Confederation would be the preference. But that's a decision for the Canadian people to make.

PHILLIPS: In the event, however, of Confederation splitting, would the United States recognize a sovereign state of Quebec?

CARTER: Well, I don't know how it could; we'll cross that bridge when we come to it.

PHILLIPS: Well, maybe that's a bridge that will never have to be crossed. Has the United States got a policy on the subject? It's all pretty new for us and I presume just as new for you, but have you got any studies going on in the State Department for the Defence Department, or are you going to have any made or have you had any made on the consequences due to the United States economy and the United States generally?

CARTER: No. We observe the Canadian political scene with great interest, and we obviously want to see the will of the Canadian people expressed accurately and in a peaceful and orderly fashion. But I see nothing, yet, that would cause me any concern about the future on that score, and all I know is what I get from meeting briefings and from reading the news and watching the television, and that is, on what happens in the future, the friendship between our people is a stabilizing force. And, as I said, I'm not concerned about what might happen.

PHILLIPS: Does this apply a judgment on your part that nothing very serious is likely to happen?

CARTER: That's my judgment.

PHILLIPS: That is your judgment.

CARTER: Yes.

PHILLIPS: Do you think that the country will not separate based on your own intelligence.

CARTER: Well, I'm not going to make a prediction about that, but I've always expressed, I hope clearly, perhaps not, that if I were making my own preferences it would be that Confederation continued, but that's a judgment for the Canadian people to make, and I trust that judgment.

PHILLIPS: I'd like to ask you a somewhat broader question, President Carter, about the future of the North American continent. How do you see the whole continental picture developing—particularly in the context of the energy problems and the raw materials that we're obviously running into. Do you think that there should be a more concerted and cooperative approach to the exploitation of our resources?

CARTER: Well, I'd hope that every major decision that you make in the future, at least, will bring oil and natural gas to help our north shore, and Alaska, to be made with the full knowledge and after close consultation with the Canadian government leaders, both the provinces and the national government. The independence and autonomy of our nations have got to be maintained, if we're to deal with these questions on an exactly equal basis, which is the way it has been in the past. But I think that this is a great opportunity for cooperation in imports, exports, in exchange of energy sources, so that we don't go to an enormous expense, acting, in an isolated way, then those expenses might be drastically reduced, and conservation measures might be more effective if we cooperate. This is one of the subjects obviously that Prime Minister Trudeau and I, well, we'll be discussing in this two-day period. And, if I'm obviously keeping an open mind and all our options clear about the arrival of the future pipelines, and an interchange of energy materials, as something that each nation will have to decide, [it is] basically what's best for one's own people.

PHILLIPS: If there are any outstanding problems in the relations between these two countries, which do think is the most important one?

CARTER: I would guess at this point, that our relationship with Canada has the least number of problem areas, at least in my memory. We have a close inner relationship, constant consultation at the top levels of government, and I think there's a growing realization of an interested share—problems that are mutual. The laws of the sea, fishing rights, St. Lawrence Seaway tolls, mutual investments in one another's country—we share in the future responsibilities for energy exchange in the mutual defence of our people, a common interest in the freedom of the people who live in Western Europe under the NATO treaty. All these things tie us together and they are potentially divisive. But because of the goodwill that exists between our people and the Canadian people, they have not been disruptive at all. One interesting thing was that a recent public opinion poll, run by Mr. Gallup, showed that among American people, the two nations that they admire most are the United States and Canada …

PHILLIPS: A lot of Americans, and Canadians too, for that matter, say that there's effectively no difference between us. Do you think there's a difference?

CARTER: Well, I think there is a great difference between the background heritage, language and structure of government, climate—there is a great deal of difference. And their individuality and the uniqueness of each nation, I think that it is important and something that ought to be preserved.

PHILLIPS: Vive la difference, so to speak.

Welcoming Ceremony for Prime Minister Pierre Trudeau

The White House
21 February 1977

THE PRESIDENT: To Prime Minister Trudeau and his beautiful wife, Margaret, to the people of Canada who come to be with us this afternoon, and to all of our own welcomers who have come here on this occasion to make our neighbours feel at home:

I am very grateful to be here, to welcome to the White House and to our country a man who shares with me the tremendous friendship that has always existed between the United States of America and the people of Canada to the north.

We share a common border, more than 5,000 miles. We share a common defence of our own people. We share the human and natural resources of an entire continent. We share a great respect and friendship for each other. We share a commitment to human decency and to personal freedom. We share a historical belief in the principles of democracy, and these principles have been tangibly demonstrated by our governments for generations. And we share a common commitment to world peace.

Canada is our most important trade partner. We have many common purposes and common concerns, common problems, and also the potential for common solutions to those problems. The next two days I will spend with Prime Minister Trudeau, and he will have a chance to visit with our top officials and to let the Canadian officials share these discussions. We will be talking about defense and peace. We will be talking about the world economy and our nations' great contribution to that economy.

Prime Minister Trudeau has been recognized for many years as one of the developed nations' leading negotiators and understander of the problems of the developing nations of the world. Because of his commitment to humanitarian purposes, he has the trust and confidence of people who are not quite so fortunate as are we. He is a senior statesman of the North Atlantic Treaty Organization, having been in office now for more than eight years. And his common and unique and persistent commitment to the principles of the democratic nations of the world has made him a leader even from the first days when he was in office.

He made a comment recently that I think is important for all of us to remember, which typifies his own attitude toward human beings. He said it is not enough to measure a nation's product in our gross national financial product, but we should think about the outcome and the output of our nation on the basis of a net human benefit, how well the people find a better life because of the activities and decisions of government.

So, because of all these reasons, in a personal way and as a leader of our great nation, I want to welcome to our country Prime Minister Trudeau and his wife, Margaret.

Welcome, Mr. Prime Minister.

THE PRIME MINISTER: Mr. President, Mrs. Carter, and American friends:

First, I wanted to tell you, Mr. President, that I brought the greetings of some twenty-two million Canadians. But I see that by the flags over on the lawn there that a lot of them have preceded me here. The greetings are warm nonetheless.

I want to tell you, also, that we bring you our great, good wishes as you assume the very arduous, important office of president of this great nation.

Canadians are looking forward to this period of good relationships with you at the head of this great nation. With your dedication, your hard work, your discipline, your sense of morality, we feel that these are great days for our relationship and for the world.

We are particularly grateful and honoured, sir, that you invited your North American neighbours very early in the term of your office. I am sure I can speak for President Lopez Portillo—I certainly speak for myself and for Canadians—when I say that we have great expectations that this continental neighbourhood will flourish and develop because of the great personal interest you have shown in it.

The links between our countries are so numerous, the cooperation that we are involved in is so deep that this kind of meeting is as natural as it is friendly. As I look through the enormous briefing books that I had, sir, and I am sure it happened to you, too, I just felt that there is perhaps nothing that our countries can do which doesn't involve one another. There are so many associations, so many committees, so many clubs, so many links between us of all kinds that I believe they are absolutely legion. I tried to get a count and I was told it wasn't possible. And I can well understand it.

We have been such old friends and our links are so deep that this number of associations together can only rest on the deep friendship between our peoples.

The International Women's Year, sir, has only passed in history for fourteen months now. It seems that our wives, Mrs. Carter and Margaret, have already met and established a good agenda for the discussions. You and I are only meeting this moment. But I am quite convinced that we will, in a friendly way, rivalize with their achievements and catch up to their friendly relations.

I want to thank you, sir, for your very warm hospitality to all the visiting Canadians and to have received us in this beautiful garden and this nice sun. It makes me feel that Canadians, now as they are buried deep in snow, they have hope. They hope that when that snow melts there will still be grass there on earth.

Sir, we hope with the same faith that you will favour us with your visit and Mrs. Carter's to Canada one of these days.

Thank you very, very much, I am looking forward to our talk.

Visit of Prime Minister Trudeau
Toasts of the President and the Prime Minister at a Dinner Honouring the Prime Minister

The White House
21 February 1977

THE PRESIDENT: In preparing for this visit, I learned that we have some very serious and very intense competition with our friends in the north. Dr. George Gallup ran a poll recently, and he asked the people who live in the United States to name their favorite nations. The United States got 95 percent; Canada got 91 percent. [Laughter] So, I feel that I'm in an intense and constant and very challenging competition with Pierre Trudeau for the hearts of my own people.

I think this does indicate the great compatibility and friendship and sense of warmth and mutual admiration that has always existed among American people toward Canada. We share a border that's more than 5,200 miles long. And for two hundred years, our people have lived—with one very brief interval around 1812—in a spirit of friendship. And that's important to us. Even more than we think, in our daily lives, we are dependent on Canada for many things.

Canada has about twenty-two million people. And every year, sixty million people cross the border. And there is a kinship and a sharing of delight and challenge and enjoyment of life that transcends the political realities of a modern, fast-changing, technological world.

Of course, the technologies are important as well. We are now beginning to see that many of the things that we took for granted—the purity of water in the Great Lakes, an unlimited supply of oil and gas, security in our borders, free of possible direct attack in a time of war—those things are now no longer sure. And I think, in a way, that's bound us even closer together.

I know that on the other side of the border, the Canadians feel what we are. The last time Prime Minister Trudeau came to our country, he said that being a neighbour to the United States was like sleeping with an elephant—[laughter]—that you could very quickly detect every twitch or grunt. Well, the elephants [symbol of the Republican party] are gone. The donkeys [symbol of the Democratic party] are here—[laughter]—and the donkeys are much more companionable beasts, I think.

I do want to thank the Canadian people and Prime Minister Trudeau for their gracious offer during this time of energy shortage for our people, for their offer to help us. They exported some of their cold weather, but they followed it up with all the natural gas.

And we had a very delightful meeting this afternoon to discuss some of the international problems that face us both. Tomorrow, we're going to talk about some things that affect both Canada and us in a bilateral fashion.

Prime Minister Trudeau's wife, Margaret, came a couple of weeks ago to visit Rosalynn and to open up a display in one of our famous art galleries of contemporary Canadian art. And I think this indicated, first of all, that we are interested in the same things, but also, that our nations are distinctive.

Although we live in close proximity, we are quite different. And the differences are carefully preserved. There is an understandable determination not to be dominated and not to be pressured and to be unique and to maintain individuality. And that's a sign of strength on our side and their side of the border that is precious to us both.

I feel that we have approached an era of recognition, of mutual purpose and ideals and hopes and dreams and aspirations and also, concerns and problems that might bind us even closer together now than in the past. And in a way, I'm thankful for it. I'm proud of the personal friendship that was almost instantaneous when I met Pierre Trudeau this afternoon. I had a sense of relaxation and a sense of compatibility that I hope will be an accurate indication on a permanent basis of what our nations feel towards one another.

I would like to close by saying that we have been close in time of war. And quite often, when our own nation had made a mistake because of an excessive dependence on our own military strength, Canada and its people have maintained kind of a standard of ethics and morality and commitment to unchanging truths that were a subtle reminder to us to reassess our own position.

So, we learn from one another. And I'm very grateful to our visitors for coming to honour us with their presence.

I'd like to propose a toast: To the Queen of Canada, to the Prime Minister of Canada, and to the people of Canada.

THE PRIME MINISTER: Mr. President, Mrs. Carter, friends:

I want to thank you, first of all, for your very warm hospitality and for the informality of the dinner that we are attending tonight. The informality was to be expected from a household where you have a child of school age and a puppy, I understand, and the hospitality and the warmth of it was to be expected from you, sir, and from your very charming wife.

I want to say that I am always a little bit moved and perhaps even intimidated when I am in the White House. It has such history; it has such great memories of remarkable statesmen, American leaders.

And it is particularly moving to be here on George Washington's birthday. I find some consolation in that, because I was told an anecdote about George Washington when he was retiring from office. The *Philadelphia Aurora*—there was then a paper called that name, I don't know if it still exists—but it had been rather unkind to President Washington during his term of office. And when he retired, they had an editorial saying that if ever there was a day for great rejoicing, this was it. I feel, sir, that an old politician like myself takes some consolation in feeling that times never change. [Laughter]

You don't have to seek solace in this type of anecdote. But indeed, you added to the sense of hospitality when you were good enough to quote this finding of Dr. Gallup, of which I knew nothing. And it makes me feel that if ever I get in trouble in Canada politically, maybe I'll come down here. [Laughter] I can assure you that if you are ever in trouble, which I pray will never happen, you would be very handily chosen to be the leader of the Canadian people.

Your generous remarks are something which are very much in keeping with the friendship and the long history of cooperation between our peoples. It began, I think, around 1781, when the Articles of Confederation proposed that Canada be admitted, be invited to join the Confederation, just by applying. I believe other colonies had to have the consent of nine states in order to be admitted, but Canada was to be admitted just on invitation and acceptance. Well, whether it is good or not that we didn't accept in those days, is perhaps very hard to speculate upon except to say that if Canada had accepted, I'm sure we wouldn't be having such a fine dinner here tonight. [Laughter]

Apart from that very short incident of hostilities to which you alluded very gently, we have since then—since the past 165 years, I guess it is—had very good neighbourhood relations, indeed. We've cooperated in many, many ways. We've built together some of the greatest of men's enterprises. We've maintained democracy alive within our countries, and we've cooperated in assisting wherever we could around the world in helping other nations in one way or another.

And I think it's fair to say that if in those days, one hundred and fifty years ago, we were the hope of the new world, a large part of the hope of the new world, I would think that today, perhaps, in large part, we represent the hope of the Third World. This joins many of the discussions we had this afternoon.

And I must say on behalf of the Canadian government and people that we are more than delighted—we are excited with the generous approach that your ideas convey as regards the world order, which would be based on equality and justice.

In our case, sir, we have done our part. In terms of foreign aid, Canada is amongst the top four or five nations of assistance to the Third World, in terms of our proportion of our GNP. Since the end of the Second World War, we have admitted more refugees, political refugees, to Canada than any other nation barring the United States. You have a slight edge on us. But they have come to Canada by the tens of thousands from Czechoslovakia, from Hungary, from Tibet, from Uganda, from Chile, and many, many other places.

So, we do try to, as Canadians, show this hospitality to the world which corresponds to the generosity of the Canadian people. I was telling you this afternoon, sir, that though we have been a nuclear power for some thirty years, and though we have the technology and the financial means of building a bomb, we have chosen not to do so. We have tried to put our technology towards a more creative and fraternal use.

We, with the United States, are the only members of NATO which has troops on both sides of the Atlantic. We're into our fourth term in the Security Council. We have been in every peacekeeping operation, United Nations peacekeeping operation, since the end of the Second World War. We were in Korea. We were in the four Indochina Control Commissions.

I say these things, sir, partly to be slightly chauvinistic, but also because we in Canada today tend to be a little bit cynical towards the role of Canada in the world and towards its generosity. And I think that you won't be angry at me for using this occasion and these hidden microphones to talk a little bit about Canada's contribution, because these things would not have been possible without a strong and united Canada. And I just want to assure you, sir, that we intend to keep Canada that way.

It is said that Daniel Boone, when giving advice to those who wanted to join him on the frontier, said that there were three essentials—to have a good gun, a good horse, and a good wife.

Well, now the frontier has changed in kind. We are still very much living on a new kind of a frontier. And in these days when changing values in the world and the increasing closeness of mankind to each other and where a new, special kind of brotherhood is called for, I think we could replace Daniel Boone's three essentials by three others. I would say it is to have good goals, good discipline, and good friends.

Well, I know we have good goals, and we discussed them a great deal this afternoon. We found that together, we shared many, many of the goals in foreign relations and, indeed, in internal affairs.

In terms of having good friends, well, you have shown us tonight through your hospitality and your friendship that that is a reality.

What has to be achieved is good discipline. I speak for Canada, and I feel that it is a virtue that we can do with a bit more of—if I can twist my grammar that way. We are going through a period now when discipline, self-discipline, is being understood as the only substitute for discipline from the outside or discipline from the state. And I must say that I personally was very, very enthusiastic to see the measure of discipline that appears in your thoughts, sir, in your approach to problems, and in your way of life.

I would propose a toast, not to the friendship that we have, and not to the goals that we share, but to the disciplines of our people—may it increase, and to President Carter and to Mrs. Carter, who will help President Carter in imparting some of those disciplines on the industrialized democracies.

Prime Minister Pierre Trudeau Address to the US Congress

Washington, 22 February 1977

For much more than a century, individual Canadians, in countless ways and on countless occasions, have expressed to Americans their friendship. Today, as prime minister, I am given the opportunity to express those feelings collectively before the elected representatives of the American people. I do so with pride, and with conviction. The friendship between our two countries is so basic that it has long since been regarded by others as the standard for enlightened international relations. No Canadian leader would be permitted by his electorate consciously to weaken it. Indeed, no Canadian leader would wish to, and certainly not this one. Simply stated, our histories record that for more than a century millions upon millions of

Canadians and Americans have known one another, liked one another, and trusted one another. Canadians are not capable of living in isolation from you any more than we are desirous of doing so. We have benefited from your stimulus; we have profited from your vitality.

Throughout your history, you have been inspired by a remarkably large number of gifted leaders who have displayed stunning foresight, oft-times in the face of then popular sentiments. In this city, which bears his name, on the anniversary of his birthday, George Washington's words bear remembering. In a message familiar to all of you in this chamber, he said: It is of infinite moment that you should properly estimate the immense value of your national union to your collective and individual happiness. At a moment in the history of mankind when men and women cannot escape from the knowledge that the only hope for humanity is the willingness of people of differing complexions and cultures and beliefs to live peaceably together, you have not forgotten Washington's high standards. You have chosen to declare your beliefs in the protection of minorities, in the richness of diversity, in the necessity of accommodation. You have contributed new fibre to that seamless fabric we call the history of mankind: that stumbling, incoherent quest by individuals and by nations for freedom and dignity.

Liberty and the pursuit of happiness have not been theoretical concepts for Americans nor have they been regarded as elusive goals. You have sought each with vigour, and shared with all mankind the joy and the creativity, which are the products of freedom. You have illustrated throughout your history the resilience, the dedication and the inherent decency of American society.

The United States achievement in recent years of conducting a great social revolution, in overcoming difficulties of immense complication and obdurateness, and doing so through the democratic process, is surely a model for all nations devoted to the dignity of the human condition. Freedom-loving men and women everywhere are the beneficiaries of your example. Not the least among them are Canadians, for whom the United States has long since been the single most important external influence, the weather only excepted.

We in Canada, facing internal tensions with roots extending back to the seventeenth century, have much to gain from the wisdom and discipline and patience with you, in this country, in this generation have brought to bear to reduce racial tensions, to broaden legal rights, and to provide opportunity to all.

Canadians long ago determined to govern themselves by a parliamentary system that favours the flowering of basic aspirations for freedom, for justice, for individual dignity. The rule of law, sovereignty of parliament, a broad sharing of power with the provinces, and official support of the pluralistic nature of Canadian society have combined to create in Canada a community where freedom thrives to an extent not exceeded anywhere else, a community where equality of opportunity between people and between regions is a constant goal.

The success of our efforts in the first century following confederation was great, but by no means complete. We created a society of individual liberty and of respect for human rights. We produced an economic standard of living that approaches your own. We have not yet, however, created a condition in which French-speaking Canadians have felt they were fully equal or could fully develop the richness of the culture they had inherited. And therein is the source of our central problem today. This is why a small minority of the people of Quebec feel they should leave Canada and strike out in a country of their own. The newly elected government of that province asserts a policy that reflects that minority view despite the fact that during the election campaign it sought a mandate for good government, and not a mandate for the separation from Canada.

The accommodation of two vigorous language groups has been, in varying fashion, the policy of every Canadian government since confederation. The reason is clear. Within Quebec, over 80 percent of the population speak French as their first or only language. In Canada as a whole, nearly one fifth of the people speak no language but French. Thus from generation to generation there has been handed down the belief that a country could be built in freedom and equality with two languages and a multitude of cultures.

I am confident it can be done. I say to you with all the certainty I can command that Canadian unity will not be fractured. Revisions will take place. Accommodations will be made; we shall succeed. There will have to be changes in some of our attitudes; there will have to be a greater comprehension of one another across the barrier of language difference. Both English-speaking and French-speaking Canadians will have to become more aware of the richness that diversity brings and less irritated by the problems it presents. We may have to revise some aspects of our constitution so that the Canadian federation can be seen by six and half million French-speaking Canadians to be the strongest bulwark against submersion by some two hundred and twenty million English-speaking North Americans. These very figures illustrate dramatically the sense of insecurity of French

Canada. But separation would not alter the arithmetic; it would merely increase the exposure. Nor would the separation of Quebec contribute in any fashion to the confidence of the many cultural minorities of various origins who dwell throughout Canada. These communities have been encouraged for decades to retain their own identities and to preserve their own cultures. They have done so and flourished, nowhere more spectacularly than in the prairie provinces of Alberta, Saskatchewan and Manitoba. The sudden departure of Quebec could signify the tragic failure of our pluralist dream, the fracturing of our cultural mosaic, and would likely remove much of the determination of Canadians to protect their cultural minorities. Problems of this magnitude cannot be wished away. They can be solved, however, by the institutions we have created for our own governance. Those institutions belong to all Canadians, to me as a Quebecer as much as to my fellow citizens from the other provinces. And because those institutions are democratically structured, because their members are freely elected, they are capable of reflecting changes and of responding to the popular will.

I am confident that we in Canada are well along in the course of devising a society as free of prejudice and fear as full of understanding and generosity, as respectful of individuality and beauty, as receptive to change and innovation, as exists anywhere.

Our nation is the very encounter of two of the most important cultures of Western civilization, to which countless other strains are being added. Most Canadians understand that the rupture of their country would be an aberrant departure from the norms they themselves have set, a crime against the history of mankind; for I am immodest enough to suggest that a failure of this always-varied, often illustrious Canadian experiment would create shock waves of disbelief among those all over the world who are committed to the proposition that among man's noblest endeavours are those communities in which persons of diverse origins live, love, work, and find mutual benefit. Canadians are conscious of the effort required of them to maintain in healthy working order not only their own nation, but as well the North American neighbourhood in which they flourish. A wholesome relationship with our mutual friend, Mexico, and a robust partnership with the United States are both, in our eyes, highly desirable. To those ends we have contributed much energy. And you in this country have reciprocated to the point where our relationship forms a model admired by much of the world, one moulded from the elements of mutual respect and supported by the vigour of disciplined cooperation.

We have built together one of the world's largest and most efficient, transportation and power generating systems in the form of the St. Lawrence Seaway. We have conceived and established the world's oldest, continuously functioning, binational arbitral tribunal: the International Joint Commission. We have joined together in many parts of the world in the defence of freedom and in the relief of want. We have created oft-times original techniques of environmental management, of emergency and disaster assistance; of air and sea traffic control, of movements of people, goods and services, the latter so successfully that the value of our trade and the volume of visitors back and forth exceeds several times over that of any other two countries in the world. It is no wonder that we are each so interested in the continued social stability and economic prosperity of the other. Nor should we be surprised that the desire of the American and Canadian peoples to understand and help one another sometimes adopts unusual forms. In what other two countries in the world could be there be reproduced the scene of tens of thousand of people in a Montreal baseball park identifying totally with one team against the other, forgetting all the while that every single player on each is American, and a similar scene in the Washington hockey arena where thousand of spectators identify totally with one team against another, forgetting that virtually every player on the ice is Canadian.

Thus do the images blur, and sometimes do they lead to chafing. Yet, how civilized are the responses! How temperate the replies! We threaten to black out your television commercials? You fire volleys of antitrust proceedings! Such admirable substitutes for hostility! More important than the occasional incident of disagreement is the continuing process of management that we have successfully incorporated into our relationship. It is a process which succeeds through careful attention, through consultation, and through awareness on both sides of the border that problems can arise which are attributable neither to intent nor neglect, but to the disproportionate size of our two populations and the resulting imbalance of our economic strength.

Those differences will likely always lead us in Canada to attempt to ensure that there be maintained a climate for the expression of Canadian culture. We will surely also be sensitive to the need for the domestic control of our economic environment. As well, in a country visited annually by extreme cold over its entire land mass, I just met the representative from Florida and I hear it also happens in your country. But in our country, a country so far-flung that transportation has always posed almost insuperable problems, the wise conservation of our energy resources assumes a compelling dimension. And for a people devoted throughout their history to accommodating themselves with the harshness, as well as the beauty, of their natural surroundings, we will respond with vigour to any threat of pollution or despoliation, be it from an indigenous or from an external source.

Our continent, however, is not the world. Increasingly it is evident, that the same sense of neighbourhood that has served so well our North American interests must be extended to all parts of the globe and to all members of the human race. Increasingly, the welfare and the dignity of others will be the measurement of our own condition. I share with President Carter his belief that in this activity also we will achieve success. However, even as we have moved away from the Cold War era of political and military confrontation, there exists another danger; one of rigidity in our response to the current challenges of poverty, hunger, environmental degradation, and nuclear proliferation. Our ability to respond adequately to these issues will in some measure be determined by our willingness to recognize them as the new obstacles to peace. Yet, sadly, our pursuit of peace in these respects has all too often been little more imaginative that was our sometimes-blind grappling with absolutes in the international political sphere. Moreover, we have failed to mobilize adequately the full support of our electorates for the construction of a new world order. The reasons are not hard to find. In these struggles there is no single tyrant, no simple ideological contest. We are engaged in complex issues of overwhelming proportions yet with few identifiable labels. Who, after all, feels stirred to oratorical heights at the mention of commodity price stabilization or of full fuel cycle nuclear safeguards or of special drawing rights? Yet these are the kind of issues that will determine the stability of tomorrow's world. They will require imaginative solutions and cooperative endeavour, for these struggles are not against human beings; they are struggles with and for human beings, in a common cause of global dimensions.

It is to the United States that the world looks for leadership in these vital activities. It has been in large measure your fervour and your direction that has inspired a quarter century of far-flung accomplishment in political organization, industrial development and international trade. Without your dedicated participation, the many constructive activities now in one stage or another in the several fields of energy, economics, trade, disarmament, development—these activities will not flourish as they must.

My message today is not a solicitous plea for continued United States involvement. It is an enthusiastic pledge of spirited Canadian support in the pursuit of those causes in which we both believe. It is as well an encouragement to our mutual rededication at this important moment in our histories to a global ethic of confidence in our fellow man. Mr. Speaker, Mr. President, in that same address to which I referred some minutes ago, George Washington warned against the insidious wiles of foreign influence and the desirability of steering clear of permanent alliances with any portion of the foreign world. Yet here I stand, ladies and gentlemen, a foreigner, endeavouring whether insidiously or not, you will have to judge, to urge the United States ever more permanently into new alliances. That I dare do so is a measure not only of the bond that links Canadians to you, but as well of the spirit of America. Thomas Paine's words of two centuries ago are as valid today as when he uttered them: "My country is the world, and my religion is to do good." In your continued quest of those ideals, ladies and gentlemen, all Canadians wish you Godspeed.

United States–Canada Agreement on a Natural Gas Pipeline

Remarks of the President and Prime Minister Trudeau Announcing the Agreement

8 September 1977

THE PRESIDENT: Good morning, everybody.

I think a joint statement has already been issued to you just recently, concerning a very important agreement that Prime Minister Trudeau and I have approved this morning in principle, that our countries will undertake the largest, single, privately financed, energy project in history, an Alcan Highway pipeline to carry Alaskan natural gas through Canada to the lower forty-eight states.

This joint United States and Canadian system could deliver more than three and a half billion cubic feet per day of Alaskan and, later on, Canadian gas to both our countries.

The cost of this transportation system will be significantly lower than under the alternative pipeline, the El Paso line down due south through Alaska and then by ship into California.

The savings to the American consumers over the first twenty years of the project could total about $5 billion. The Alcan route is preferable to the El Paso route, which was the other one that we were considering, because it is more economical, it's safer, and has less damage to the environment, and because it will deliver gas more directly to the American markets where the gas is needed, in the northern mid-western part of our country, with perhaps a spur later on over to the California region.

The project will benefit Canada by facilitating development of its own gas reserves, particularly in the frontier region to the Mackenzie Delta area.

We have agreed in principle not to build the route diversion to Dawson originally required by the Canadian National Energy Board. But in exchange, the United States has agreed to share the cost of a Dempster Highway lateral from Dawson to Whitehorse if and when it is constructed. This lateral line would connect at Whitehorse with the main pipeline so that additional gas from the Mackenzie Delta could be brought to market.

The exact share of the US cost for the extension will be determined by the percentage of cost overruns on construction of the main pipeline in Canada.

This formula will provide incentives for the most efficient construction of the pipeline. Both countries recognize the benefits from increased cooperation in developing our energy supplies. This agreement brings great benefits to both countries. We will continue to cooperate to our mutual benefit in many other matters of importance to our two nations as has always been the case between ourselves and Canada.

Once the agreement is signed, probably next week, Prime Minister Trudeau and I will then seek approval of the Alcan project from our respective legislative bodies. I hope the US Congress will approve this critical energy project before the close of the session.

Once approved, I believe the project will be expeditiously built consistent with sound environmental practices.

Under the provisions of the *Alaska Natural Gas Transportation Act* passed by Congress last year, I will appoint a strong Federal construction coordinator and inspector to insure effective project design and management.

Again I want to express my deep appreciation to Prime Minister Pierre Trudeau and to the negotiators, and I look forward to another opportunity to demonstrate to the world and to our own people that our sharing of mutual projects and mutual purposes and a common philosophy about the future is a very valuable thing to our people and constantly demonstrates the good neighbourship that exists across our borders.

Pierre, I do thank you very much for your cooperation. And I believe that when the details of the agreement are described within the next few days, that the Americans and Canadians will be pleased at the progress that we have made. It's a dramatic breakthrough, thanks to you and the cooperation of the Canadian government.

THE PRIME MINISTER: Thank you, Jimmy.

I do want, Mr. President, to associate myself with these feelings. It's certain that what we have done and agreed upon in principle this morning is certainly in line with the spirit of good neighbourliness that our countries have always attempted to practice.

We were successful in one other giant project a generation ago on the Seaway. This one is even bigger. In terms of energy, it's certainly more important.

And I am very happy to say that the spirit that you and I defined last February at our meeting of attempting to solve all these problems—not to one's greatest possible advantage at the disadvantage of the other, but so that both sides get the maximum amount of advantage—I am very glad that that spirit has underlined all the negotiations, and that I think in the process of them there was only one phone call that you and I had to make to insure that our people were negotiating in a spirit of complete openness, that both sides were endeavouring to make sure that the other side was operating on the same facts.

We weren't trying to hide things from each other in order to get maximum advantage from the other, but we were trying to make a project which would be to the advantage of the American people and to the Canadian people.

From our side, we are very happy with the cooperation that you, Mr. President, and your people have shown. It remains, as you say, to sign the fine print next week. But I am certain that with the agreed-upon principles that there will be no difficulty there.

We will have to, apart from going to our legislature—we'll want to make sure that transmission of the energy itself is in keeping with the high principles as we have set for ourselves in terms of protecting the environment, making sure that the interests of the native peoples will be guarded in every way, and that, of course, our provinces and our Yukon Council will be involved in the execution of this. But that is for us to follow up on. And so far as our bilateral negotiations are concerned, I am very happy with the spirit that pervaded them.

THE PRESIDENT: Thank you, Pierre.

I might say that I congratulated Prime Minister Trudeau on the tough negotiators that the Canadians have proven themselves to be. And I am now in the process of asking him to help us negotiate agreements with other nations; they've done so well in this particular project. [Laughter]

But we are proud of this. There has never been a larger project in the history of the world. And for two nations who have intense domestic political problems involving environment, involving cost to consumers, involving assured supplies of energy in the future, to look twenty or forty years ahead and to undertake this project with friendship and mutual trust is a major step forward.

And I think, again, it demonstrates vividly the longstanding friendship that exists between ourselves and the Canadians. We've had many other potential disagreements in recent months concerning the oceans, fisheries, and in every instance we've been able to work these potential problems out harmoniously.

And we still have some problems concerning United States and Canadian tax laws, extraterritorial questions concerning antitrust enforcements. But, again, we are trying—and I am sure with assured eventual success—to resolve these very important matters for our people in harmony and a spirit of cooperation.

But I want to reemphasize my thanks to you, Pierre, for your friendship and cooperation.

THE PRIME MINISTER: Well, Jimmy, I am very grateful for these final words. If I can help you with your elections at any point, I would like to—[laughter]—

Meeting With Prime Minister Pierre Elliott Trudeau of Canada
Remarks on the Departure of the Prime Minister

3 March 1979

THE PRESIDENT: Good afternoon, everybody.

Recently, Prime Minister Trudeau and I were scheduled to meet this evening in New York to attend the performance of the Winnipeg Symphony Orchestra. We were not able to do so, but we had a delightful lunch today and maybe made some good music together.

We were able to discuss international and bilateral issues concerning the economy. We spent a considerable portion of our time talking about energy matters. We both are resolved to work much more closely in the future even than we have in the past. We discussed the possibility of establishing a consultative mechanism so that we might exchange ideas on energy on a continuing basis.

We had a general review of world political problems, some of the fast-changing developments that are of interest both to us and to Canada and others who want peace and stability and a better quality of life throughout the world. We share with Canada, as you know, the longest open border in the world. We benefit from the stable and reliable and very valuable friendship that we have with the Canadian people. And I think it's accurate to say that the relationship that we have with the great Prime Minister of Canada, Pierre Trudeau, is accurately mirrored in this same context.

We've been successful in recent months in resolving some potentially very difficult issues concerning the exact border between our two countries and the open seas and also resolving fisheries agreements. These kinds of issues are ones that we discussed and resolved successfully as a matter of routine.

And I'm very grateful and honoured and pleased to have Prime Minister Trudeau come and visit us for this substantive discussion. I think it is an indication of our past excellent relationships and, I think, an accurate precursor or prediction that our relationships will be equally favourable in the future for both countries.

Pierre, we're glad to have you again in our home.

THE PRIME MINISTER: Thank you. Well, I feel fortunate to have been able to meet with President Carter at this time. Naturally, there will be a lot of disappointed Canadians in New York who were hoping to see the president and myself hearing these great Canadian and international artists. But from the point of view of the timing and the substance, I feel it fortunate that it worked out this way, because I am meeting President Carter at a very important time in the development of international relations in the midst of his meetings with the Prime Minister of Israel, following shortly after his meeting with the Vice Premier of China and on the eve, I hope, of the successful conclusion of SALT II, to which Canada and, I'm sure, all peace-loving peoples attach very, very great importance. And we're very supportive of the initiatives taken by the president and by Mr. Brezhnev in bringing the SALT II treaty, hopefully, close to a successful conclusion.

As the president said, apart from these international problems in which I was mainly the listener—and a willing listener—we did discuss a number of bilateral issues which are of great importance to both countries.

I feel that those discussions were well in the direction that we had set together a couple of years ago at our first meeting, in ensuring the political will of solving many of these issues. And we talked about the very ones which are coming now to a successful conclusion of the MTN negotiations, many of the environmental border issues, the fisheries dispute, which then seemed almost unsolvable and which we have solved in a successful way, at least on the east coast; and the fact that the areas which remain unsolved, particularly the border areas, have been referred or will be referred to arbitration as an indication of the confidence that exists between our two countries and administrations, that we trust each other enough to sort of say, "Well, if we can't agree, let's get a third party to agree for us." There's no browbeating and pushing around. It's a fair bargain between friends.

So, on all these issues, we have seen progress between our countries in the past few years.

I'm very grateful for the understanding of the Canadian points of view. We feel in some cases they got a better deal, but the president was telling me that he thought it was the contrary. So, it means both sides are pretty happy, I think, with the way in which we've settled the disputes in the MTN and the fisheries areas, in particular.

On energy, there is the major question of the Foothills Pipeline. And I was reassured that President Carter insisted that there was a desire on the part of the US government that it be proceeded with and that no one, certainly in his administration, had any doubts about that.

But there are a lot of secondary but important issues which have to be solved, having to do with our excess capacity in the east coast of refining capacity, having to do with what we do with the surplus of gas which was found in the West and Canada, the eventual disposition of the liquefied natural gas that we are planning for the Arctic, and so on.

And these issues do call for a much more direct and ongoing consultation between the two administrations. And I think the proposition was made to have an ongoing group of officials monitor it and report to us on a more frequent basis. It's a very good one, and I think in the short time ahead, it will prove of significant benefit to both our countries.

So, everything that I had hoped to talk about, including the Auto Pact, was covered in our talks. And I think it's fair to say that the lunch was pleasant, not only for the food but for the friendship between us and the results which were achieved, hopefully, to the benefit of our two countries.

And I'm very grateful to you, President Carter, for having received me at this very busy time.

Prime Minister Trudeau and President Carter at the White House, 3 March 1979. *Canadian Press photo by Peter Bregg.*

Meeting With Prime Minister Trudeau of Canada Joint Communiqué

Released by the White House and Prime Minister's Office
3 March 1979

Energy

During their discussion today over lunch at the White House, the prime minister and the president discussed the world energy situation and noted that increased energy self-reliance is a major objective of both their governments. They reaffirmed that enhanced bilateral cooperation in the field of energy will serve the interests of both countries. They also agreed that maximizing the supplies of domestic energy available to each country was a common and shared objective.

Recent international events have served to underline the vulnerability of the USA and Canada and other oil-consuming countries to oil supply and pricing disruptions. The president and the prime minister endorsed the coordinated undertaking of March 2 by the member countries of the International Energy Agency to reduce demand for oil on the world market on an urgent basis in response to the current global supply situation. The prime minister noted that Canada is raising its oil production and that production in the first quarter of 1979 will be some 13 percent above the previous year, a portion of it being used to offset domestic shortfalls resulting from the Iranian situation. The United States plans to take appropriate action to increase its oil production to offset the world supply shortfall.

The prime minister outlined to the president the progress already achieved in Canada toward construction of the Northern Gas Pipeline. The president affirmed his government's strong commitment to the completion of the line, which will bring Alaskan gas to the lower forty-eight states and eventually Mackenzie Delta gas to Canadian markets. He noted that he is sending a reorganization plan to the Congress no later than April 1, establishing the Office of the Federal Pipeline Inspector. He also stated his determination to ensure that the US regulatory process on all aspects of the Northern Gas Pipeline proceeds as quickly as possible.

The two leaders agreed to seek ways whereby any additional Canadian gas exports, should they be authorized, could facilitate timely construction of the entire Northern Gas Pipeline.

In order to enhance the already close and timely cooperation in other bilateral energy areas, the two leaders agreed to establish a consultative

mechanism at the sub-cabinet level which would function at least to the end of 1979. This consultative mechanism is charged with:
- ensuring that decision-making processes in each country on the matter of a delivery system to transport Alaskan crude oil to the northern tier and other inland states proceed in a parallel and timely manner;
- developing options for decision by each government on a number of operational issues in bilateral energy relations, including oil supplies and oil exchanges, strategic petroleum storage, the utilization of surplus Canadian refinery capacity, electricity exchanges, possibilities for liquefied and synthetic natural gas exports to the US, and other energy-related tasks as may be appropriate.

The president and the prime minister will designate promptly senior officials from their respective governments to serve on this consultative mechanism.

Multilateral Trade Negotiations

The prime minister and the president expressed satisfaction over progress achieved between them in the Multilateral Trade Negotiations. They agreed that timely completion of a balanced MTN agreement involving all the participants would make a notable contribution to reducing inflation and improving the prospects for sustained and balanced growth in the world economy.

Strategic Arms Limitation Talks

The president and the prime minister discussed prospects for the conclusion of a SALT II treaty with the Soviet Union and agreed that such a treaty would be a significant step forward in the important task of restraining the nuclear arms race and of developing a more stable basis for maintaining world peace and security. The president acknowledged the prime minister's contribution to the nuclear arms control debate and expressed his appreciation for Canada's support for the US pursuit of SALT II negotiations.

President Jimmy Carter on the Return of Six Americans From Iran

Telephone Discussion with Prime Minister Joe Clark of Canada

31 January 1980

PRESIDENT CARTER: Mr. Prime Minister, good morning to you. Where are you?

[The prime minister responds.]

Well, I know. I called as you know, we've had a series of communications back and forth privately, sometimes almost in verbal code, on the telephone and otherwise but I wanted to call, now that our six Americans are back in this country and safe, publicly and on behalf of all the American people, Joe, to thank you and Ambassador Taylor and the Canadian government and people for a tremendous exhibition of friendship and support and, I think, personal and political courage.

You've probably seen the outpouring of appreciation that has come from the American people of their own volition. And it's typical of the way we all feel. I might point out that the congressional parliamentarians tell me that the action taken by our Congress yesterday toward the Canadian government is the first time in the history of our nation that the Congress has ever expressed its thanks personally to another government for an act of friendship and heroism. And I just wanted to relay that historical note to you as well.

[The prime minister responds.]

Well, I thank you. I don't believe that the revelation of their departure will be damaging to the well being of our other hostages. You're nice and very perceptive to express that concern. I think it was a remarkable demonstration of mutual trust that the fact of the existence of those Americans was kept confidential so long, and the fact that it was not revealed publicly until after they'd already left is very good.

But Joe, good luck to you. And I hope that you'll not only send a copy of my letter to Ambassador Taylor but also publicly express to the people of Canada my deep appreciation, both to you, to Ambassador Taylor, to all of the embassy officials, and indeed to your whole country. We are deeply grateful for this, a new demonstration of the closeness that is very beneficial to us.

[The prime minister responds.]

Same to you, Joe. Have a good 1980. Goodbye.

PRESIDENT CARTER TO REPORTERS: Well, he's very nice. He expressed his hope that the revelation of their departure was not in any way going to endanger our own hostages still being held, and pointed out accurately that they've been very supportive of us from the very beginning of the Iranian crisis.

President Carter and Prime Minister Joe Clark sip saki with fellow G7 leaders at the 1979 Tokyo summit. *Canadian Press photo by Peter Bregg.*

Prime Minister Joe Clark to Reporters While on the Campaign Trail

1 February 1980

REPORTER: Mr. Clark, I wonder if you could tell us if President Carter made any reference to the release of the news [about the escape of the hostages] coming from a Canadian journalist in Washington, and the fear that many people have expressed, that the fact that this news has come out might in some way endanger the fifty hostages still being held in Tehran?

PRIME MINISTER CLARK: No, the president did not raise that matter, although I raised the matter directly. I told him that the only concern I had about the entire episode was that I would not want the release of the news at this time to jeopardize the safety or the security of the Americans still held hostage. He said that in his judgment the publication of the news at this time did not jeopardize the Americans who are still hostages and that there should be no undue concern about their situation being adversely affected by the fact that good journalists did their job and had the news out.[2]

Declassified US Intelligence Report

February 1980 (From the Jimmy Carter Library)
The Canadian Elections

SUMMARY: Canada's unexpected, unwanted, and unusual election campaign ends on 18 February. The outgoing Parliament, elected last May, has sat for a shorter period than any in Canadian history; the confidence vote that brought down Prime Minister Clark's government in December was almost an accident; and former prime minister Pierre Trudeau has had to return from retirement to lead the Liberal Party in the campaign.

As in May, campaign debate centres on the leadership qualities of Trudeau and Joe Clark. In the last election, the voters decided that they disliked Trudeau enough to take a chance on Clark, but in the interven-

---

2 Former Prime Minister Clark graciously allowed the editor access to his private papers, currently restricted to researchers, in Library and Archives Canada for the purpose of searching for any notes or Canadian records of his side of this historic telephone call from President Carter. While no private notes were discovered, this search, undertaken by the LAC's Maureen Hoogenraad, did locate a transcript of Prime Minister Clark's press conference of 1 February 1980, from which I have been able to give readers at least some detail of our prime minister's side of part of the conversation with President Carter. The editor would like to publicly acknowledge and thank Mr. Clark and Ms. Hoogenraad for their assistance.

ing months the electorate seems to have changed its mind. Polls taken two weeks before the election show the Liberals seventeen points ahead of Clark's Progressive Conservatives and well over three times as many people picking Trudeau over Clark as "the most competent leader." Even New Democratic Party leader Ed Broadbent came in ahead of Clark.

The crucial area for any party to win is Ontario. Even though polls indicate a swing to the Liberals in this province, the Conservatives have not given up. A large portion of the electorate is undecided, and Conservatives claims that the purported Liberal support is "soft." The Conservatives, however, probably do not have enough time to reverse the current trend.

In the wake of recent events in Iran and Afghanistan, both candidates have scrambled to demonstrate solidarity with the United States and NATO. Notwithstanding this unanimity of opinion on the international front, Trudeau can be expected to institute more nationalistic economic policies with respect to foreign investment and energy exports than would a Clark government.

The Tory Campaign

Less than seven months after its election last May, the Progressive Conservative minority government of Prime Minister Joe Clark lost a vote of confidence over its austerity budget. The upset came as a distinct surprise. Even on the afternoon of the vote, the Liberals were uncertain whether they wanted to defeat the government. Encouraged, however, by a growing lead in public opinion polls and by hints that some of Clark's supporters might abstain; the Liberals were unable to resist the opportunity.

Despite the defeat, the Tories insist in their campaign platform that Clark's tough austerity policies remain essential. Clark says he will, if re-elected, reintroduce the same budget, which sets a priority on attacking longstanding budget and current account deficits through higher energy taxes at a short-term cost of higher inflation and slower growth.

The Conservatives are sensitive to charges that they broke campaign promises, and they outline "139 promises" in twenty different areas which "have been honoured to date" by the Tory government. But the Tories' campaign slogan "real change deserves a fair chance"—implicitly acknowledges that they made little headway on major legislation before the government fell. They point out that work was under way on a broad range of subjects, including economic development, financial integrity, regional projects, improvement of federal relations with Quebec and other provinces, and freedom of information legislation.

Recent international developments, particularly in Iran and Afghanistan, have made foreign policy an issue in this election. Tories list the increased defence equipment budget, revised armed forces salaries, the reaffirmation of Canadian support for NATO among the major accomplishments of their six months in office. Clark can also point to Canada's higher profile on human rights.

But the major advantage foreign policy holds for Clark is that it gives him a forum for demonstrating his leadership abilities. He has held weekly press conferences devoted largely to announcements on decisive Canadian actions in response to the Soviet invasion of Afghanistan or in support of US initiatives on Iran. The Canadian rescue of American officials from Tehran was especially opportune, and Clark has been making the most of it.

Clark is still having image problems, however, and he knows it. He has so far been unable to dispel deep-seated public doubts about his ability to be an effective prime minister. Except in the prairie provinces and British Columbia, Trudeau is considered better able to handle problems such as inflation, unemployment, energy, and the national unity questions raised by Quebec's aspirations for increased independence. Even the rescue of Americans from Iran, much lauded and redounding to Clark's credit, has not done much to change this perception. Polls taken after the rescue show that voters who drifted away from the Liberals moved into the undecided, rather than the Tory, column.

The Liberal Campaign

The Liberal Party entered the campaign with no leader, no program, and no money. The party is still short of money, but it persuaded former prime minister Pierre Trudeau to withdraw his resignation as party leader, announced only the month before. Trudeau insists that this will be his last campaign but leaves open how far into his next term of office he would wait before calling a leadership convention.

Trudeau has changed his campaign style radically. He now reads set speeches, holds press conferences only rarely, and refuses to debate other party leaders on television. Party strategists are aware that the dislike of Trudeau built up over his eleven years as prime minister was a major reason for the Liberal loss last May. Their aim is to keep Trudeau from making blunders, which could cut into the twenty-point lead the Liberals had in the polls in December. No party, however, has ever lost a Canadian election if it started the campaign more than five or six points ahead.

The Liberal program, introduced at midcampaign, promised:

- Greater oil self-sufficiency, but at a lower price to the consumer than proposed by the Tories.
- A reduction of foreign ownership and control of Canadian petroleum assets to 50 percent by 1990.
- Rigorous control of government spending to keep its growth below the growth of the gross national product.
- Job creation through aid to industry.
- Greater regional economic strength.
- More financial assistance to individuals below the poverty line.

The program avoids the problem of Quebec separatism. Despite Trudeau's strong opposition to the independence movement, he refused to comment on Quebec Liberal leader Claude Ryan's January proposals for changing the Canadian federation, calling it a "provincial issue." This stems partly from a desire not to undercut Ryan's chances of defeating the separatist Parti Quebecois in the province but even more from the realization that this is a relatively unimportant subject—although an irritating one—to voters outside Quebec.

The program is incidental to the campaign, however, and, except for the oil pricing scheme, is not new. The Liberals' campaign revolves mainly around leadership, and they hammer away at Clark, depicting him as an inept fumbler who reverses himself on issues, breaks campaign promises, and bungles the conduct of foreign affairs. Trudeau, on the other hand, is portrayed as a strong, dynamic leader who knows what to do and how to do it and who is, in addition, highly regarded in the international arena.

A secondary, but telling, Liberal theme is that Clark's plan to raise oil and gasoline prices is unnecessarily drastic. Such a pocketbook issue weighs heavily in Ontario.

Minor Parties

Two other parties will also elect deputies to parliament—the Social Credit Party led by Fabien Roy and the New Democratic Party led by Ed Broadbent. The Socreds are a tiny Quebec-based party. It elected only six deputies last May and is likely to do even worse this time around. Its principal importance came from the winning margin it provided Clark in confidence votes—until the last one.

The New Democrats are potentially important as the balance of support should the Liberals win with less than a full majority. The New Democrats elected twenty-seven deputies from across Canada to the last Parliament, and they hope for more this time. Broadbent is well respected—he was named by 20 percent of respondents in a January poll as the man who would "make the best prime minister for Canada," a better score than Clark received. The NDP platform is both socialist and nationalist; it repeats the party's longstanding opposition to NATO, nuclear proliferation, and trade with South Africa, while supporting Third World economic aspirations.

The New Democrats' chances for significant gains are diminished by the electorate's desire for a stable, majority government. After a period of minority rule, such as Canada has experienced under Clark, the vote generally swings back to the major parties.

Implications for the United States

Outlook and voter sentiment does not seem to have shifted greatly since last May.

The western provinces overwhelmingly support the Tories; Quebec over-whelmingly supports the Liberals—so much so that it skews national poll results—and the Atlantic provinces are split. But in Ontario—the province that controls national elections—a shift is likely. In Parliament, 95 of the 282 seats are elected from Ontario, and the Conservatives won their plurality last May on the basis of results in that province. Polling midway through the present campaign indicates a swing back to the Liberals, but there is an unusually high number of undecided voters. Factors such as a marked anti-Trudeau bias in the press, the return of Ontario Premier Davis from vacation to campaign for Clark, and the public euphoria over Canada's role in rescuing American diplomats in Iran could still hurt the Liberals in the province.

Should Joe Clark win reelection, he will continue his present policies with a strongly pro-US, pro-NATO stance. For example, Canada will maintain support for US initiatives related to Iran and Afghanistan, such as a boycott of the Olympic games in Moscow.

In the likelier event of a Liberal victory, Trudeau will also support US initiatives in Iran and Afghanistan. He has even attacked Clark for not doing enough in support of the United States. He, too, advocates an Olympic boycott as long as other Western allies go along. Trudeau's support for Western solidarity reflects his desire to be identified with an issue with strong popular support in Canada.

Trudeau would differ from Clark mainly on economic policy—he would definitely be a more difficult bargaining partner for the United States. Trudeau demands that at least 50 percent of the country's petroleum industry assets—now about 75 percent are controlled by foreign multinationals—be under Canadian control by the end of the decade. He has also scored the agreement to sell the United States additional natural gas at a time when winter fuel shortages were possible in Canada. He claimed he would not have done so without guarantees that the Alaska pipeline would be built and "without fully exploring the possibility of future replacement of exports with Alaska gas."

If Trudeau is elected with a minority government, he would most likely try to obtain support from the leftish NDP as he did from 1972 to 1974. In such a case, nationalist economic policies would probably be even more in evidence. The New Democrats' platform calls for limits on foreign economic control, an industrial strategy based on the development of Canadian resources by Canadians, the cancellation of the gas export deal approved by the Tories, and the creation of a publicly owned bank that would purchase supplies of natural gas in the ground and leave it there for future domestic use. The party would also like to renegotiate the 1965 pact that regulates trade between the United States and Canada in automobiles and automobile parts.

Our Nation's Past and Future:

Address Accepting the Presidential Nomination at the Democratic National Convention in New York City

15 July 1976

My name is Jimmy Carter, and I'm running for president.

It's been a long time since I said those words the first time, and now I've come here after seeing our great country to accept your nomination.

I accept it, in the words of John F. Kennedy, with a full and grateful heart and with only one obligation: to devote every effort of body, mind and spirit to lead our party back to victory and our nation back to greatness.

It's a pleasure to be here with all you Democrats and to see that our Bicentennial celebration and our Bicentennial convention has been one of decorum and order without any fights or free-for-alls. Among Democrats that can only happen once every two hundred years. With this kind of a united Democratic Party, we are ready, and eager, to take on the Republicans—whichever Republican Party they decide to send against us in November.

Nineteen seventy-six will not be a year of politics as usual. It can be a year of inspiration and hope, and it will be a year of concern, of quiet and sober reassessment of our nation's character and purpose. It has already been a year when voters have confounded the experts. And I guarantee you that it will be the year when we give the government of this country back to the people of this country.

There is a new mood in America. We have been shaken by a tragic war abroad and by scandals and broken promises at home. Our people are searching for new voices and new ideas and new leaders.

Although government has its limits and cannot solve all our problems, we Americans reject the view that we must be reconciled to failures and mediocrity, or to an inferior quality of life. For I believe that we can come through this time of trouble stronger than ever. Like troops who have been in combat, we have been tempered in the fire; we have been disciplined, and we have been educated.

Guided by lasting and simple moral values, we have emerged idealists without illusions, realists who still know the old dreams of justice and liberty, of country and of community.

This year we have had thirty state primaries—more than ever before—making it possible to take our campaign directly to the people of America:

Main Street, Plains, September 2008. *Photo by Frances O'Malley.*

The Carter election headquarters, Plains, Georgia. *Photo by Peter O'Malley.*

to homes and shopping centres, to factory shift lines and colleges, to beauty parlors and barbershops, to farmers markets and union halls.

This has been a long and personal campaign—a humbling experience, reminding us that ultimate political influence rests not with the power brokers but with the people. This has been a time of tough debate on the important issues facing our country. This kind of debate is part of our tradition, and as Democrats we are heirs to a great tradition.

I have never met a Democratic president, but I have always been a Democrat.

Years ago, as a farm boy sitting outdoors with my family on the ground in the middle of the night, gathered close around a battery radio connected to the automobile battery and listening to the Democratic conventions in far-off cities, I was a long way from the selection process. I feel much closer to it tonight.

Ours is the party of the man who was nominated by those distant conventions and who inspired and restored this nation in its darkest hours—Franklin D. Roosevelt.

Ours is the party of a fighting Democrat who showed us that a common man could be an uncommon leader—Harry S. Truman.

Ours is the party of a brave young president who called the young at heart, regardless of age, to seek a "New Frontier" of national greatness—John F. Kennedy.

And ours is also the party of a great-hearted Texan who took office in a tragic hour and who went on to do more than any other president in this century to advance the cause of human rights—Lyndon Johnson.

Our party was built out of the sweatshops of the old Lower East Side, the dark mills of New Hampshire, the blazing hearths of Illinois, the coal mines of Pennsylvania, the hard-scrabble farms of the southern coastal plains, and the unlimited frontiers of America.

Ours is the party that welcomed generations of immigrants—the Jews, the Irish, the Italians, the Poles, and all the others, enlisted them in its ranks and fought the political battles that helped bring them into the American mainstream.

And they have shaped the character of our party.

That is our heritage. Our party has not been perfect. We have made mistakes, and we have paid for them. But ours is a tradition of leadership and compassion and progress.

Our leaders have fought for every piece of progressive legislation, from RFD and REA to Social Security and civil rights. In times of need, the Democrats were there.

But in recent years our nation has seen a failure of leadership. We have been hurt, and we have been disillusioned. We have seen a wall go up that separates us from our own government.

We have lost some precious things that historically have bound our people and our government together. We feel that moral decay has weakened our country, that it is crippled by a lack of goals and values, and that our public officials have lost faith in us.

We have been a nation adrift too long. We have been without leadership too long. We have had divided and deadlocked government too long. We have been governed by veto too long. We have suffered enough at the hands of a tired and worn-out administration without new ideas, without youth or vitality, without vision and without the confidence of the American people. There is a fear that our best years are behind us. But I say to you that our nation's best is still ahead.

Our country has lived through a time of torment. It is now a time for healing. We want to have faith again. We want to be proud again. We just want the truth again.

It is time for the people to run the government, and not the other way around.

It is the time to honour and strengthen our families and our neighbourhoods and our diverse cultures and customs.

We need a Democratic president and a Congress to work in harmony for a change, with mutual respect for a change. And next year we are going to have that new leadership. You can depend on it!

It is time for America to move and to speak not with boasting and belligerence but with a quiet strength, to depend in world affairs not merely on the size of an arsenal but on the nobility of ideas, and to govern at home not by confusion and crisis but with grace and imagination and common sense.

Too many have had to suffer at the hands of a political economic elite who have shaped decisions and never had to account for mistakes or to suffer from injustice. When unemployment prevails, they never stand in line looking for a job.

When deprivation results from a confused and bewildering welfare system, they never do without food or clothing or a place to sleep. When the public schools are inferior or torn by strife, their children go to exclusive private schools. And when the bureaucracy is bloated and confused, the powerful always manage to discover and occupy niches of special influence and privilege. An unfair tax structure serves their needs. And tight secrecy always seems to prevent reform.

All of us must be careful not to cheat each other. Too often unholy, self-perpetuating alliances have been formed between money and politics, and the average citizen has been held at arm's length.

Each time our nation has made a serious mistake the American people have been excluded from the process. The tragedy of Vietnam and Cambodia, the disgrace of Watergate, and the embarrassment of the CIA revelations could have been avoided if our government had simply reflected the sound judgment and good common sense and the high moral character of the American people.

It is time for us to take a new look at our own government, to strip away the secrecy, to expose the unwarranted pressure of lobbyists, to eliminate waste, to release our civil servants from bureaucratic chaos, to provide tough management, and always to remember that in any town or city the mayor, the governor, and the president represent exactly the same constituents.

As a governor, I had to deal each day with the complicated and confused and overlapping and wasteful federal government bureaucracy. As president, I want you to help me evolve an efficient, economical, purposeful, and manageable government for our nation. Now, I recognize the difficulty, but if I'm elected, it's going to be done. And you can depend on it!

We must strengthen the government closest to the people. Business, labour, agriculture, education, science, and government should not struggle in isolation from one another but should be able to strive toward mutual goals and shared opportunities. We should make major investments in people and not in buildings and weapons. The poor, the aged, the weak, the afflicted must be treated with respect and compassion and with love.

I have spoken a lot of times this year about love. But love must be aggressively translated into simple justice. The test of any government is not how popular it is with the powerful but how honestly and fairly it deals with those who must depend on it.

It is time for a complete overhaul of our income tax system. I still tell you: It is a disgrace to the human race. All my life I have heard promises about tax reform, but it never quite happens. With your help, we are finally going to make it happen. And you can depend on it.

Here is something that can really help our country: It is time for universal voter registration.

It is time for a nationwide comprehensive health program for all our people.

It is time to guarantee an end to discrimination because of race or sex by full involvement in the decision-making process of government by those who know what it is to suffer from discrimination. And they'll be in the government if I am elected.

It is time for the law to be enforced. We cannot educate children, we cannot create harmony among our people, we cannot preserve basic human freedom unless we have an orderly society.

Crime and lack of justice are especially cruel to those who are least able to protect themselves. Swift arrest and trial, fair and uniform punishment, should be expected by anyone who would break our laws.

It is time for our government leaders to respect the law no less than the humblest citizen, so that we can end once and for all a double standard of justice.

I see no reason why big-shot crooks should go free and the poor ones go to jail.

A simple and a proper function of government is just to make it easy for us to do good and difficult for us to do wrong.

As an engineer, a planner, a businessman, I see clearly the value to our nation of a strong system of free enterprise based on increase productivity and adequate wages. We Democrats believe that competition is better than regulation, and we intend to combine strong safeguards for consumers with minimal intrusion of government in our free economic system.

I believe that anyone who is able to work ought to work—and ought to have a chance to work. We will never have an end to the inflationary spiral, we will never have a balanced budget—which I am determined to see—as long as we have eight or nine million Americans out of work who cannot find a job. Any system of economics is bankrupt if it sees either value or virtue in unemployment. We simply cannot check inflation by keeping people out of work.

The foremost responsibility of any president, above all else, is to guarantee the security of our nation—a guarantee of freedom from the threat of successful attack or blackmail, and the ability with our allies to maintain peace.

But peace is not the mere absence of war. Peace is action to stamp out international terrorism. Peace is the unceasing effort to preserve human rights.

Peace is a combined demonstration of strength and good will. We will pray for peace and we will work for peace, until we have removed from all nations for all time the threat of nuclear destruction.

America's birth opened a new chapter in mankind's history. Ours was the first nation to dedicate itself clearly to basic moral and philosophical principles: that all people are created equal and endowed with inalienable rights to life, liberty, and the pursuit of happiness, and that the power of government is derived from the consent of the governed.

This national commitment was a singular act of wisdom and courage, and it brought the best and the bravest from other nations to our shores. It was a revolutionary development that captured the imagination of mankind. It created a basis for a unique role of America—that of a pioneer in shaping more decent and just relations among people and among societies.

Today, two hundred years later, we must address ourselves to that role, both in what we do at home and how we act abroad among people everywhere who have become politically more alert, socially more congested, and increasingly impatient with global inequities, and who are now organized, as you know, into some one hundred and fifty different nations. This calls for nothing less than a sustained architectural effort to shape an international framework of peace within which our own ideals gradually can become a global reality.

Our nation should always derive its character directly from the people and let this be the strength and the image to be presented to the world—the character of the American people.

To our friends and allies I say that what unites us through our common dedication to democracy is much more important than that which occasionally divides us on economics or politics. To the nations that seek to lift themselves from poverty I say that America shares your aspirations and extends its hand to you. To those nation-states that wish to compete with us I say that we neither fear competition nor see it as an obstacle to wider cooperation. To all people I say that after two hundred years America still remains confident and youthful in its commitment to freedom and equality, and we always will be.

During this election year we candidates will ask you for your votes, and from us will be demanded our vision.

My vision of this nation and its future has been deepened and matured during the nineteen months that I have campaigned among you for president. I have never had more faith in America than I do today. We have an America that, in Bob Dylan's phrase, is busy being born, not busy dying.

We can have an America that has reconciled its economic needs with its desire for an environment that we can pass on with pride to the next generation.

We can have an America that provides excellence in education to my child and your child and every child.

We can have an America that encourages and takes pride in our ethnic diversity, our religious diversity, our cultural diversity—knowing that out of this pluralistic heritage has come the strength and the vitality and the creativity that has made us great and will keep us great.

We can have an American government that does not oppress or spy on its own people but respects our dignity and our privacy and our right to be let alone.

We can have an America where freedom, on the one hand, and equality, on the other hand, are mutually supportive and not in conflict, and where the dreams of our nation's first leaders are fully realized in our own day and age.

And we can have an America which harnesses the idealism of the student, the compassion of a nurse or the social worker, the determination of a farmer, the wisdom of a teacher, the practicality of the business leader, the experience of the senior citizen, and the hope of a labourer to build a better life for us all. And we can have it, and we're going to have it!

As I've said many times before, we can have an American president who does not govern with negativism and fear of the future, but with vigour and vision and aggressive leadership—a president who's not isolated from the people, but who feels your pain and shares your dreams and takes his strength and his wisdom and his courage from you.

I see an America on the move again, united, a diverse and vital and tolerant nation, entering our third century with pride and confidence, an America that lives up to the majesty of our Constitution and the simple decency of our people.

This is the America we want. This is the America that we will have.

We will go forward from this convention with some differences of opinion perhaps, but nevertheless united in a calm determination to make our country large and driving and generous in spirit once again, ready to embark on great national deeds. And once again, as brothers and sisters, our hearts will swell with pride to call ourselves Americans.

Inaugural Address

Washington, D.C., 20 January 1977

For myself and for our nation, I want to thank my predecessor (Gerald R. Ford) for all he has done to heal our land.

In this outward and physical ceremony, we attest once again to the inner and spiritual strength of our Nation. As my high school teacher, Miss Julia Coleman, used to say, "We must adjust to changing times and still hold to unchanging principles."

Here before me is the Bible used in the inauguration of our first president in 1789, and I have just taken the oath of office on the Bible my mother gave me just a few years ago, opened to a timeless admonition from the ancient prophet Micah: "He hath showed thee, O man, what is good; and what doth the Lord require of thee, but to do justly, and to love mercy, and to walk humbly with thy God."

This inauguration ceremony marks a new beginning, a new dedication within our government, and a new spirit among us all. A president may sense and proclaim that new spirit, but only a people can provide it.

Two centuries ago, our nation's birth was a milestone in the long quest for freedom. But the bold and brilliant dream which excited the founders of this nation still awaits its consummation. I have no new dream to set forth today, but rather urge a fresh faith in the old dream.

Ours was the first society openly to define itself in terms of both spirituality and human liberty. It is that unique self-definition which has given us an exceptional appeal, but it also imposes on us a special obligation to take on those moral duties which, when assumed, seem invariably to be in our own best interests.

You have given me a great responsibility—to stay close to you, to be worthy of you, and to exemplify what you are. Let us create together a new national spirit of unity and trust. Your strength can compensate for my weakness, and your wisdom can help to minimize my mistakes.

Let us learn together and laugh together and work together and pray together, confident that in the end we will triumph together in the right.

The American dream endures. We must once again have full faith in our country—and in one another. I believe America can be better. We can be even stronger than before.

Let our recent mistakes bring a resurgent commitment to the basic principles of our nation, for we know that if we despise our own government, we have no future. We recall in special times when we have stood briefly, but magnificently, united. In those times no prize was beyond our grasp.

But we cannot dwell upon remembered glory. We cannot afford to drift. We reject the prospect of failure or mediocrity or an inferior quality of life for any person. Our government must at the same time be both competent and compassionate.

We have already found a high degree of personal liberty, and we are now struggling to enhance equality of opportunity. Our commitment to human rights must be absolute, our laws fair, our national beauty preserved; the powerful must not persecute the weak, and human dignity must be enhanced.

We have learned that more is not necessarily better, that even our great nation has its recognized limits, and that we can neither answer all questions nor solve all problems. We cannot afford to do everything, nor can we afford to lack boldness as we meet the future. So, together, in a spirit of individual sacrifice for the common good, we must simply do our best.

Our nation can be strong abroad only if it is strong at home. And we know that the best way to enhance freedom in other lands is to demonstrate here that our democratic system is worthy of emulation.

To be true to ourselves, we must be true to others. We will not behave in foreign places so as to violate our rules and standards here at home, for we know that the trust which our nation earns is essential to our strength.

The world itself is now dominated by a new spirit. Peoples more numerous and more politically aware are craving, and now demanding, their place in the sun—not just for the benefit of their own physical condition, but for basic human rights.

The passion for freedom is on the rise. Tapping this new spirit, there can be no nobler nor more ambitious task for America to undertake on this day of a new beginning than to help shape a just and peaceful world that is truly humane.

We are a strong nation, and we will maintain strength so sufficient that it need not be proven in combat—a quiet strength based not merely on the size of an arsenal but on the nobility of ideas.

We will be ever vigilant and never vulnerable, and we will fight our wars against poverty, ignorance, and injustice, for those are the enemies against which our forces can be honourably marshalled.

We are a proudly idealistic nation, but let no one confuse our idealism with weakness.

Because we are free, we can never be indifferent to the fate of freedom elsewhere. Our moral sense dictates a clear-cut preference for those societies which share with us an abiding respect for individual human rights. We do not seek to intimidate, but it is clear that a world which others can dominate with impunity would be inhospitable to decency and a threat to the well-being of all people.

The world is still engaged in a massive armaments race designed to ensure continuing equivalent strength among potential adversaries. We pledge perseverance and wisdom in our efforts to limit the world's armaments to those necessary for each nation's own domestic safety. And we will move this year a step toward our ultimate goal—the elimination of all nuclear weapons from this earth. We urge all other people to join us, for success can mean life instead of death.

Within us, the people of the United States, there is evident a serious and purposeful rekindling of confidence. And I join in the hope that when my time as your president has ended, people might say this about our nation:

—that we had remembered the words of Micah and renewed our search for humility, mercy, and justice;

—that we had torn down the barriers that separated those of different race and region and religion, and where there had been mistrust, built unity, with a respect for diversity;

—that we had found productive work for those able to perform it;

—that we had strengthened the American family, which is the basis of our society;

—that we had ensured respect for the law and equal treatment under the law, for the weak and the powerful, for the rich and the poor; and

—that we had enabled our people to be proud of their own government once again.

I would hope that the nations of the world might say that we had built a lasting peace, based not on weapons of war but on international policies which reflect our own most precious values.

These are not just my goals—and they will not be my accomplishments—but the affirmation of our nation's continuing moral strength and our belief in an undiminished, ever-expanding American dream.

Thank you very much.

United Nations Address Before the General Assembly

17 March 1977

Last night I was in Clinton, Massachusetts, at a Town Hall meeting where people of that small town decide their political and economic future.

Tonight I speak to a similar meeting where people representing nations all over the world come here to decide their political and economic future.

I am proud to be with you tonight in this house where the shared hopes of the world can find a voice. I have come here to express my own support and the continuing support of my country for the ideals of the United Nations.

We are proud that for the thirty-two years since its creation, the United Nations has met on American soil. And we share with you the commitments of freedom, self-government, human dignity, mutual toleration, and the peaceful resolution of disputes—which the founding principles of the United Nations and also Secretary General Kurt Waldheim so well represent.

No one nation by itself can build a world which reflects all these fine values. But the United States, my own country, has a reservoir of strength—economic strength, which we are willing to share; military strength, which we hope never to use again; and the strength of ideals, which are determined fully to maintain the backbone of our own foreign policy.

It is now eight weeks since I became president. I have brought to office a firm commitment to a more open foreign policy. And I believe that the American people expect me to speak frankly about the policies that we intend to pursue, and it is in that spirit that I speak to you tonight about our own hopes for the future.

I see a hopeful world, a world dominated by increasing demands for basic freedoms, for fundamental rights, for higher standards of human existence. We are eager to take part in the shaping of that world.

But in seeking such a better world, we are not blind to the reality of disagreement, nor to the persisting dangers that confront us all. Every headline reminds us of bitter divisions, of national hostilities, of territorial conflicts, of ideological competition.

In the Middle East, peace is a quarter of a century overdue. A gathering racial conflict threatens southern Africa; new tensions are rising in the Horn of Africa. Disputes in the eastern Mediterranean remain to be resolved.

Perhaps even more ominous is the staggering arms race. The Soviet Union and the United States have accumulated thousands of nuclear weapons. Our two nations now have five times more missile warheads today than we had just eight years ago. But we are not five times more secure. On the contrary, the arms race has only increased the risk of conflict.

We can only improve this world if we are realistic about its complexities. The disagreements that we face are deeply rooted, and they often raise difficult philosophical as well as territorial issues. They will not be solved easily. They will not be solved quickly. The arms race is now embedded in the very fabric of international affairs and can only be contained with the greatest difficulty. Poverty and inequality are of such monumental scope that it will take decades of deliberate and determined effort even to improve the situation substantially.

I stress these dangers and these difficulties because I want all of us to dedicate ourselves to a prolonged and persistent effort designed first to maintain peace and to reduce the arms race; second, to build a better and a more cooperative international economic system; and third, to work with potential adversaries as well as our close friends to advance the cause of human rights.

In seeking these goals, I realize that the United States cannot solve the problems of the world. We can sometimes help others resolve their differences, but we cannot do so by imposing our own particular solutions.

In the coming months, there is important work for all of us in advancing international cooperation and economic progress in the cause of peace.

Later this spring, the leaders of several industrial nations of Europe, North America, and Japan will confer at a summit meeting in London on a broad range of issues. We must promote the health of the industrial economies. We must seek to restrain inflation and bring ways of managing our own domestic economies for the benefit of the global economy.

We must move forward with multilateral trade negotiations in Geneva.

The United States will support the efforts of our friends to strengthen the democratic institutions in Europe, and particularly in Portugal and Spain.

We will work closely with our European friends on the forthcoming Review Conference on Security and Cooperation in Europe. We want to make certain that the provisions of the Helsinki agreement are fully implemented and that progress is made to further East-West cooperation.

In the Middle East we are doing our best to clarify areas of disagreement, to surface underlying consensus, and to help to develop mutually acceptable principles that can form a flexible framework for a just and a permanent settlement.

In southern Africa, we will work to help attain majority rule through peaceful means. We believe that such fundamental transformation can be achieved, to the advantage of both the blacks and whites who live in that region of the world. Anything less than that may bring a protracted racial war, with devastating consequences to all.

This week the government of the United States took action to bring our country into full compliance with United Nations sanctions against the illegal regime in Rhodesia. And I will sign that bill Friday in Washington.

We will put our relations with Latin America on a more constructive footing, recognizing the global character of the region's problems.

We are also working to resolve in amicable negotiations the future of the Panama Canal.

We will continue our efforts to develop further our relationships with the People's Republic of China. We recognize our parallel strategic interests in maintaining stability in Asia, and we will act in the spirit of the Shanghai Communiqué.

In Southeast Asia and in the Pacific, we will strengthen our association with our traditional friends, and we will seek to improve relations with our former adversaries.

We have a mission now in Vietnam seeking peaceful resolution of the differences that have separated us for so long.

Throughout the world, we are ready to normalize our relationships and to seek reconciliation with all states which are ready to work with us in promoting global progress and global peace.

Above all, the search for peace requires a much more deliberate effort to contain the global arms race. Let me speak in this context, first, of the US–Soviet Union relationship, and then of the wider need to contain the proliferation of arms throughout the global community.

I intend to pursue the strategic arms limitation talks between the United States and the Soviet Union with determination and with energy. Our Secretary of State will visit Moscow in just a few days.

SALT is extraordinarily complicated. But the basic fact is that while negotiations remain deadlocked, the arms race goes on; the security of both countries and the entire world is threatened.

My preference would be for strict controls or even a freeze on new types and new generations of weaponry and with a deep reduction in the strategic arms of both sides. Such a major step towards not only arms limitation, but arms reduction would be welcomed by mankind as a giant step towards peace.

Alternatively, and perhaps much more easily, we could conclude a limited agreement based on those elements of the Vladivostok accord on which we can find complete consensus, and set aside for prompt consideration and subsequent negotiations the more contentious issues and also the deeper reductions in nuclear weapons which I favour.

We will also explore the possibility of a total cessation of nuclear testing. While our ultimate goal is for all nuclear powers to end testing, we do not regard this as a prerequisite for the suspension of tests by the two principal nuclear powers, the Soviet Union and the United States.

We should, however, also pursue a broad, permanent multilateral agreement on this issue.

We will also seek to establish Soviet willingness to reach agreement with us on mutual military restraint in the Indian Ocean, as well as on such matters as arms exports to the troubled areas of the world.

In proposing such accommodations I remain fully aware that American-Soviet relations will continue to be highly competitive—but I believe that our competition must be balanced by cooperation in preserving peace, and thus our mutual survival.

I will seek such cooperation with the Soviet Union—earnestly, constantly, and sincerely.

However, the effort to contain the arms race is not a matter just for the United States and Soviet Union alone. There must be a wider effort to reduce the flow of weapons to all the troubled spots of this globe.

Accordingly, we will try to reach broader agreements among producer and consumer nations to limit the export of conventional arms, and we, ourselves, will take the initiative on our own because the United States has become one of the major arms suppliers of the world.

We are deeply committed to halting the proliferation of nuclear weapons. And we will undertake a new effort to reach multilateral agreements designed to provide legitimate supplies of nuclear fuels for the production of energy, while controlling the poisonous and dangerous atomic wastes.

Working with other nations represented here, we hope to advance the cause of peace. We will make a strong and a positive contribution at the upcoming Special Session on Disarmament which I understand will commence next year.

But the search for peace also means the search for justice. One of the greatest challenges before us as a nation, and therefore one of our greatest opportunities, is to participate in moulding a global economic system which will bring greater prosperity to all the people of all countries.

I come from a part of the United States which is largely agrarian and which for many years did not have the advantages of adequate transportation or capital or management skills or education which were available in the industrial states of our country.

So, I can sympathize with the leaders of the developing nations, and I want them to know that we will do our part.

To this end, the United States will be advancing proposals aimed at meeting the basic human needs of the developing world and helping them to increase their productive capacity. I have asked Congress to provide $7.5 billion of foreign assistance in the coming year, and I will work to ensure sustained American assistance as the process of global economic development continues. I am also urging the Congress of our country to increase our contributions to the United Nations Development Program and meet in full our pledges to multilateral lending institutions, especially the International Development Association of the World Bank.

We remain committed to an open international trading system, one which does not ignore domestic concerns in the United States. We have extended duty-free treatment to many products from the developing countries. In the multilateral trade agreements in Geneva we have offered substantial trade concessions on the goods of primary interest to developing countries. And in accordance with the Tokyo Declaration, we are also examining ways to provide additional consideration for the special needs of developing countries.

The United States is willing to consider, with a positive and open attitude, the negotiation on agreements to stabilize commodity prices, including the establishment of a common funding arrangement for financing buffer stocks where they are a part of individual negotiated agreements.

I also believe that the developing countries must acquire fuller participation in the global economic decision-making process. Some progress has already been made in this regard by expanding participation of developing countries in the International Monetary Fund.

We must use our collective natural resources wisely and constructively. We've not always done so. Today our oceans are being plundered and defiled. With a renewed spirit of cooperation and hope, we join in the Conference of the Law of the Sea in order to correct past mistakes of generations gone by and to ensure that all nations can share the bounties of the eternal oceans in the future.

We must also recognize that the world is facing serious shortages of energy. This is truly a global problem. For our part, we are determined to reduce waste and to work with others toward a fair and proper sharing of the benefits and costs of energy resources.

The search for peace and justice also means respect for human dignity. All the signatories of the UN Charter have pledged themselves to observe and to respect basic human rights. Thus, no member of the United Nations can claim that mistreatment of its citizens is solely its own business. Equally, no member can avoid its responsibilities to review and to speak when torture or unwarranted deprivation occurs in any part of the world.

The basic thrust of human affairs points toward a more universal demand for fundamental human rights. The United States has a historical birthright to be associated with this process.

We in the United States accept this responsibility in the fullest and the most constructive sense. Ours is a commitment, and not just a political posture. I know perhaps as well as anyone that our own ideals in the area of human rights have not always been attained in the United States, but the American people have an abiding commitment to the full realization of these ideals. And we are determined, therefore, to deal with our deficiencies quickly and openly. We have nothing to conceal.

To demonstrate this commitment, I will seek congressional approval and sign the UN covenants on economic, social, and cultural rights, and the covenants on civil and political rights. And I will work closely with our own Congress in seeking to support the ratification not only of these two instruments but the United Nations Genocide Convention and the Treaty for the Elimination of All Forms of Racial Discrimination, as well. I have just removed all restrictions on American travel abroad, and we are moving now to liberalize almost completely travel opportunities to America.

The United Nations is a global forum dedicated to the peace and well-being of every individual—no matter how weak, no matter how poor. But we have allowed its human rights machinery to be ignored and sometimes politicized. There is much that can be done to strengthen it.

The Human Rights Commission should be prepared to meet more often. And all nations should be prepared to offer its fullest cooperation to the Human Rights Commission, to welcome its investigations, to work with its officials, and to act on its reports.

I would like to see the entire United Nations Human Rights Division moved back here to the central headquarters, where its activities will be in the forefront of our attention and where the attention of the press corps can stimulate us to deal honestly with this sensitive issue. The proposal made twelve years ago by the Government of Costa Rica, to establish a

United Nations High Commission[er] for Human Rights, also deserves our renewed attention and our support.

Strengthened international machinery will help us to close the gap between promise and performance in protecting human rights. When gross or widespread violation takes place—contrary to international commitments—it is of concern to all. The solemn commitments of the United Nations Charter, of the United Nations Universal Declaration for Human Rights, of the Helsinki Accords, and of many other international instruments must be taken just as seriously as commercial or security agreements.

This issue is important in itself. It should not block progress on other important matters affecting the security and well-being of our people and of world peace. It is obvious that the reduction of tension, the control of nuclear arms, the achievement of harmony in the troubled areas of the world, and the provision of food, good health, and education will independently contribute to advancing the human condition.

In our relationships with other countries, these mutual concerns will be reflected in our political, our cultural, and our economic attitudes.

These, then, are our basic priorities as we work with other members to strengthen and to improve the United Nations.

First, we will strive for peace in the troubled areas of the world; second, we will aggressively seek to control the weaponry of war; third, we will promote a new system of international economic progress and cooperation; and fourth, we will be steadfast in our dedication to the dignity and well-being of people throughout the world.

I believe that this is a foreign policy that is consistent with my own nation's historic values and commitments. And I believe that it is a foreign policy that is consonant with the ideals of the United Nations.

University of Notre Dame
Address at Commencement Exercises at the University

22 May 1977

I want to speak to you today about the strands that connect our actions overseas with our essential character as a nation. I believe we can have a foreign policy that is democratic, that is based on fundamental values, and that uses power and influence, which we have, for humane purposes. We can also have a foreign policy that the American people both support and, for a change, know about and understand.

I have a quiet confidence in our own political system. Because we know that democracy works, we can reject the arguments of those rulers who deny human rights to their people.

We are confident that democracy's example will be compelling, and so we seek to bring that example closer to those from whom in the past few years we have been separated and who are not yet convinced about the advantages of our kind of life.

We are confident that the democratic methods are the most effective, and so we are not tempted to employ improper tactics here at home or abroad.

We are confident of our own strength, so we can seek substantial mutual reductions in the nuclear arms race.

And we are confident of the good sense of American people, and so we let them share in the process of making foreign policy decisions. We can thus speak with the voices of 215 million, and not just of an isolated handful.

Democracy's great recent successes—in India, Portugal, Spain, Greece—show that our confidence in this system is not misplaced. Being confident of our own future, we are now free of that inordinate fear of communism which once led us to embrace any dictator who joined us in that fear. I'm glad that that's being changed.

For too many years, we've been willing to adopt the flawed and erroneous principles and tactics of our adversaries, sometimes abandoning our own values for theirs. We've fought fire with fire, never thinking that fire is better quenched with water. This approach failed, with Vietnam the best example of its intellectual and moral poverty. But through failure we have now found our way back to our own principles and values, and we have regained our lost confidence.

By the measure of history, our nation's two hundred years are very brief, and our rise to world eminence is briefer still. It dates from 1945, when Europe and the old international order lay in ruins. Before then, America was largely on the periphery of world affairs. But since then, we have inescapably been at the centre of world affairs.

Our policy during this period was guided by two principles: a belief that Soviet expansion was almost inevitable but that it must be contained, and the corresponding belief in the importance of an almost exclusive alliance among non-Communist nations on both sides of the Atlantic. That system could not last forever unchanged. Historical trends have weakened its foundation. The unifying threat of conflict with the Soviet Union has become less intensive, even though the competition has become more extensive.

The Vietnamese war produced a profound moral crisis, sapping worldwide faith in our own policy and our system of life, a crisis of confidence made even more grave by the covert pessimism of some of our leaders.

In less than a generation, we've seen the world change dramatically. The daily lives and aspirations of most human beings have been transformed. Colonialism is nearly gone. A new sense of national identity now exists in almost one hundred new countries that have been formed in the last generation. Knowledge has become more widespread. Aspirations are higher. As more people have been freed from traditional constraints, more have been determined to achieve, for the first time in their lives, social justice.

The world is still divided by ideological disputes, dominated by regional conflicts, and threatened by danger that we will not resolve the differences of race and wealth without violence or without drawing into combat the major military powers. We can no longer separate the traditional issues of war and peace from the new global questions of justice, equity, and human rights.

It is a new world, but America should not fear it. It is a new world, and we should help to shape it. It is a new world that calls for a new American foreign policy—a policy based on constant decency in its values and on optimism in our historical vision.

We can no longer have a policy solely for the industrial nations as the foundation of global stability, but we must respond to the new reality of a politically awakening world.

We can no longer expect that the other one hundred and fifty nations will follow the dictates of the powerful, but we must continue—confidently—our efforts to inspire, to persuade, and to lead.

Our policy must reflect our belief that the world can hope for more than simple survival and our belief that dignity and freedom are fundamental spiritual requirements. Our policy must shape an international system that will last longer than secret deals.

We cannot make this kind of policy by manipulation. Our policy must be open; it must be candid; it must be one of constructive global involvement, resting on five cardinal principles.

I've tried to make these premises clear to the American people since last January. Let me review what we have been doing and discuss what we intend to do.

First, we have reaffirmed America's commitment to human rights as a fundamental tenet of our foreign policy. In ancestry, religion, color, place of origin, and cultural background, we Americans are as diverse a nation as the world has even seen. No common mystique of blood or soil unites us. What draws us together, perhaps more than anything else, is a belief in human freedom. We want the world to know that our nation stands for more than financial prosperity.

This does not mean that we can conduct our foreign policy by rigid moral maxims. We live in a world that is imperfect and which will always be imperfect—a world that is complex and confused and which will always be complex and confused.

I understand fully the limits of moral suasion. We have no illusion that changes will come easily or soon. But I also believe that it is a mistake to undervalue the power of words and of the ideas that words embody. In our own history, that power has ranged from Thomas Paine's *Common Sense* to Martin Luther King, Jr.'s "I Have a Dream."

In the life of the human spirit, words are action; much more so than many of us may realize who live in countries where freedom of expression is taken for granted. The leaders of totalitarian nations understand this very well. The proof is that words are precisely the action for which dissidents in those countries are being persecuted.

Nonetheless, we can already see dramatic, worldwide advances in the protection of the individual from the arbitrary power of the state. For us to ignore this trend would be to lose influence and moral authority in the world. To lead it will be to regain the moral stature that we once had.

The great democracies are not free because we are strong and prosperous. I believe we are strong and influential and prosperous because we are free.

Throughout the world today, in free nations and in totalitarian countries as well, there is a preoccupation with the subject of human freedom, human rights. And I believe it is incumbent on us in this country to keep that discussion, that debate, that contention alive. No other country is as well-qualified as we to set an example. We have our own shortcomings and faults, and we should strive constantly and with courage to make sure that we are legitimately proud of what we have.

Second, we've moved deliberately to reinforce the bonds among our democracies. In our recent meetings in London, we agreed to widen our economic cooperation, to promote free trade, to strengthen the world's monetary system, to seek ways of avoiding nuclear proliferation. We prepared constructive proposals for the forthcoming meetings on North-South problems of poverty, development, and global well-being. And we agreed on joint efforts to reinforce and to modernize our common defence.

You may be interested in knowing that at this NATO meeting, for the first time in more than twenty-five years, all members are democracies. Even more important, all of us reaffirmed our basic optimism in the future of the democratic system. Our spirit of confidence is spreading. Together, our democracies can help to shape the wider architecture of global cooperation.

Third, we've moved to engage the Soviet Union in a joint effort to halt the strategic arms race. This race is not only dangerous, it's morally deplorable. We must put an end to it.

I know it will not be easy to reach agreements. Our goal is to be fair to both sides, to produce reciprocal stability, parity, and security. We desire a freeze on further modernization and production of weapons and a continuing, substantial reduction of strategic nuclear weapons as well. We want a comprehensive ban on all nuclear testing, a prohibition against all chemical warfare, no attack capability against space satellites, and arms limitations in the Indian Ocean.

We hope that we can take joint steps with all nations toward a final agreement eliminating nuclear weapons completely from our arsenals of death. We will persist in this effort.

Now, I believe in detente with the Soviet Union. To me it means progress toward peace. But the effects of detente should not be limited to our own two countries alone. We hope to persuade the Soviet Union that one country cannot impose its system of society upon another, either through direct military intervention or through the use of a client state's military force, as was the case with Cuban intervention in Angola.

Cooperation also implies obligation. We hope that the Soviet Union will join with us and other nations in playing a larger role in aiding the developing world, for common aid efforts will help us build a bridge of mutual confidence in one another.

Fourth, we are taking deliberate steps to improve the chances of lasting peace in the Middle East. Through wide-ranging consultation with leaders of the countries involved—Israel, Syria, Jordan, and Egypt—we have found some areas of agreement and some movement toward consensus. The negotiations must continue.

Through my own public comments, I've also tried to suggest a more flexible framework for the discussion of the three key issues which have so far been so intractable: the nature of a comprehensive peace—what is peace; what does it mean to the Israelis; what does it mean to their Arab neighbours; secondly, the relationship between security and borders—how can the dispute over border delineations be established and settled with a feeling of security on both sides; and the issue of the Palestinian homeland.

The historic friendship that the United States has with Israel is not dependent on domestic politics in either nation; it's derived from our common respect for human freedom and from a common search for permanent peace.

We will continue to promote a settlement which all of us need. Our own policy will not be affected by changes in leadership in any of the countries in the Middle East. Therefore, we expect Israel and her neighbours to continue to be bound by United Nations Resolutions 242 and 338, which they have previously accepted.

This may be the most propitious time for a genuine settlement since the beginning of the Arab-Israeli conflict almost thirty years ago. To let this opportunity pass could mean disaster not only for the Middle East but, perhaps, for the international political and economic order as well.

And fifth, we are attempting, even at the risk of some friction with our friends, to reduce the danger of nuclear proliferation and the worldwide spread of conventional weapons.

At the recent summit, we set in motion an international effort to determine the best ways of harnessing nuclear energy for peaceful use while reducing the risks that its products will be diverted to the making of explosives.

We've already completed a comprehensive review of our own policy on arms transfers. Competition in arms sales is inimical to peace and destructive of the economic development of the poorer countries.

We will, as a matter of national policy now in our country, seek to reduce the annual dollar volume of arms sales, to restrict the transfer of advanced weapons, and to reduce the extent of our coproduction arrangements about weapons with foreign states. And just as important, we are trying to get other nations, both free and otherwise, to join us in this effort.

But all of this that I've described is just the beginning. It's a beginning aimed towards a clear goal: to create a wider framework of international cooperation suited to the new and rapidly changing historical circumstances.

We will cooperate more closely with the newly influential countries in Latin America, Africa, and Asia. We need their friendship and cooperation in a common effort as the structure of world power changes.

More than one hundred years ago, Abraham Lincoln said that our nation could not exist half slave and half free. We know a peaceful world cannot long exist one-third rich and two-thirds hungry.

Most nations share our faith that, in the long run, expanded and equitable trade will best help the developing countries to help themselves. But the immediate problems of hunger, disease, illiteracy, and repression are here now.

The Western democracies, the OPEC nations, and the developed Communist countries can cooperate through existing international institutions in providing more effective aid. This is an excellent alternative to war.

We have a special need for cooperation and consultation with other nations in this hemisphere—to the north and to the south. We do not need another slogan. Although these are our close friends and neighbours, our links with them are the same links of equality that we forge for the rest of the world. We will be dealing with them as part of a new, worldwide mosaic of global, regional, and bilateral relations.

It's important that we make progress toward normalizing relations with the People's Republic of China. We see the American and Chinese relationship as a central element of our global policy and China as a key force for global peace. We wish to cooperate closely with the creative Chinese people on the problems that confront all mankind. And we hope to find a formula which can bridge some of the difficulties that still separate us.

Finally, let me say that we are committed to a peaceful resolution of the crisis in southern Africa. The time has come for the principle of majority rule to be the basis for political order, recognizing that in a democratic system the rights of the minority must also be protected.

To be peaceful, change must come promptly. The United States is determined to work together with our European allies and with the concerned African states to shape a congenial international framework for the rapid and progressive transformation of southern African society and to help protect it from unwarranted outside interference.

Let me conclude by summarizing: Our policy is based on a historical vision of America's role. Our policy is derived from a larger view of global change. Our policy is rooted in our moral values, which never change. Our policy is reinforced by our material wealth and by our military power. Our policy is designed to serve mankind. And it is a policy that I hope will make you proud to be Americans.

United Nations Address Before the General Assembly

4 October 1977

Thirty-two years ago, in the cold dawn of the Atomic Age, this organization came into being. Its first and its most urgent purpose has been to secure peace for an exhausted and ravaged world.

Present conditions in some respects appear quite hopeful, yet the assurance of peace continues to elude us. Before the end of this century, a score of nations could possess nuclear weapons. If this should happen, the world that we leave our children will mock our own hopes for peace.

The level of nuclear armaments could grow by tens of thousands, and the same situation could well occur with advanced conventional weapons. The temptation to use these weapons, for fear that someone else might do it first, would be almost irresistible.

The ever-growing trade in conventional arms subverts international commerce from a force for peace to a caterer for war.

Violence, terrorism, assassination, undeclared wars all threaten to destroy the restraint and the moderation that must become the dominant characteristic of our age.

Unless we establish a code of international behaviour in which the resort to violence becomes increasingly irrelevant to the pursuit of national interests, we will crush the world's dreams for human development and the full flowering of human freedom.

We have already become a global community, but only in the sense that we face common problems and we share for good or evil a common future. In this community, power to solve the world's problems, particularly economic and political power, no longer lies solely in the hands of a few nations.

Power is now widely shared among many nations with different cultures and different histories and different aspirations. The question is whether we will allow our differences to defeat us or whether we will work together to realize our common hopes for peace.

Today I want to address the major dimensions of peace and the role the United States intends to play in limiting and reducing all armaments, controlling nuclear technology, restricting the arms trade, and settling disputes by peaceful means.

When atomic weapons were used for the first time, Winston Churchill described the power of the atom as a revelation long, mercifully, withheld from man. Since then we have learned in Dürrenmatt's chilling words that "what has once been thought can never be un-thought."

If we are to have any assurance that our children are to live out their lives in a world which satisfies our hope—or that they will have a chance to live at all—we must finally come to terms with this enormous nuclear force and turn it exclusively to beneficial ends.

Peace will not be assured until the weapons of war are finally put away. While we work toward that goal, nations will want sufficient arms to preserve their security.

The United States' purpose is to ensure peace. It is for that reason that our military posture and our alliances will remain as strong as necessary to deter attack. However, the security of the global community cannot forever rest on a balance of terror.

In the past, war has been accepted as the ultimate arbiter of disputes among nations. But in the nuclear era we can no longer think of war as merely a continuation of diplomacy by other means. Nuclear war cannot be measured by the archaic standards of victory or defeat.

This stark reality imposes on the United States and the Soviet Union an awesome and special responsibility. The United States is engaged, along with other nations, in a broad range of negotiations. In strategic arms limitation talks, we and the Soviets are within sight of a significant agreement in limiting the total numbers of weapons and in restricting certain categories of weapons of special concern to each of us. We can also start the crucial process of curbing the relentless march of technological development which makes nuclear weapons ever more difficult to control.

We must look beyond the present and work to prevent the critical threats and instabilities of the future. In the principles of self-restraint, reciprocity, and mutual accommodation of interests, if these are observed, then the United States and the Soviet Union will not only succeed in limiting weapons but will also create a foundation of better relations in other spheres of interest.

The United States is willing to go as far as possible, consistent with our security interest, in limiting and reducing our nuclear weapons. On a reciprocal basis we are willing now to reduce them by 10 percent or 20 percent, even 50 percent. Then we will work for further reductions to a world truly free of nuclear weapons.

The United States also recognizes a threat of continued testing of nuclear explosives.

Negotiations for a comprehensive ban on nuclear explosions are now being conducted by the United States, the United Kingdom, and the Soviet Union. As in other areas where vital national security interests are engaged, agreements must be verifiable and fair. They must be seen by all the parties as serving a longer term interest that justifies the restraints of the moment.

The longer term interest in this instance is to close one more avenue of nuclear competition and thereby demonstrate to all the world that the major nuclear powers take seriously our obligations to reduce the threat of nuclear catastrophe.

My country believes that the time has come to end all explosions of nuclear devices, no matter what their claimed justification, peaceful or military, and we appreciate the efforts of other nations to reach this same goal.

During the past nine months, I have expressed the special importance that we attach to controlling nuclear proliferation. But I fear that many do not understand why the United States feels as it does.

Why is it so important to avoid the chance that one or two or ten other nations might acquire one or two or ten nuclear weapons of their own?

Let me try to explain why I deeply believe that this is one of the greatest challenges that we face in the next quarter of a century.

It's a truism that nuclear weapons are a powerful deterrent. They are a deterrent because they threaten. They could be used for terrorism or blackmail as well as for war. But they threaten not just the intended enemy, they threaten every nation, combatant or noncombatant alike. That is why all of us must be concerned.

Let me be frank. The existence of nuclear weapons in the United States and the Soviet Union, in Great Britain, France, and China, is something that we cannot undo except by the painstaking process of negotiation. But the existence of these weapons does not mean that other nations need to develop their own weapons any more than it provides a reason for those of us who have them to share them with others.

Rather, it imposes two solemn obligations on the nations which have the capacity to export nuclear fuel and nuclear technology—the obligations to meet legitimate energy needs and, in doing so, to ensure that nothing that we export contributes directly or indirectly to the production of nuclear explosives. That is why the supplier nations are seeking a common policy, and that is why the United States and the Soviet Union, even as we struggle to find common ground in the SALT talks, have already moved closer toward agreement and cooperation in our efforts to limit nuclear proliferation.

I believe that the London Suppliers Group must conclude its work as it's presently constituted so that the world security will be safeguarded from the pressures of commercial competition. We have learned it is not enough to safeguard just some facilities or some materials. Full-scope, comprehensive safeguards are necessary.

Two weeks from now in our own country, more than thirty supplier and consuming nations will convene for the International Fuel Cycle Evaluation, which we proposed last spring. For the next several years experts will work together on every facet of the nuclear fuel cycle.

The scientists and the policymakers of these nations will face a tremendous challenge. We know that by the year 2000, nuclear power reactors could be producing enough plutonium to make tens of thousands of bombs every year.

I believe from my own personal knowledge of this issue that there are ways to solve the problems that we face. I believe that there are alternative fuel cycles that can be managed safely on a global basis. I hope, therefore, that the International Fuel Cycle Evaluation will have the support and the encouragement of every nation.

I've heard it said that efforts to control nuclear proliferation are futile, that the genie is already out of the bottle. I do not believe this to be true. It should not be forgotten that for twenty-five years the nuclear club did not expand its membership. By genuine cooperation, we can make certain that this terrible club expands no further.

Now, I've talked about the special problems of nuclear arms control and nuclear proliferation at length. Let me turn to the problem of conventional arms control, which affects potentially or directly every nation represented in this great hall. This is not a matter for the future, even the near future, but of the immediate present. Worldwide military expenditures are now in the neighbourhood of $300 billion a year.

Last year the nations of the world spent more than sixty times as much—*sixty times as much*—equipping each soldier as we spent educating each child. The industrial nations spent the most money, but the rate of growth in military spending is faster in the developing world.

While only a handful of states produce sophisticated weapons, the number of nations which seek to purchase these weapons is expanding rapidly.

The conventional arms race both causes and feeds on the threat of larger and more deadly wars. It levies an enormous burden on an already troubled world economy.

For our part, the United States has now begun to reduce its arms exports. Our aim is to reduce both the quantity and the deadliness of the weapons that we sell. We have already taken the first few steps, but we cannot go very far alone. Nations whose neighbours are purchasing large quantities of arms feel constrained to do the same. Supplier nations who practice restraint in arms sales sometimes find that they simply lose valuable commercial markets to other suppliers.

We hope to work with other supplier nations to cut back on the flow of arms and to reduce the rate at which the most advanced and sophisticated weapon technologies spread around the world. We do not expect this task to be easy or to produce instant results. But we are committed to stop the spiral of increasing sale of weapons.

Equally important, we hope that purchaser nations, individually and through regional organizations, will limit their arms imports. We are ready to provide to some nations the necessary means for legitimate self-defence, but we are also eager to work with any nation or region in order to decrease the need for more numerous, more deadly, and ever more expensive weapons.

Fourteen years ago one of my predecessors spoke in this very room under circumstances that in certain ways resembled these. It was a time, he said, of comparative calm, and there was an atmosphere of rising hope about the prospect of controlling nuclear energy.

The first specific step had been taken to limit the nuclear arms race—a test ban treaty signed by nearly a hundred nations.

But the succeeding years did not live up to the optimistic prospect John F. Kennedy placed before this assembly, because as a community of nations, we failed to address the deepest sources of potential conflict among us.

As we seek to establish the principles of detente among the major nuclear powers, we believe that these principles must also apply in regional conflicts.

The United States is committed to the peaceful settlement of differences. We are committed to the strengthening of the peacemaking capabilities of the United Nations and regional organizations, such as the Organization of African Unity and the Organization of American States.

The United States supports Great Britain's efforts to bring about a peaceful, rapid transition to majority rule and independence in Zimbabwe. We have joined other members of the Security Council last week and also the Secretary General in efforts to bring about independence and democratic rule in Namibia. We are pleased with the level of cooperation that we have achieved with the leaders of the nations in the area, as well as those people who are struggling for independence.

We urge South Africa and other nations to support the proposed solution to the problems in Zimbabwe and to cooperate still more closely in providing for a smooth and prompt transition in Namibia. But it is essential that all outside nations exercise restraint in their actions in Zimbabwe and Namibia so that we can bring about this majority rule and avoid a widening war that could engulf the southern half of the African continent.

Of all the regional conflicts in the world, none holds more menace than the Middle East. War there has already carried the world to the edge of nuclear confrontation. It has already disrupted the world economy and imposed severe hardships on the people in the developed and the developing nations alike.

So, true peace—peace embodied in binding treaties—is essential. It will be in the interest of the Israelis and the Arabs. It is in the interest of the American people. It is in the interest of the entire world.

The United Nations Security Council has provided the basis for peace in Resolutions 242 and 338, but negotiations in good faith by all parties is needed to give substance to peace.

Such good faith negotiations must be inspired by a recognition that all nations in the area—Israel and the Arab countries—have a right to exist in peace, with early establishment of economic and cultural exchange and of normal diplomatic relations. Peace must include a process in which the bitter divisions of generations, even centuries, hatreds and suspicions can be overcome. Negotiations cannot be successful if any of the parties harbour the deceitful view that peace is simply an interlude in which to prepare for war.

Good faith negotiations will also require acceptance by all sides of the fundamental rights and interests of everyone involved.

For Israel this means borders that are recognized and secure. Security arrangements are crucial to a nation that has fought for its survival in each of the last four decades. The commitment of the United States to Israel's security is unquestionable.

For the Arabs, the legitimate rights of the Palestinian people must be recognized. One of the things that binds the American people to Israel is our shared respect for human rights and the courage with which Israel has defended such rights. It is clear that a true and lasting peace in the Middle East must also respect the rights of all peoples of the area. How these rights are to be defined and implemented is, of course, for the interested parties to decide in detailed negotiations and not for us to dictate.

We do not intend to impose, from the outside, a settlement on the nations of the Middle East.

The United States has been meeting with the foreign ministers of Israel and the Arab nations involved in the search for peace. We are staying in close contact with the Soviet Union, with whom we share responsibility for reconvening the Geneva conference.

As a result of these consultations, the Soviet Union and the United States have agreed to call for the resumption of the Geneva conference before the end of this year.

While a number of procedural questions remain, if the parties continue to act in good faith, I believe that these questions can be answered.

The major powers have a special responsibility to act with restraint in areas of the world where they have competing interests, because the association of these interests with local rivalries and conflicts can lead to serious confrontation.

In the Indian Ocean area, neither we nor the Soviet Union has a large military presence, nor is there a rapidly mounting competition between us.

Restraint in the area may well begin with a mutual effort to stabilize our presence and to avoid an escalation in military competition. Then both sides can consider how our military activities in the Indian Ocean, this whole area, might be even further reduced.

The peaceful settlement of differences is, of course, essential. The United States is willing to abide by that principle, as in the case of the recently signed Panama Canal treaties. Once ratified, these treaties can transform the US–Panama relationship into one that permanently protects the interests and respects the sovereignty of both our countries.

We have all survived and surmounted major challenges since the United Nations was founded. But we can accelerate progress even in a world of ever-increasing diversity.

A commitment to strengthen international institutions is vital. But progress lies also in our own national policies. We can work together to form a community of peace if we accept the kind of obligations that I have suggested today.

To summarize: first, an obligation to remove the threat of nuclear weaponry, to reverse the buildup of armaments and their trade, and to conclude bilateral and multilateral arms control agreements that can bring security to all of us. In order to reduce the reliance of nations on nuclear weaponry, I hereby solemnly declare on behalf of the United States that we will not use nuclear weapons except in self-defense; that is, in circumstances of an actual nuclear or conventional attack on the United States, our territories, or Armed Forces, or such an attack on our allies.

In addition, we hope that initiatives by the Western nations to secure mutual and balanced force reductions in Europe will be met by equal response from the Warsaw Pact countries.

Second, an obligation to show restraint in areas of tension, to negotiate disputes and settle them peacefully, and to strengthen peacemaking capabilities of the United Nations and regional organizations.

And finally, an effort by all nations, East as well as West, North as well as South, to fulfill mankind's aspirations for human development and human freedom. It is to meet these basic demands that we build governments and seek peace.

We must share these obligations for our own mutual survival and our own mutual prosperity.

We can see a world at peace. We can work for a world without want. We can build a global community dedicated to these purposes and to human dignity.

The view that I have sketched for you today is that of only one leader in only one nation. However wealthy and powerful the United States may be, however capable of leadership, this power is increasingly only relative. The leadership increasingly is in need of being shared.

No nation has a monopoly of vision, of creativity, or of ideas. Bringing these together from many nations is our common responsibility and our common challenge. For only in these ways can the idea of a peaceful global community grow and prosper.

United States Naval Academy Address at the Commencement Exercises

7 June 1978

Today I want to discuss one of the most important aspects of that international context—the relationship between the world's two greatest powers, the United States of America and the Soviet Union.

We must realize that for a very long time our relationship with the Soviet Union will be competitive. That competition is to be constructive if we are successful. Instead it could be dangerous and politically disastrous. Then our relationship must be cooperative as well.

We must avoid excessive swings in the public mood in our country—from euphoria when things are going well, to despair when they are not; from an exaggerated sense of compatibility with the Soviet Union, to open expressions of hostility.

Detente between our two countries is central to world peace. It's important for the world, for the American public, and for you as future leaders of the Navy to understand the complex and sensitive nature.

The word "detente" can be simplistically defined as "the easing of tension between nations." The word is in practice however, further defined by experience, as those nations evolve new means by which they can live with each other in peace.

To be stable, to be supported by the American people, and to be a basis for widening the scope of cooperation, then detente must be broadly defined and truly reciprocal. Both nations must exercise restraint in troubled areas and in troubled times. Both must honour meticulously those agreements which have already been reached to widen cooperation, naturally and mutually limit nuclear arms production, permit the free movement of people and the expression of ideas, and to protect human rights.

Neither of us should entertain the notion that military supremacy can be attained, or that transient military advantage can be politically exploited.

Our principal goal is to help shape a world which is more responsive to the desire of people everywhere for economic well-being, social justice, political self-determination, and basic human rights.

We seek a world of peace. But such a world must accommodate diversity—social, political, and ideological. Only then can there be a genuine cooperation among nations and among cultures.

We desire to dominate no one. We will continue to widen our cooperation with the positive new forces in the world.

We want to increase our collaboration with the Soviet Union, but also with the emerging nations, with the nations of Eastern Europe, and with the People's Republic of China. We are particularly dedicated to genuine self-determination and majority rule in those areas of the world where these goals have not yet been attained.

Our long-term objective must be to convince the Soviet Union of the advantages of cooperation and of the costs of disruptive behaviour.

We remember that the United States and the Soviet Union were allies in the Second World War. One of the great historical accomplishments of the US Navy was to guide and protect the tremendous shipments of armaments and supplies from our country to Murmansk and to other Soviet ports in support of a joint effort to meet the Nazi threat.

In the agony of that massive conflict, twenty million Soviet lives were lost. Millions more who live in the Soviet Union still recall the horror and the hunger of that time.

I'm convinced that the people of the Soviet Union want peace. I cannot believe that they could possibly want war.

Through the years, our nation has sought accommodation with the Soviet Union, as demonstrated by the Austrian Peace Treaty, the Quadripartite Agreement concerning Berlin, the termination of nuclear testing in the atmosphere, joint scientific explorations in space, trade agreements, the antiballistic missile treaty, the interim agreement on strategic offensive armaments, and the limited test ban agreement.

Efforts still continue with negotiations toward a SALT II agreement, a comprehensive test ban against nuclear explosives, reductions in conventional arms transfers to other countries, the prohibition against attacks on satellites in space, an agreement to stabilize the level of force deployment in the Indian Ocean, and increased trade and scientific and cultural exchange. We must be willing to explore such avenues of cooperation despite the basic issues which divide us. The risks of nuclear war alone propel us in this direction.

The numbers and destructive potential of nuclear weapons has been increasing at an alarming rate. That is why a SALT agreement which enhances the security of both nations is of fundamental importance. We and the Soviet Union are negotiating in good faith almost every day because we both know that a failure to succeed would precipitate a resumption of a massive nuclear arms race.

I'm glad to report to you today that the prospects for a SALT II agreement are good.

Beyond this major effort, improved trade and technological and cultural exchange are among the immediate benefits of cooperation between our two countries. However, these efforts to cooperate do not erase the significant differences between us.

What are these differences?

To the Soviet Union, detente seems to mean a continuing aggressive struggle for political advantage and increased influence in a variety of ways. The Soviet Union apparently sees military power and military assistance as the best means of expanding their influence abroad. Obviously, areas of instability in the world provide a tempting target for this effort, and all too often they seem ready to exploit any such opportunity.

As became apparent in Korea, in Angola, and also, as you know, in Ethiopia more recently, the Soviets prefer to use proxy forces to achieve their purposes.

To other nations throughout the world, the Soviet military buildup appears to be excessive, far beyond any legitimate requirement to defend themselves or to defend their allies. For more than fifteen years, they have maintained this program of military growth, investing almost 15 percent of their total gross national product in armaments, and this sustained growth continues.

The abuse of basic human rights in their own country, in violation of the agreement which was reached at Helsinki, has earned them the condemnation of people everywhere who love freedom. By their actions, they've demonstrated that the Soviet system cannot tolerate freely expressed ideas or notions of loyal opposition and the free movement of peoples.

The Soviet Union attempts to export a totalitarian and repressive form of government, resulting in a closed society. Some of these characteristics and goals create problems for the Soviet Union.

Outside a tightly controlled bloc, the Soviet Union has difficult political relations with other nations. Their cultural bonds with others are few and frayed. Their form of government is becoming increasingly unattractive to other nations, so that even Marxist-Leninist groups no longer look on the Soviet Union as a model to be imitated.

Many countries are becoming very concerned that the nonaligned movement is being subverted by Cuba, which is obviously closely aligned with the Soviet Union and dependent upon the Soviets for economic sustenance and for military and political guidance and direction.

Although the Soviet Union has the second largest economic system in the world, its growth is slowing greatly, and its standard of living does not compare favourably with that of other nations at the same equivalent stage of economic development.

Agricultural production still remains a serious problem for the Soviet Union, so that in times of average or certainly adverse conditions for crop production, they must turn to us or turn to other nations for food supplies.

We in our country are in a much more favourable position. Our industrial base and our productivity are unmatched. Our scientific and technological capability is superior to all others. Our alliances with other free nations are strong and growing stronger, and our military capability is now and will be second to none.

In contrast to the Soviet Union, we are surrounded by friendly neighbours and wide seas. Our societal structure is stable and cohesive, and our foreign policy enjoys bipartisan public support, which gives it continuity.

We are also strong because of what we stand for as a nation: the realistic chance for every person to build a better life; protection by both law and custom from arbitrary exercise of government power; the right of every individual to speak out, to participate fully in government, and to share political power. Our philosophy is based on personal freedom, the most powerful of all ideas, and our democratic way of life warrants the admiration and emulation by other people throughout the world.

Our work for human rights makes us part of an international tide, growing in force. We are strengthened by being part of it.

Our growing economic strength is also a major political factor, potential influence for the benefit of others. Our gross national product exceeds that of all nine nations combined in the European Economic Community and is twice as great as that of the Soviet Union. Additionally, we are now learning how to use our resources more wisely, creating a new harmony between our people and our environment.

Our analysis of American military strength also furnishes a basis for confidence. We know that neither the United States nor the Soviet Union can launch a nuclear assault on the other without suffering a devastating counterattack which could destroy the aggressor nation. Although the Soviet Union has more missile launchers, greater throw-weight, and more continental air defense capabilities, the United States has more warheads, generally greater accuracy, more heavy bombers, a more balanced nuclear force, better missile submarines, and superior antisubmarine warfare capability.

A successful SALT II agreement will give both nations equal but lower ceilings on missile launchers and also on missiles with multiple warheads. We envision in SALT III an even greater mutual reduction in nuclear weapons.

With essential nuclear equivalence, relative conventional force strength has now become more important. The fact is that the military capability of the United States and its allies is adequate to meet any foreseeable threat.

It is possible that each side tends to exaggerate the military capability of the other. Accurate analyses are important as a basis for making decisions for the future. False or excessive estimates of Soviet strength or American weakness contributes to the effectiveness of the Soviet propaganda effort.

For example, recently alarming news reports of the military budget proposals for the US Navy ignored the fact that we have the highest defense budget in history and that the largest portion of this will go to the Navy.

You men are joining a long tradition of superior leadership, seamanship, tactics, and ship design. And I'm confident that the US Navy has no peer, no equal, on the high seas today, and that you, I, and others will always keep the Navy strong.

Let there be no doubt about our present and future strength. This brief assessment which I've just made shows that we need not be overly concerned about our ability to compete and to compete successfully. Certainly there is no cause for alarm. The healthy self-criticism and the free debate which are essential in a democracy should never be confused with weakness or despair or lack of purpose.

What are the principal elements of American foreign policy to the Soviet Union? Let me outline them very briefly.

We will continue to maintain equivalent nuclear strength, because we believe that in the absence of worldwide nuclear disarmament, such equivalency is the least threatening and the most stable situation for the world.

We will maintain a prudent and sustained level of military spending, keyed to a stronger NATO, more mobile forces, and undiminished presence in the Pacific. We and our allies must and will be able to meet any foreseeable challenge to our security from either strategic nuclear forces or from conventional forces. America has the capability to honour this commitment without excessive sacrifice on the part of our citizens, and that commitment to military strength will be honoured.

Looking beyond our alliances, we will support worldwide and regional organizations which are dedicated to enhancing international peace, like the United Nations, the Organization of American States, and the Organization for African Unity.

In Africa, we and our African friends want to see a continent that is free of the dominance of outside powers, free of the bitterness of racial injustice, free of conflict, and free of the burdens of poverty and hunger and disease. We are convinced that the best way to work toward these objectives is through affirmative policies that recognize African realities and that recognize aspirations.

The persistent and increasing military involvement of the Soviet Union and Cuba in Africa could deny this hopeful vision. We are deeply concerned about the threat to regional peace and to the autonomy of countries within which these foreign troops seem permanently to be stationed. That is why I've spoken up on this subject today. And this is why I and the American people will support African efforts to contain such intrusion, as we have done recently in Zaire.

I urge again that all other powers join us in emphasizing works of peace rather than the weapons of war. In their assistance to Africa, let the Soviet Union now join us in seeking a peaceful and a speedy transition to majority rule in Rhodesia and in Namibia. Let us see efforts to resolve peacefully the disputes in Eritrea and in Angola. Let us all work, not to divide and to seek domination in Africa, but to help those nations to fulfill their great potential.

We will seek peace, better communication and understanding, cultural and scientific exchange, and increased trade with the Soviet Union and with other nations.

We will attempt to prevent the proliferation of nuclear weapons among those nations not now having this capability.

We will continue to negotiate constructively and persistently for a fair strategic arms limitation agreement. We know that no ideological victories can be won by either side by the use of nuclear weapons.

We have no desire to link this negotiation for a SALT agreement with other competitive relationships nor to impose other special conditions on the process. In a democratic society, however, where public opinion is an integral factor in the shaping and implementation of foreign policy, we do recognize that tensions, sharp disputes, or threats to peace will complicate the quest for a successful agreement. This is not a matter of our preference but a simple recognition of fact.

The Soviet Union can choose either confrontation or cooperation. The United States is adequately prepared to meet either choice.

We would prefer cooperation through a detente that increasingly involves similar restraint for both sides; similar readiness to resolve disputes by negotiations, and not by violence; similar willingness to compete peacefully, and not militarily. Anything less than that is likely to undermine detente. And this is why I hope that no one will underestimate the concerns which I have expressed today.

A competition without restraint and without shared rules will escalate into graver tensions, and our relationship as a whole with the Soviet Union will suffer. I do not wish this to happen, and I do not believe that Mr. Brezhnev desires it. And this is why it is time for us to speak frankly and to face the problems squarely.

By a combination of adequate American strength, of quiet self-restraint in the use of it, of a refusal to believe in the inevitability of war, and of a patient and persistent development of all the peaceful alternatives, we hope eventually to lead international society into a more stable, more peaceful, and a more hopeful future.

You and I leave here today to do our common duty—protecting our nation's vital interests by peaceful means if possible, by resolute action if necessary. We go forth sobered by these responsibilities, but confident of our strength. We go forth knowing that our nation's goals—peace, security, liberty for ourselves and for others—will determine our future and that we together can prevail.

To attain these goals, our nation will require exactly those qualities of courage, self-sacrifice, idealism, and self-discipline which you as midshipmen have learned here at Annapolis so well. That is why your nation expects so much of you, and that is why you have so much to give.

I leave you now with my congratulations and with a prayer to God that both you and I will prove worthy of the task that is before us and the nation which we have sworn to serve.

Remarks of the President, President Anwar al-Sadat of Egypt, and Prime Minister Menachem Begin of Israel

at the Conclusion of the Camp David Meeting on the Middle East

17 September 1978

PRESIDENT CARTER: When we first arrived at Camp David, the first thing upon which we agreed was to ask the people of the world to pray that our negotiations would be successful. Those prayers have been answered far beyond any expectations. We are privileged to witness tonight a significant achievement in the cause of peace, an achievement none thought possible a year ago, or even a month ago, an achievement that reflects the courage and wisdom of these two leaders.

Through thirteen long days at Camp David, we have seen them display determination and vision and flexibility which was needed to make this agreement come to pass. All of us owe them our gratitude and respect. They know that they will always have my personal admiration.

There are still great difficulties that remain and many hard issues to be settled. The questions that have brought warfare and bitterness to the Middle East for the last thirty years will not be settled overnight. But we should all recognize the substantial achievements that have been made.

One of the agreements that President Sadat and Prime Minister Begin are signing tonight is entitled, "A Framework for Peace in the Middle East."

This framework concerns the principles and some specifics, in the most substantive way, which will govern a comprehensive peace settlement. It deals specifically with the future of the West Bank and Gaza and the need to resolve the Palestinian problem in all its aspects. The framework document proposes a five-year transitional period in the West Bank and Gaza during which the Israeli military government will be withdrawn and a self-governing authority will be elected with full autonomy. It also provides for Israeli forces to remain in specified locations during this period to protect Israel's security.

The Palestinians will have the right to participate in the determination of their own future, in negotiations which will resolve the final status of the West Bank and Gaza, and then to produce an Israeli-Jordanian peace treaty.

These negotiations will be based on all the provisions and all the principles of United Nations Security Council Resolution 242. And it provides that Israel may live in peace, within secure and recognized borders. And this great aspiration of Israel has been certified without constraint, with the greatest degree of enthusiasm, by President Sadat, the leader of one of the greatest nations on earth.

The other document is entitled, "Framework for the Conclusion of a Peace Treaty Between Egypt and Israel."

It provides for the full exercise of Egyptian sovereignty over the Sinai. It calls for the full withdrawal of Israeli forces from the Sinai and, after an interim withdrawal which will be accomplished very quickly, the establishment of normal, peaceful relations between the two countries, including diplomatic relations.

Together with accompanying letters, which we will make public tomorrow, these two Camp David agreements provide the basis for progress and peace throughout the Middle East.

There is one issue on which agreement has not been reached. Egypt states that the agreement to remove Israeli settlements from Egyptian territory is a prerequisite to a peace treaty. Israel states that the issue of the Israeli settlements should be resolved during the peace negotiations. That's a substantial difference. Within the next two weeks, the Knesset will decide on the issue of these settlements.

Tomorrow night, I will go before the Congress to explain these agreements more fully and to talk about their implications for the United States and for the world. For the moment, and in closing, I want to speak more personally about my admiration for all of those who have taken part in this process and my hope that the promise of this moment will be fulfilled.

During the last two weeks, the members of all three delegations have spent endless hours, day and night, talking, negotiating, grappling with problems that have divided their people for thirty years. Whenever there was a danger that human energy would fail, or patience would be exhausted or good will would run out—and there were many such moments—these two leaders and the able advisers in all delegations found the resources within them to keep the chances for peace alive.

Well, the long days at Camp David are over. But many months of difficult negotiations still lie ahead. I hope that the foresight and the wisdom that have made this session a success will guide these leaders and the leaders of all nations as they continue the progress toward peace. Thank you very much.

PRESIDENT SADAT: Dear President Carter: In this historic moment, I would like to express to you my heartfelt congratulations and appreciation. For long days and nights, you devoted your time and energy to the pursuit of peace. You have been most courageous when you took the gigantic step of convening this meeting. The challenge was great and the risks were high, but so was your determination. You made a commitment to be a full partner in the peace process. I'm happy to say that you have honoured your commitment.

The signing of the framework for the comprehensive peace settlement has a significance far beyond the event. It signals the emergence of a new peace initiative, with the American nation in the heart of the entire process.

In the weeks ahead, important decisions have to be made if we are to proceed on the road to peace. We have to reaffirm the faith of the Palestinian people in the ideal of peace.

The continuation of your active role is indispensable. We need your help and the support of the American people. Let me seize this opportunity to thank each and every American for his genuine interest in the cause of people in the Middle East.

Dear friend, we came to Camp David with all the good will and faith we possessed, and we left Camp David a few minutes ago with a renewed sense of hope and inspiration. We are looking forward to the days ahead with an added determination to pursue the noble goal of peace.

Your able assistants spared no effort to bring out this happy conclusion. We appreciate their spirit and dedication. Our hosts at Camp David and the State of Maryland were most generous and hospitable. To each one of them and to all those who are watching this great event, I say thank you.

Let us join in a prayer to God Almighty to guide our path. Let us pledge to make the spirit of Camp David a new chapter in the history of our nations.

Thank you, Mr. President.

PRIME MINISTER BEGIN: Mr. President of the United States, Mr. President of the Arab Republic of Egypt, ladies and gentlemen:

The Camp David conference should be renamed. It was the Jimmy Carter conference. [Laughter]

The president undertook an initiative most imaginative in our time and brought President Sadat and myself and our colleagues and friends and advisers together under one roof. In itself, it was a great achievement. But the president took a great risk for himself and did it with great civil courage. And it was a famous French field commander who said that it is much more difficult to show civil courage than military courage.

And the president worked. As far as my historic experience is concerned, I think that he worked harder than our forefathers did in Egypt building the pyramids. [Laughter]

Yes, indeed, he worked day and night—

PRESIDENT CARTER: Amen.

PRIME MINISTER BEGIN: —day and night. We used to go to bed at Camp David between 3 and 4 o'clock in the morning, arise, as we are used to since our boyhood, between 5 and 6, and continue working.

The president showed interest in every section, every paragraph, every sentence, every word, every letter of the framework agreements.

We had some difficult moments as usually there are some crises in negotiations, as usually somebody gives a hint that perhaps he would like to pick up and go home. [Laughter] It's all usual. But ultimately, ladies and gentlemen, the president of the United States won the day. And peace now celebrates a great victory for the nations of Egypt and Israel and for all mankind.

Mr. President, we, the Israelis, thank you from the bottom of our hearts for all you have done for the sake of peace, for which we prayed and yearned more than thirty years. The Jewish people suffered much, too much. And, therefore, peace to us is a striving, coming innermost from our heart and soul.

Now, when I came here to the Camp David conference, I said, perhaps as a result of our work, one day people will, in every corner of the world, be able to say, *Habemus pacem*, in the spirit of these days. Can we say so tonight? Not yet. We still have to go a road until my friend President Sadat and I sign the peace treaties.

We promised each other that we shall do so within three months. Mr. President [referring to President Sadat], tonight, at this celebration of the great historic event, let us promise each other that we shall do it earlier than within three months.

Mr. President, you inscribed your name forever in the history of two ancient civilized peoples, the people of Egypt and the people of Israel. Thank you, Mr. President.

PRESIDENT CARTER: Thank you very much.

PRIME MINISTER BEGIN: Oh, no, no, no. I would like to say a few words about my friend, President Sadat. We met for the first time in our lives last November in Jerusalem. He came to us as a guest, a former enemy, and during our first meeting we became friends.

In the Jewish teachings, there is a tradition that the greatest achievement of a human being is to turn his enemy into a friend, and this we do in reciprocity. Since then, we had some difficult days. [Laughter] I'm not going now to tell you the saga of those days. Everything belongs to the past. Today, I visited President Sadat in his cabin, because in Camp David you don't have houses, you only have cabins. [Laughter] And he then came to visit me. We shook hands. And, thank God, we again could have said to each other, "You are my friend."

And, indeed, we shall go on working in understanding, and in friendship, and with good will. We will still have problems to solve. Camp David proved that any problem can be solved if there is good will and understanding and some—some wisdom.

I looked for a precedent; I didn't find it. It was a unique conference, perhaps one of the most important since the Vienna Conference in the nineteenth century, perhaps.

Camp David Meeting on the Middle East Address Before a Joint Session of the Congress

18 September 1978

It's been more than 2,000 years since there was peace between Egypt and a free Jewish nation. If our present expectations are realized, this year we shall see such peace again.

The first thing I would like to do is to give tribute to the two men who made this impossible dream now become a real possibility, the two great leaders with whom I have met for the last two weeks at Camp David: first, President Anwar Sadat of Egypt, and the other, of course, is Prime Minister Menachem Begin of the nation of Israel.

I know that all of you would agree that these are two men of great personal courage, representing nations of peoples who are deeply grateful to them for the achievement which they have realized. And I am personally grateful to them for what they have done.

At Camp David, we sought a peace that is not only of vital importance to their own two nations but to all the people of the Middle East, to all the people of the United States, and, indeed, to all the world as well.

The world prayed for the success of our efforts, and I am glad to announce to you that these prayers have been answered.

I've come to discuss with you tonight what these two leaders have accomplished and what this means to all of us.

The United States has had no choice but to be deeply concerned about the Middle East and to try to use our influence and our efforts to advance the cause of peace. For the last thirty years, through four wars, the people of this troubled region have paid a terrible price in suffering and division and hatred and bloodshed. No two nations have suffered more than Egypt and Israel. But the dangers and the costs of conflicts in this region for our own nation have been great as well. We have longstanding friendships among the nations there and the peoples of the region, and we have profound moral commitments which are deeply rooted in our values as a people.

The strategic location of these countries and the resources that they possess mean that events in the Middle East directly affect people everywhere. We and our friends could not be indifferent if a hostile power were to establish domination there. In few areas of the world is there a greater risk that a local conflict could spread among other nations adjacent to them and then, perhaps, erupt into a tragic confrontation between us superpowers ourselves.

Our people have come to understand that unfamiliar names like Sinai, Aqaba, Sharm el Sheikh, Ras en Naqb, Gaza, the West Bank of Jordan, can have a direct and immediate bearing on our own wellbeing as a nation and our hope for a peaceful world. That is why we in the United States cannot afford to be idle bystanders and why we have been full partners in the search for peace and why it is so vital to our nation that these meetings at Camp David have been a success.

Through the long years of conflict, four main issues have divided the parties involved. One is the nature of peace—whether peace will simply mean that the guns are silenced, that the bombs no longer fall, that the tanks cease to roll, or whether it will mean that the nations of the Middle East can deal with each other as neighbours and as equals and as friends, with a full range of diplomatic and cultural and economic and human relations between them.

That's been the basic question. The Camp David agreement has defined such relationships, I'm glad to announce to you, between Israel and Egypt.

The second main issue is providing for the security of all parties involved, including, of course, our friends, the Israelis, so that none of them need fear attack or military threats from one another. When implemented, the Camp David agreement, I'm glad to announce to you, will provide for such mutual security.

Third is the question of agreement on secure and recognized boundaries, the end of military occupation, and the granting of self-government or else the return to other nations of territories which have been occupied by Israel since the 1967 conflict. The Camp David agreement, I'm glad to announce to you, provides for the realization of all these goals.

And finally, there is the painful human question of the fate of the Palestinians who live or who have lived in these disputed regions. The Camp David agreement guarantees that the Palestinian people may participate in the resolution of the Palestinian problem in all its aspects, a commitment that Israel has made in writing and which is supported and appreciated, I'm sure, by all the world.

Over the last eighteen months, there has been, of course, some progress on these issues. Egypt and Israel came close to agreeing about the first issue, the nature of peace. They then saw that the second and third issues, that is, withdrawal and security, were intimately connected, closely entwined. But fundamental divisions still remained in other areas—about the fate of the Palestinians, the future of the West Bank and Gaza, and the future of Israeli settlements in occupied Arab territories.

We all remember the hopes for peace that were inspired by President Sadat's initiative, that great and historic visit to Jerusalem last November that thrilled the world, and by the warm and genuine personal response of Prime Minister Begin and the Israeli people, and by the mutual promise between them, publicly made, that there would be no more war. These hopes were sustained when Prime Minister Begin reciprocated by visiting Ismailia on Christmas Day. That progress continued, but at a slower and slower pace through the early part of the year. And by early summer, the negotiations had come to a standstill once again.

It was this stalemate and the prospect for an even worse future that prompted me to invite both President Sadat and Prime Minister Begin to join me at Camp David. They accepted, as you know, instantly, without delay, without preconditions, without consultation even between them.

It's impossible to overstate the courage of these two men or the foresight they have shown. Only through high ideals, through compromises of words and not principle, and through a willingness to look deep into the human heart and to understand the problems and hopes and dreams of one another can progress in a difficult situation like this ever be made. That's what these men and their wise and diligent advisers who are here with us tonight have done during the last thirteen days.

When this conference began, I said that the prospects for success were remote. Enormous barriers of ancient history and nationalism and suspicion would have to be overcome if we were to meet our objectives. But President Sadat and Prime Minister Begin have overcome these barriers, exceeded our fondest expectations, and have signed two agreements that hold out the possibility of resolving issues that history had taught us could not be resolved.

The first of these documents is entitled, "A Framework for Peace in the Middle East Agreed at Camp David." It deals with a comprehensive settlement, comprehensive agreement, between Israel and all her neighbours, as well as the difficult question of the Palestinian people and the future of the West Bank and the Gaza area.

The agreement provides a basis for the resolution of issues involving the West Bank and Gaza during the next five years. It outlines a process of change which is in keeping with Arab hopes, while also carefully respecting Israel's vital security.

The Israeli military government over these areas will be withdrawn and will be replaced with a self-government of the Palestinians who live there. And Israel has committed that this government will have full autonomy. Prime Minister Begin said to me several times, not partial autonomy, but full autonomy.

Israeli forces will be withdrawn and redeployed into specified locations to protect Israel's security. The Palestinians will further participate in determining their own future through talks in which their own elected representatives, the inhabitants of the West Bank and Gaza, will negotiate with Egypt and Israel and Jordan to determine the final status of the West Bank and Gaza.

Israel has agreed, has committed themselves, that the legitimate rights of the Palestinian people will be recognized. After the signing of this framework last night, and during the negotiations concerning the establishment of the Palestinian self-government, no new Israeli settlements will be established in this area. The future settlements issue will be decided among the negotiating parties.

The final status of the West Bank and Gaza will be decided before the end of the five-year transitional period during which the Palestinian Arabs will have their own government, as part of a negotiation which will produce a peace treaty between Israel and Jordan specifying borders, withdrawal, all those very crucial issues.

These negotiations will be based on all the provisions and the principles of Security Council Resolution 242, with which you all are so familiar. The agreement on the final status of these areas will then be submitted to a vote by the representatives of the inhabitants of the West Bank and Gaza, and they will have the right for the first time in their history, the Palestinian people, to decide how they will govern themselves permanently.

We also believe, of course, all of us, that there should be a just settlement of the problems of displaced persons and refugees, which takes into account appropriate United Nations resolutions.

Finally, this document also outlines a variety of security arrangements to reinforce peace between Israel and her neighbours. This is, indeed, a comprehensive and fair framework for peace in the Middle East, and I'm glad to report this to you.

The second agreement is entitled, "A Framework for the Conclusion of a Peace Treaty Between Egypt and Israel." It returns to Egypt its full exercise of sovereignty over the Sinai Peninsula and establishes several security zones, recognizing carefully that sovereignty right for the protection of all parties. It also provides that Egypt will extend full diplomatic recognition to Israel at the time the Israelis complete an interim withdrawal from most of the Sinai, which will take place between three months and nine months after the conclusion of the peace treaty. And the peace treaty is to be fully negotiated and signed no later than three months from last night.

I think I should also report that Prime Minister Begin and President Sadat have already challenged each other to conclude the treaty even earlier. And I hope they [applause] … This final conclusion of a peace treaty will be completed late in December, and it would be a wonderful Christmas present for the world.

Final and complete withdrawal of all Israeli forces will take place between two and three years following the conclusion of the peace treaty.

While both parties are in total agreement on all the goals that I have just described to you, there is one issue on which agreement has not yet been reached. Egypt states that agreement to remove the Israeli settlements from Egyptian territory is a prerequisite to a peace treaty. Israel says that the issue of the Israeli settlements should be resolved during the peace negotiations themselves.

Now, within two weeks, with each member of the Knesset or the Israeli Parliament acting as individuals, not constrained by party loyalty, the Knesset will decide on the issue of the settlements. Our own government's position, my own personal position is well known on this issue and has been consistent. It is my strong hope, my prayer, that the question of Israeli settlements on Egyptian territory will not be the final obstacle to peace.

None of us should underestimate the historic importance of what has already been done. This is the first time that an Arab and an Israeli leader have signed a comprehensive framework for peace. It contains the seeds of a time when the Middle East, with all its vast potential, may be a land of human richness and fulfillment, rather than a land of bitterness and continued conflict. No region in the world has greater natural and human resources than this one, and nowhere have they been more heavily weighed down by intense hatred and frequent war. These agreements hold out the real possibility that this burden might finally be lifted.

But we must also not forget the magnitude of the obstacles that still remain. The summit exceeded our highest expectations, but we know that it left many difficult issues which are still to be resolved. These issues will require careful negotiation in the months to come. The Egyptian and Israeli people must recognize the tangible benefits that peace will bring and support the decisions their leaders have made, so that a secure and a peaceful future can be achieved for them. The American public, you and I, must also offer our full support to those who have made decisions that are difficult and those who have very difficult decisions still to make.

What lies ahead for all of us is to recognize the statesmanship that President Sadat and Prime Minister Begin have shown and to invite others in that region to follow their example. I have already, last night, invited the other leaders of the Arab world to help sustain progress toward a comprehensive peace.

We must also join in an effort to bring an end to the conflict and the terrible suffering in Lebanon. This is a subject that President Sadat discussed with me many times while I was in Camp David with him. And the first time that the three of us met together, this was a subject of heated discussion. On the way to Washington last night in the helicopter, we mutually committed ourselves to join with other nations, with the Lebanese people themselves, all factions, with President Sarkis, with Syria and Saudi Arabia, perhaps the European countries like France, to try to move toward a solution of the problem in Lebanon, which is so vital to us and to the poor people in Lebanon, who have suffered so much.

We will want to consult on this matter and on these documents and their meaning with all of the leaders, particularly the Arab leaders. And I'm pleased to say to you tonight that just a few minutes ago, King Hussein of Jordan and King Khalid of Saudi Arabia, perhaps other leaders later, but these two have already agreed to receive Secretary Vance, who will be leaving tomorrow to explain to them the terms of the Camp David agreement. And we hope to secure their support for the realization of the new hopes and dreams of the people of the Middle East.

This is an important mission, and this responsibility, I can tell you, based on my last two weeks with him, could not possibly rest on the shoulders of a more able and dedicated and competent man than Secretary (of State) Cyrus Vance.

Finally, let me say that for many years the Middle East has been a textbook for pessimism, a demonstration that diplomatic ingenuity was no match for intractable human conflicts. Today we are privileged to see the chance for one of the sometimes rare, bright moments in human history—a chance that may offer the way to peace. We have a chance for peace, because these two brave leaders found within themselves the willingness to work together to seek these lasting prospects for peace, which we all want so badly. And for that, I hope that you will share my prayer of thanks and my hope that the promise of this moment shall be fully realized.

The prayers at Camp David were the same as those of the shepherd King David, who prayed in the 85th Psalm, "Wilt thou not revive us again: that thy people may rejoice in thee? ... I will hear what God the Lord will speak: for he will speak peace unto his people, and unto his saints: but let them not return again unto folly."

And I would like to say, as a Christian, to these two friends of mine, the words of Jesus, "Blessed are the peacemakers, for they shall be the children of God."

Cairo, Egypt
Address Before the People's Assembly

10 March 1979

I also come before you in the name of God, as a partner with my great and good friend, your President, Anwar al-Sadat, to address the Egyptian people through the members of this People's Assembly of Egypt.

My heart is full as I stand before you today. I feel admiration for the land of Egypt, and I feel a profound respect for the people of Egypt and for your leader, President Sadat, a man who has reached out his strong hand to alter the very course of history.

And I also feel a deep sense of hope as I consider the future that will unfold before us if we have the will and the faith to bring peace. And we have that will and faith, and we will bring peace.

As a boy, like other schoolchildren all over the world, I studied the civilization of Egypt. In the last few days, I have at last seen the legacy of that great civilization with my own eyes. As a citizen of a very young country, I can only marvel at the seven-thousand-year heritage of the Egyptian people, whom you represent.

For most of the last five hundred years, Egypt suffered under foreign domination. But Egypt has again taken her place among the world's independent countries and has led the resurgence among the Arab people to a prominent place among the nations of the world. I'm very proud of that great achievement on your part.

Tragically, this generation of progress has also been a generation of suffering. Again and again, the energies of the peoples of the Middle East have been drained by the conflicts among you—and especially by the violent confrontations between Arabs and Israelis. Four wars have taken their toll in blood and treasure, in uprooted families, and young lives cut short by death.

Then, sixteen months ago, one man, Anwar al-Sadat, rose up and said, "Enough of war." He rose up and said, "Enough of war. It is time for peace."

This extraordinary journey of President Sadat to Jerusalem began the process which has brought me here today. Your president has demonstrated the power of human courage and human vision to create hope where there had been only despair.

The negotiations begun by President Sadat's initiative have been long and arduous. It could not have been otherwise. The issues involved are complex, and they are tangled in a web of strong emotion. But among the people of Egypt and the people of Israel alike, the most powerful emotion is not hostility. It is not hatred. It is a will to peace. And more has been accomplished in one year of talking than in thirty years of fighting.

As the peace process has moved forward—sometimes smoothly, more often with pain and difficulty—the government of Egypt has been represented by able diplomats, fully attuned to Egypt's national interests and continually mindful of Egypt's responsibilities to the rest of the Arab world.

Last September, the course of negotiations took the president of Egypt and the prime minister of Israel to Camp David, in the wooded mountains near the capital of the United States of America.

Out of our discussion there came two agreements: A framework within which peace between Israel and all her neighbours might be achieved, and the legitimate rights of the Palestinian people realized—and also an outline for a peace treaty between Egypt and Israel, in the context of a comprehensive peace for the Middle East.

Those agreements were rooted in United Nations Security Council Resolution 242, which established the basic equation between an Arab commitment to peace and Israeli withdrawal in the context of security. The treaty which is now being negotiated between Egypt and Israel reflects those principles.

Since the two agreements were signed, we have been working to bring both of them to fruition. The United States has served as a mediator, working to solve problems—not to press either party to accept provisions that are inconsistent with its basic interests.

In these negotiations, a crucial question has involved the relationship between an Egyptian-Israeli treaty and the broader peace envisioned and committed at Camp David. I believe that this body and the people of Egypt deserve to know my thinking on this subject.

When two nations conclude a treaty with one another, they have every right to expect that the terms of that treaty will be carried out faithfully and steadfastly. At the same time, there can be little doubt that the two agreements reached at Camp David—negotiated together and signed together—are related, and that a comprehensive peace remains a common objective.

Just in recent days, both Prime Minister Begin in Washington and President Sadat here in Egypt have again pledged to carry out every commitment made at Camp David.

Both leaders have reaffirmed that they do not want a separate peace between their two nations. Therefore, our current efforts to complete the treaty negotiations represent not the end of a process, but the beginning of one, for a treaty between Egypt and Israel is an indispensable part of a comprehensive peace.

I pledge to you today that I also remain personally committed to move on to negotiations concerning the West Bank and the Gaza Strip and other issues of concern to the Palestinians and also to future negotiations between Israel and all her neighbours. I feel a personal obligation in this regard.

Only the path of negotiation and accommodation can lead to the fulfillment of the hopes of the Palestinian people for peaceful self-expression. The negotiations proposed in the Camp David agreements will provide them with an opportunity to participate in the determination of their own future. We urge representative Palestinians to take part in these negotiations.

We are ready to work with any who are willing to talk peace. Those who attack these efforts are opposing the only realistic prospect that can bring real peace to the Middle East.

Let no one be deceived. The effect of their warlike slogans and their rhetoric is to make them in reality advocates of the status quo, not change; advocates of war, not peace; advocates of further suffering, not of achieving the human dignity to which long-suffering people of this region are entitled.

There is simply no workable alternative to the course that your nation and my nation are now following together. The conclusion of a treaty between Israel and Egypt will enable your government to mobilize its resources not for war, but for the provision of a better life for every Egyptian.

I know how deeply President Sadat is committed to that quest. And I believe its achievement will ultimately be his greatest legacy to the people he serves so well.

My government, for its part, the full power and influence of the United States of America, is ready to share that burden of that commitment with you. These gains which we envision will not come quickly or easily, but they will come.

The conclusion of the peace treaty that we are discussing will strengthen cooperation between Egypt and the United States in other ways. I fully share and will support President Sadat's belief that stability must be maintained in this part of the world, even while constructive change is actively encouraged. He and I recognize that the security of this vital region is being challenged. I applaud his determination to meet that challenge, and my government will stand with him.

Our policy is that each nation should have the ability to defend itself, so that it does not have to depend on external alliances for its own security. The United States does not seek a special position for itself.

If we are successful in our efforts to conclude a comprehensive peace, it will be presented, obviously, each element of it, to this body for ratification.

It is in the nature of negotiation that no treaty can be ideal or perfect from either the Egyptian or the Israeli point of view. The question we've faced all along, however, is not whether the treaty we negotiate will meet all the immediate desires of each of the two parties, but whether it will protect the vital interests of both and further the cause of peace for all the states and all the peoples of this region. That is the basic purpose and the most difficult question which we are resolved to answer.

Such a treaty, such an agreement, is within our grasp. Let us seize this opportunity while we have it.

We who are engaged in this great work, the work of peace, are of varied religious faiths. Some of us are Moslems; some are Jews; some are Christians. The forms of our faith are different. We worship the same God. And the message of Providence has always been the same.

I would like to quote the words of the Holy Quran: "If thine adversary incline towards peace, do thou also incline towards peace and trust in God, for he is the one that heareth and knoweth all things."

Now I would like to quote from the words of the Old Testament: "Depart from evil and do good; seek peace, and pursue it."

And now I would like to quote from the words of Jesus in the Sermon on the Mount: "Blessed are the peacemakers, for they shall be called the children of God."

My friends, my brothers, let us complete the work before us. Let us find peace together.

Jerusalem, Israel
Address Before the Knesset

12 March 1979

For the last twenty-four hours, I have been writing different versions of this speech. I have discarded the speech of despair; I have discarded the speech of glad tidings and celebration. I have decided to deliver the speech of concern and caution and hope.

I'm honoured to stand in this assembly of free men and women, which represents a great and an ancient people, a young and a courageous nation.

I bring with me the best wishes and the greetings of the people of the United States of America, who share with the people of Israel the love of liberty, of justice, and of peace. And I'm honoured to be in Jerusalem, this holy city described by Isaiah as a quiet habitation in which for so many of the human race the cause of brotherhood and peace are enshrined.

I am here in a cause of brotherhood and of peace. I've come to Cairo and also here to Jerusalem to try to enhance the bold, brave, and historic efforts of President Sadat and Prime Minister Begin and to demonstrate that the United States of America is as determined as these two leaders are to create lasting peace and friendship between Egypt and Israel and to put an end to war and the threat of war throughout the Middle East.

No people desire or deserve peace more than the Jewish people. None have wanted it so long. None have spoken of it more eloquently. None have suffered so much from the absence of peace. Pogrom after pogrom, war after war, Israel has buried its sons and its daughters.

Yesterday morning, at Yad Vashem, I grieved in the presence of terrible reminders of the agony and the horror of the Holocaust.

Modern Israel came into being in the wake of that historic crime, the enormity of which is almost beyond human comprehension. I know that Israel is committed and determined, above all, that nothing like it must ever, ever be permitted to happen again on earth.

Americans respect that determination, and we fully share that determination with you. And Americans recognize that for Jews over the centuries, as for Israel since its independence, caution and wariness have been a practical and a moral necessity for survival. And yet, in these past months, you've made enormous sacrifices and you've taken great risks for peace.

This sacred dedication to peace, born and fostered in Jerusalem and in Cairo, has given to men and women everywhere renewed sense of hope that human reason, good will, and faith can succeed, can break down barriers between peoples who, in our lifetimes, have only known war.

As Prime Minister Begin said after the Camp David summit, the agreements reached there proved that any problem can be solved if there is some—and he repeated, just some wisdom. Those are truthful and also reassuring words. I know from my intense, personal involvement in these negotiations that President Sadat and Prime Minister Begin have not wavered from their often-expressed commitment to peace.

President Sadat told me in Cairo that he will let nothing stand in the way of our shared goal of finishing the treaty of peace between Israel and Egypt and of making it a living testament of friendship between the two neighbouring peoples. I believe him, and I know in my heart that Prime Minister Begin and the Government of Israel are no less fervently committed to the same noble objective.

But we've not yet fully met our challenge. Despite our unflagging determination, despite the extraordinary progress of the past six months, we still fall short. It's now the somber responsibility of us all to exert our energies and our imaginations once again to contemplate the tragedy of failure and the legitimate exultation if we bring peace.

In this effort, the support of the members of the Knesset will obviously be crucial. Our vision must be as great as our goal. Wisdom and courage are required of us all, and so, too, are practicality and realism. We must not lose this moment. We must pray as if everything depended on God, and we must act as if everything depends on ourselves.

What kind of peace do we seek? Spinoza said that peace is not an absence of war; it is a virtue, a state of mind, a disposition for benevolence, for confidence, for justice. Americans share that vision and will stand beside Israel to be sure that that vision is fulfilled.

In Egypt, I saw vivid evidence of this deep longing for peace among the Egyptian people, millions of them. But like you, they worry about the uncertainties of that first crucial stage in the broad task of pounding Middle East swords into plowshares. Like you, they hope to banish forever the enmity that has existed between the neighbours, the permanent neighbours of Egypt and of Israel. Like you, they want this peace, and like you, they want it to be real and not just a sham peace.

My friends, from my own experience as president of the United States, I understand all too well that historic decisions are seldom easy, seldom without pain. Benjamin Franklin, who negotiated the treaty of peace between England and America after our own War of Independence, once said that he had never seen a peace made, even the most advantageous, that was not censured as inadequate.

Throughout the peace process, both Israel and Egypt have understood that no treaty can embody every aim of both nations. What a treaty can do, what it can do far better than the fragile status quo, and infinitely better than the insidious tensions that will build if our efforts are further stalled or fail, is to protect the vital interests of both Israel and Egypt and open up the possibility of peace for all the states and all the peoples of this troubled region.

Doubts are the stuff of great decisions, but so are dreams. We are now at the very edge of turning Israel's eternal dream of peace into reality. I will not pretend that this reality will be free from further challenges. It will not. And better than most, the Jewish people know that life is seldom easy. But we must make this beginning. We must seize this precious opportunity.

Fifty-seven years ago, the Congress of the United States of America committed itself to a Jewish homeland. Twenty-six years later, President Harry Truman recognized the new State of Israel eleven minutes after your nation was born. Seven presidents have believed and demonstrated that America's relationship with Israel is more than just a special relationship. It has been and it is a unique relationship. And it's a relationship which is indestructible, because it is rooted in the consciousness and the morals and the religion and the beliefs of the American people themselves.

Let me repeat what I said to Prime Minister Begin last year on the lawn of the White House, on the anniversary of the founding of the modern State of Israel, and I quote: "For thirty years we have stood at the side of the proud and independent nation of Israel. I can say without reservation, as president of the United States, that we will continue to do so, not just for another thirty years but forever."

We recognize the advantages to the United States of this partnership. You know that America deeply desires peace between Israel and Egypt, and that we will do everything we can to make peace possible.

The people of the two nations are ready now for peace. The people of the two nations are ready now for peace. The leaders have not yet proven that we are also ready for peace, enough to take a chance. We must persevere. But with or without a peace treaty, the United States will always be at Israel's side.

Meeting in this hall of liberty reminds us that we are bound more than in any other way by instinctive, common ideals and common commitments and beliefs. This Knesset itself is a temple to the principle and the practice of open debate. Democracy is an essential element to the very nationhood of Israel, as it is to the United States.

You've proven that democracy can be a stable form of government in a nation of great diversity and in a time and a place of danger and instability. But Israel and the United States were shaped by pioneers—my nation is also a nation of immigrants and refugees—by peoples gathered in both nations from many lands, by dreamers who, and I quote, "by the work of their hands and the sweat of their brows" transformed their dreams into the reality of nationhood.

We share the heritage of the Bible, the worship of God, of individual freedom, and we share a belief in cooperative endeavour, even in the face of apparently insurmountable obstacles.

In nations around the world where governments deny these values, millions look to us to uphold the right to freedom of speech, freedom of the press, the right to emigrate, the right to express one's political views, the right to move from one place to another, the right for families to be reunited, the right to a decent standard of material life.

These are the kinds of unbreakable ties that bind Israel and the United States together. These are the values that we offer to the whole world. Our mutual dedication to these ideals is an indispensable resource in our search for peace.

The treaty between Egypt and Israel that we hope may be placed before you for approval promises to be the cornerstone of a comprehensive structure of peace for this entire region.

We all recognize that this structure will be incomplete until the peace can be extended to include all the people who have been involved in the conflict. I know and I understand the concerns you feel as you consider the magnitude of the choices that will remain to be faced even after a peace treaty is concluded between Israel and Egypt. And as the time for these choices approaches, remember this pledge that I make to you again today: The United States will never support any agreement or any action that places Israel's security in jeopardy.

We must proceed with due caution. I understand that. But we must proceed.

As recently as two years ago, after all, these present steps that have already been taken seemed absolutely unthinkable. We know that confrontation magnifies differences. But the process of negotiation circumscribes differences, defines the differences, isolates them from the larger regions of common interests, and so makes the gaps which do exist more bridgeable. We've seen the proof of that in the last sixteen months.

At Camp David, Prime Minister Begin and President Sadat forged two frameworks for the building of that comprehensive peace. The genius of that accomplishment is that negotiations under these frameworks can go forward independently of each other, without destroying the obvious relationship between them.

They are designed to be mutually reinforcing, with the intrinsic flexibility necessary to promote the comprehensive peace that we all desire. Both will be fulfilled only when others of your Arab neighbours follow the visionary example of President Sadat, when they put ancient animosities behind them and agree to negotiate, as you desire, as you've already done with President Sadat, an honourable solution to the differences between you.

It's important that the door be kept open to all the parties to the conflict, including the Palestinians, with whom, above all, Israel shares a common interest in living in peace and living with mutual respect.

Peace in the Middle East, always important to the security of the entire region, in recent weeks has become an even more urgent concern.

Israel's security will rest not only on how the negotiations affect the situation on your own borders but also on how it affects the forces of stability and moderation beyond your borders.

I'm convinced that nothing can do more to create a hospitable atmosphere for those more distant forces in the long run than an equitable peace treaty between Israel and Egypt.

The risks of peace between you and your Egyptian neighbours are real. But America is ready to reduce any risks and to balance them within the bounds of our strength and our influence.

I came to Israel representing the most powerful country on Earth. And I can assure you that the United States intends to use that power in the pursuit of a stable and a peaceful Middle East.

We've been centrally involved in this region, and we will stay involved politically, economically, and militarily. We will stand by our friends. We are ready to place our strength at Israel's side when you want it to ensure Israel's security and well-being.

We know Israel's concern about many issues. We know your concern for an adequate oil supply. In the context of peace, we are ready to guarantee that supply. I've recommitted our nation publicly to this commitment, as you know, only in recent days in my own country.

We know Israel's concern that the price of peace with Egypt will exacerbate an already difficult economic situation and make it more difficult to meet your country's essential security requirements. In the context of peace, we are prepared to see Israel's economic and military relationship with the United States take on new and strong and more meaningful dimensions, even than already exist.

We will work not only to attain peace but to maintain peace, recognizing that it's a permanent challenge of our time.

We will rededicate ourselves to the ideals that our peoples share. These ideals are the course not only of our strength but of our self-respect as nations, as leaders, and as individuals.

I'm here today to reaffirm that the United States will always recognize, appreciate, and honour the mutual advantages of the strength and security of Israel. And I'm here to express my most heartfelt and passionate hope that we may work together successfully to make this peace.

The Midrash tells us that, and I quote, "Peace is the wisp of straw that binds together the sheaf of blessings." But the wisp of straw, we know, is fragile and easily broken.

Let us pray to God to guide our hand. Millions of men, women, and children, in Israel and Egypt and beyond, in this generation and in generations to come, are relying on our skill and relying on our faith.

In the words of a Sabbath prayer, "May He who causes peace to reign in the high heavens let peace descend on us, on all Israel, and on all the world."

Address Delivered Before a Joint Session of the Congress on the Vienna Summit Meeting

18 June 1979

The truth of the nuclear age is that the United States and the Soviet Union must live in peace, or we may not live at all.

From the beginning of history, the fortunes of men and nations were made and unmade in unending cycles of war and peace. Combat was often the measure of human courage. Willingness to risk war was the mark of statecraft. My fellow Americans, that pattern of war must now be broken forever.

Between nations armed with thousands of thermonuclear weapons—each one capable of causing unimaginable destruction—there can be no more cycles of both war and peace. There can only be peace.

About two hours ago, I returned from three days of intensive talks with President Leonid Brezhnev of the Soviet Union. I come here tonight to meet with you in a spirit of patience, of hope, and of reason and responsibility.

Patience—because the way is long and hard, and the obstacles ahead are at least as great as those that have been overcome in the last thirty years of diligent and dedicated work.

Hope—because I'm thankful to be able to report to you tonight that real progress has been made.

Reason and responsibility—because both will be needed in full measure if the promise which has been awakened in Vienna is to be fulfilled and the way is to be opened for the next phase in the struggle for a safe and a sane earth.

Nothing will more strongly affect the outcome of that struggle than the relationship between the two predominant military powers in the world, the United States of America and the Soviet Union.

The talks in Vienna were important in themselves. But their truest significance was as a part of a process—a process that, as you well know, began long before I became president.

This is the tenth time since the end of World War II when the leader of the United States and the leader of the Soviet Union have met at a summit conference. During these past three days, we've moved closer to a goal of stability and security in Soviet-American relationships.

That has been the purpose of American policy ever since the rivalry between the United States and the Soviet Union became a central fact in international relations more than a generation ago at the end of World War II.

With the support of the Congress of the United States and with the support of the people of this nation, every president throughout this period has sought to reduce the most dangerous elements of the Soviet-American competition.

While the United States still had an absolute nuclear monopoly, President Truman sought to place control of the atomic bomb under international authority. President Eisenhower made the first efforts to control nuclear testing. President Kennedy negotiated with the Soviet Union prohibition against atmospheric testing of nuclear explosives. President Johnson broadened the area of negotiations for the first time to include atomic weapons themselves. President Nixon concluded the first strategic arms limitation agreement, SALT I. President Ford negotiated the Vladivostok accords. You can see that this is a vital and a continuing process.

Later this week I will deliver to the United States Senate the complete and signed text of the second strategic arms limitation agreement, SALT II.

This treaty is the product of seven long years of tough, painstaking negotiation under the leadership of three different presidents. When ratified, it will be a truly national achievement—an achievement of the Executive and of the Congress, an achievement of civilians and of our military leaders, of liberals and conservatives, of Democrats and Republicans.

Of course, SALT II will not end the competition between the United States and the Soviet Union. That competition is based on fundamentally different visions of human society and human destiny. As long as that basic difference persists, there will always be some degree of tension in the relationship between our two countries. The United States has no fear of this rivalry. But we want it to be peaceful.

In any age, such rivalry risks degeneration into war. But our age is unique, for the terrible power of nuclear weapons has created an incentive that never existed before for avoiding war. This tendency transcends even the very deep differences of politics and philosophy. In the age of the hydrogen bomb, there is no longer any meaningful distinction between global war and global suicide.

Our shared understanding of these realities has given the world an interval of peace—a kind of a strange peace—marked by tension, marked by danger, marked even sometimes by regional conflict, but a kind of peace nonetheless. In the twenty-seven years before Hiroshima, the leading powers of the world were twice engulfed in total war. In the thirty-four years since Hiroshima, humanity has by no means been free of armed conflict. Yet, at least we have avoided a world war.

Yet this kind of twilight peace carries the ever-present danger of a catastrophic nuclear war, a war that in horror and destruction and massive death would dwarf all the combined wars of man's long and bloody history.

We must prevent such a war. We absolutely must prevent such a war.

To keep the peace, to prevent the war, we must have strong military forces, we must have strong alliances, we must have a strong national resolve—so strong that no potential adversary would dare be tempted to attack our country. We have that strength. And the strength of the United States is not diminishing; the strength of our great country is growing, and I thank God for it.

Yet, for these same reasons—in order to keep the peace—we must prevent an uncontrolled and pointless nuclear arms race that would damage the security of all countries, including our own, by exposing the world to an ever greater risk of war through instability and through tension and through uncertainty about the future. That's why the new strategic arms limitation treaty is so important.

SALT II will undoubtedly become the most exhaustively discussed and debated treaty of our time, perhaps of all times. The Secretary of State, the Secretary of Defense, the members of the Joint Chiefs of Staff, the Director of the Arms Control and Disarmament Agency, and many others who hammered out this treaty will testify for it before the Senate, in detail and in public. As president of our country, I will explain it throughout our nation to every American who will listen. This treaty will withstand the most severe scrutiny because it is so clearly in the interest of American security and of world peace.

SALT II is the most detailed, far-reaching, comprehensive treaty in the history of arms control. Its provisions are interwoven by the give-and-take of the long negotiating process. Neither side obtained everything it sought. But the package that did emerge is a carefully balanced whole, and it will make the world a safer place for both sides.

The restrictions on strategic nuclear weapons are complex, because these weapons represent the highest development of the complicated technical skills of two great nations. But the basic realities underlying this treaty and the thrust of the treaty itself are not so complex. When all is said and done, SALT II is a matter of common sense.

The SALT II treaty reduces the danger of nuclear war. For the first time, it places equal ceilings on the strategic arsenals of both sides, ending a previous numerical imbalance in favour of the Soviet Union.

SALT II preserves our options to build the forces we need to maintain that strategic balance. The treaty enhances our own ability to monitor what the Soviet Union is doing. And it leads directly to the next step in more effectively controlling nuclear weapons.

Again, SALT II does not end the arms competition. But it does make that competition safer and more predictable, with clear rules and verifiable limits, where otherwise there would be no rules and there would be no limits.

It's in our interest because it slows down—it even reverses—the momentum of the Soviet arms buildup that has been of such great concern to all of us. Under this new treaty, the Soviet Union will be held to a third fewer strategic missile launchers and bombers by 1985 than they would have simply by continuing to build at their present rate.

With SALT II, the numbers of warheads on missiles, their throw-weight, and the qualitative development of new missiles will all be limited. The Soviet Union will have to destroy or dismantle some two hundred and fifty strategic missile systems—systems such as nuclear submarines armed with relatively new missiles, built in the early 1970s, and aircraft will have to be destroyed by the Soviet Union carrying their largest multi-megaton bomb. Once dismantled, under the provisions of SALT II, these systems cannot be replaced.

By contrast, no operational United States forces will have to be reduced.

For one Soviet missile alone—the SS18—the SALT II limits will mean that some six thousand fewer Soviet nuclear warheads can be built and aimed at our country. SALT II limits severely for the first time the number of warheads that can be mounted on these very large missiles of the Soviet Union, cutting down their actual potential by six thousand.

With or without SALT II, we must modernize and strengthen our own strategic forces—and we are doing so—but SALT II will make this task easier, surer, and less expensive.

The agreement constrains none of the reasonable programs we've planned to improve our own defenses. Moreover, it helps us to respond more effectively to our most pressing strategic problem—the prospective vulnerability in the 1980s of our land-based silo missiles. The MX missile, which has been so highly publicized, is permitted under SALT II. Yet its verifiable mobile development system will enhance stability as it deprives an attacker of the confidence that a successful first strike could be launched against the United States ICBMs, or intercontinental ballistic missiles.

Without the SALT II limits, the Soviet Union could build so many warheads that any land-based system, fixed or mobile, could be jeopardized.

With SALT II, we can concentrate more effort on preserving the balance in our own conventional and NATO forces. Without the SALT II treaty, we would be forced to spend extra billions and billions of dollars each year in a dangerous, destabilizing, unnecessary nuclear arms race.

As I have said many times, SALT II is not based on trust. Compliance will be assured by our own nation's means of verification, including extremely sophisticated satellites, powerful electronic systems, and a vast intelligence network. Were the Soviet Union to take enormous risk of trying to violate this treaty in any way that might affect the strategic balance, there is no doubt that we would discover it in time to respond fully and effectively.

It's the SALT II agreement itself which forbids concealment measures—many of them for the first time—forbids interference with our monitoring, and forbids the encryption or the encoding of crucial missile-test information. A violation of this part of the agreement—which we would quickly detect—would be just as serious as a violation of the limits on strategic weapons themselves.

Consider these prospects for a moment. Suppose the Soviet leaders build a thousand additional missiles, above and beyond the ones they have now, many new, advanced, and of a formidable design. This can happen only if the SALT II treaty is defeated.

Suppose the Soviet leaders wanted to double the number of warheads on all their existing missiles; suppose they wanted to triple the annual production rate of the Backfire bomber and greatly improve its characteristics in range and payload. These kinds of things can happen only if the SALT II treaty is defeated.

Suppose the Soviet Union leaders encrypt all data on their missile tests; suppose they conceal their nuclear launcher deployment rate and hide all their existing missile systems. Those things can happen only if the SALT II treaty is defeated.

SALT II is very important. But it's more than a single arms control agreement; it's part of a long, historical process of gradually reducing the danger of nuclear war—a process that we in this room must not undermine.

The SALT II treaty must be judged on its own merits. And on its own merits, it is a substantial gain for national security for us and the people who we represent, and it's a gain for international stability. But it would be the height of irresponsibility to ignore other possible consequences of a failure to ratify this treaty.

These consequences would include: greatly increased spending for strategic nuclear arms which we do not need; greater uncertainty about the strategic balance between ourselves and the Soviet Union; vastly increased danger of nuclear proliferation among other nations of the world who do not presently have nuclear explosives; increased political tension between the East and the West, with greater likelihood that other inevitable problems would escalate into serious superpower confrontations.

Rejection would also be a damaging blow to the Western Alliance. All of our European and other allies, including especially those who are most directly and courageously facing Soviet power, all of them strongly support SALT II. If the Senate were to reject the treaty, America's leadership of this alliance would be compromised, and the alliance itself would be severely shaken.

In short, SALT II is not a favour we are doing for the Soviet Union. It's a deliberate, calculated move that we are making as a matter of self-interest for the United States—a move that happens to serve the goals of both security and survival, that strengthens both the military position of our own country and the cause of world peace.

And, of course, SALT II is the absolutely indispensable precondition for moving on to much deeper and more significant cuts under SALT III.

Although we will not begin negotiations on SALT III until SALT II goes into effect, I discussed other nuclear control issues with President Brezhnev, such as much deeper mutual reductions in nuclear weapon inventories, stricter limit on the production of nuclear warheads and launchers, enhanced survivability and stability of missile systems that are authorized under existing SALT agreement, pre-notification about missile tests and mass use or exercises of strategic bombers, and limits and controls on types of missiles which are not presently covered under any SALT agreement

Though SALT is the most important single part of the complex relationship between the United States and the Soviet Union, it is only a part. The US–Soviet relationship covers a broad range of issues, some of which bear directly on our joint responsibility to reduce the possibility of war. President Brezhnev and I discussed these issues in Vienna this morning in a long private session with only the interpreters present.

I undertook all these discussions with a firm confidence in the strength of America. Militarily, our power is second to none. I'm determined that it will remain so. We will continue to have military power to deter any possible aggression, to maintain security of our country, and to permit the continuing search for peace and for the control of arms from a position of strength. We must have that strength so that we will never be afraid to negotiate for peace.

Economically, despite serious problems of energy and inflation, we are by far the most productive nation on earth. Along with our allies, our economic strength is three times greater than that of the Soviet Union and all its allies.

Diplomatically, we've strengthened our friendships with Western Europe and Japan, with China and India, with Israel and Egypt, and with the countries of the Third World. Our alliances are stronger because they are based not on force, but on common interests and often on common values.

Politically, our democratic system is an enormous advantage, not only to each of us as individuals who enjoy freedom but to all of us together because our nation is stronger. Our support of human rights, backed by the concrete example of the American society, has aligned us with peoples all over the world who yearn for freedom.

These strengths are such that we need fear no other country. This confidence in our nation helped me in Vienna as we discussed specific areas of potential, either direct or indirect, confrontation around the world, including places like southern Africa or the Middle East.

For instance, I made it clear to President Brezhnev that Cuban military activities in Africa, sponsored by or supported by the Soviet Union, and also the growing Cuban involvement in the problems of Central America and the Caribbean can only have a negative impact on US–Soviet relations.

Our strength, our resolve, our determination, our willingness to protect our own interests, our willingness to discuss these problems with others are the best means by which we can resolve these differences and alleviate these tests successfully for our people.

Despite disagreements, our exchange in Vienna was useful, because it enabled us to clarify our positions directly to each other, face-to-face, and, thus, to reduce the chances of future miscalculations on both sides.

And, finally, I would like to say to you that President Brezhnev and I developed a better sense of each other as leaders and as men. The responsibility for many decisions involving the very future of the world rests on me as the leader of this great country, and it's vital that my judgments be based on as much firsthand knowledge and experience as possible.

In these conversations, I was careful to leave no doubt about either my desire for peace or my determination to defend the interests of the United States and of our allies. I believe that together we laid a foundation on which we can build a more stable relationship between our two countries.

We will seek to broaden the areas of cooperation, and we will compete where and when we must. We know how determined the Soviet leaders are to secure their interests, and we are equally determined to protect and to advance our own.

We look to the future—all of us Americans look to the future—with anticipation and with confidence, not only because of the vast material powers of our nation but because of the power of our nation's ideas and ideals and principles. The ultimate future of the human race lies not with tyranny, but with freedom; not with war, but with peace.

With that kind of vision to sustain us, we must now complete the work of ratifying this treaty, a major step in the limitation of nuclear weapons and a major step toward world peace. And then we may turn our energies not only to further progress along that path but also more urgently to our own domestic agenda in the knowledge that we have strengthened the security of a nation which we love and also strengthened peace for all the world.

Address to the Nation on Energy and National Goals:
'The Malaise Speech'

15 July 1979

Good evening.

This is a special night for me. Exactly three years ago, on July 15, 1976, I accepted the nomination of my party to run for president of the United States. I promised you a president who is not isolated from the people, who feels your pain, and who shares your dreams and who draws his strength and his wisdom from you.

During the past three years I've spoken to you on many occasions about national concerns, the energy crisis, reorganizing the government, our nation's economy, and issues of war and especially peace. But over those years the subjects of the speeches, the talks, and the press conferences have become increasingly narrow, focused more and more on what the isolated world of Washington thinks is important. Gradually, you've heard more and more about what the government thinks or what the government should be doing and less and less about our nation's hopes, our dreams, and our vision of the future.

Ten days ago I had planned to speak to you again about a very important subject: energy. For the fifth time I would have described the urgency of the problem and laid out a series of legislative recommendations to the Congress.

But as I was preparing to speak, I began to ask myself the same question that I now know has been troubling many of you. Why have we not been able to get together as a nation to resolve our serious energy problem?

It's clear that the true problems of our nation are much deeper—deeper than gasoline lines or energy shortages, deeper even than inflation or recession. And I realize more than ever that as president I need your help. So, I decided to reach out and listen to the voices of America.

I invited to Camp David people from almost every segment of our society—business and labour, teachers and preachers, governors, mayors, and private citizens. And then I left Camp David to listen to other Americans, men and women like you. It has been an extraordinary ten days, and I want to share with you what I've heard.

First of all, I got a lot of personal advice. Let me quote a few of the typical comments that I wrote down.

This from a southern governor: "Mr. President, you are not leading this nation, instead you're just managing the government."

"You don't see the people enough any more."

"Some of your Cabinet members don't seem loyal. There is not enough discipline among your disciples."

"Don't talk to us about politics or the mechanics of government, but about an understanding of our common good."

"Mr. President, we're in trouble. Talk to us about blood and sweat and tears."

"If you lead, Mr. President, we will follow."

Many people talked about themselves and about the condition of our nation. This from a young woman in Pennsylvania: "I feel so far from government. I feel like ordinary people are excluded from political power."

And this from a young Chicano: "Some of us have suffered from recession all our lives."

"Some people have wasted energy, but others haven't had anything to waste."

And this from a religious leader: "No material shortage can touch the important things like God's love for us or our love for one another."

And I like this one particularly from a black woman who happens to be the mayor of a small Mississippi town: "The big-shots are not the only ones who are important. Remember, you can't sell anything on Wall Street unless someone digs it up somewhere else first."

This kind of summarized a lot of other statements: "Mr. President, we are confronted with a moral and a spiritual crisis."

Several of our discussions were on energy, and I have a notebook full of comments and advice. I'll read just a few.

"We can't go on consuming 40 percent more energy than we produce. When we import oil we are also importing inflation plus unemployment."

"We've got to use what we have. The Middle East has only 5 percent of the world's energy, but the United States has 24 percent."

And this is one of the most vivid statements: "Our neck is stretched over the fence and OPEC has a knife."

"There will be other cartels and other shortages. American wisdom and courage right now can set a path to follow in the future."

This was a good one: "Be bold, Mr. President. We may make mistakes, but we are ready to experiment."

And this one from a labour leader got to the heart of it: "The real issue is freedom. We must deal with the energy problem on a war footing."

And the last that I'll read: "When we enter the moral equivalent of war, Mr. President, don't issue us BB guns."

These ten days confirmed my belief in the decency and the strength and the wisdom of the American people, but it also bore out some of my long-standing concerns about our nation's underlying problems.

I know, of course, being president, that government actions and legislation can be very important. That's why I've worked hard to put my campaign promises into law—and I have to admit, with just mixed success. But after listening to the American people I have been reminded again that all the legislation in the world can't fix what's wrong with America. So, I want to speak to you first tonight about a subject even more serious than energy or inflation. I want to talk to you right now about a fundamental threat to American democracy.

I do not mean our political and civil liberties. They will endure. And I do not refer to the outward strength of America, a nation that is at peace tonight everywhere in the world, with unmatched economic power and military might.

The threat is nearly invisible in ordinary ways. It is a crisis of confidence. It is a crisis that strikes at the very heart and soul and spirit of our national will. We can see this crisis in the growing doubt about the meaning of our own lives and in the loss of a unity of purpose for our nation.

The erosion of our confidence in the future is threatening to destroy the social and the political fabric of America.

The confidence that we have always had as a people is not simply some romantic dream or a proverb in a dusty book that we read just on the Fourth of July. It is the idea which founded our nation and has guided our development as a people. Confidence in the future has supported everything else—public institutions and private enterprise, our own families, and the very Constitution of the United States. Confidence has defined our course and has served as a link between generations. We've always believed in something called progress. We've always had a faith that the days of our children would be better than our own.

Our people are losing that faith, not only in government itself but in the ability as citizens to serve as the ultimate rulers and shapers of our democracy. As a people we know our past and we are proud of it. Our progress has been part of the living history of America, even the world. We always believed that we were part of a great movement of humanity itself called democracy, involved in the search for freedom, and that belief has always strengthened us in our purpose. But just as we are losing our confidence in the future, we are also beginning to close the door on our past.

In a nation that was proud of hard work, strong families, close-knit communities, and our faith in God, too many of us now tend to worship self-indulgence and consumption. Human identity is no longer defined by what one does, but by what one owns. But we've discovered that owning things and consuming things does not satisfy our longing for meaning. We've learned that piling up material goods cannot fill the emptiness of lives which have no confidence or purpose.

The symptoms of this crisis of the American spirit are all around us. For the first time in the history of our country a majority of our people believe that the next five years will be worse than the past five years. Two-thirds of our people do not even vote. The productivity of American workers is actually dropping, and the willingness of Americans to save for the future has fallen below that of all other people in the Western world.

As you know, there is a growing disrespect for government and for churches and for schools, the news media, and other institutions. This is not a message of happiness or reassurance, but it is the truth and it is a warning.

These changes did not happen overnight. They've come upon us gradually over the last generation, years that were filled with shocks and tragedy.

We were sure that ours was a nation of the ballot, not the bullet, until the murders of John Kennedy and Robert Kennedy and Martin Luther King, Jr. We were taught that our armies were always invincible and our causes were always just, only to suffer the agony of Vietnam. We respected the presidency as a place of honour until the shock of Watergate.

We remember when the phrase "sound as a dollar" was an expression of absolute dependability, until ten years of inflation began to shrink our dollar and our savings. We believed that our nation's resources were limitless until 1973, when we had to face a growing dependence on foreign oil.

These wounds are still very deep. They have never been healed.

Looking for a way out of this crisis, our people have turned to the federal government and found it isolated from the mainstream of our nation's life. Washington, D.C. has become an island. The gap between our citizens and our government has never been so wide. The people are looking for honest answers, not easy answers; clear leadership, not false claims and evasiveness and politics as usual.

What you see too often in Washington and elsewhere around the country is a system of government that seems incapable of action. You see a Congress twisted and pulled in every direction by hundreds of well-financed and powerful special interests. You see every extreme position defended to the last vote, almost to the last breath by one unyielding group or another. You often see a balanced and a fair approach that demands sacrifice, a little sacrifice from everyone, abandoned like an orphan without support and without friends.

Often you see paralysis and stagnation and drift. You don't like it, and neither do I. What can we do?

First of all, we must face the truth, and then we can change our course. We simply must have faith in each other, faith in our ability to govern ourselves, and faith in the future of this nation. Restoring that faith and that confidence to America is now the most important task we face. It is a true challenge of this generation of Americans.

One of the visitors to Camp David last week put it this way: "We've got to stop crying and start sweating, stop talking and start walking, stop cursing and start praying. The strength we need will not come from the White House, but from every house in America."

We know the strength of America. We are strong. We can regain our unity. We can regain our confidence. We are the heirs of generations who survived threats much more powerful and awesome than those that challenge us now. Our fathers and mothers were strong men and women who shaped a new society during the Great Depression, who fought world wars, and who carved out a new charter of peace for the world.

We ourselves are the same Americans who just ten years ago put a man on the moon. We are the generation that dedicated our society to the pursuit of human rights and equality. And we are the generation that will win the war on the energy problem and in that process rebuild the unity and confidence of America.

We are at a turning point in our history. There are two paths to choose. One is a path I've warned about tonight, the path that leads to fragmentation and self-interest. Down that road lies a mistaken idea of freedom; the right to grasp for ourselves some advantage over others. That path would be one of constant conflict between narrow interests ending in chaos and immobility. It is a certain route to failure.

All the traditions of our past, all the lessons of our heritage, all the promises of our future point to another path, the path of common purpose and the restoration of American values. That path leads to true freedom for our nation and ourselves. We can take the first steps down that path as we begin to solve our energy problem.

Energy will be the immediate test of our ability to unite this nation, and it can also be the standard around which we rally. On the battlefield of energy we can win for our nation a new confidence, and we can seize control again of our common destiny.

In little more than two decades we've gone from a position of energy independence to one in which almost half the oil we use comes from foreign countries, at prices that are going through the roof. Our excessive dependence on OPEC has already taken a tremendous toll on our economy and our people. This is the direct cause of the long lines which have made millions of you spend aggravating hours waiting for gasoline. It's a cause of the increased inflation and unemployment that we now face. This intolerable dependence on foreign oil threatens our economic independence and the very security of our nation.

The energy crisis is real. It is worldwide. It is a clear and present danger to our nation. These are facts and we simply must face them:

What I have to say to you now about energy is simple and vitally important.

Point one: I am tonight setting a clear goal for the energy policy of the United States. Beginning this moment, this nation will never use more foreign oil than we did in 1977—never. From now on, every new addition to our demand for energy will be met from our own production and our own conservation. The generation-long growth in our dependence on foreign oil will be stopped dead in its tracks right now and then reversed as we move through the 1980s, for I am tonight setting the further goal of cutting our dependence on foreign oil by one-half by the end of the next decade—a saving of over four and a half million barrels of imported oil per day.

Point two: To ensure that we meet these targets, I will use my presidential authority to set import quotas. I'm announcing tonight that for 1979 and 1980, I will forbid the entry into this country of one drop of foreign oil more than these goals allow. These quotas will ensure a reduction in imports even below the ambitious levels we set at the recent Tokyo summit.

Point three: To give us energy security, I am asking for the most massive peacetime commitment of funds and resources in our nation's history to develop America's own alternative sources of fuel—from coal, from oil shale, from plant products for gasohol, from unconventional gas, from the sun.

I propose the creation of an energy security corporation to lead this effort to replace two and a half million barrels of imported oil per day by 1990. The corporation will issue up to $5 billion in energy bonds, and I especially want them to be in small denominations so that average Americans can invest directly in America's energy security.

Just as a similar synthetic rubber corporation helped us win World War II, so will we mobilize American determination and ability to win the energy war. Moreover, I will soon submit legislation to Congress calling for the creation of this nation's first solar bank, which will help us achieve the crucial goal of 20 percent of our energy coming from solar power by the year 2000.

These efforts will cost money, a lot of money, and that is why Congress must enact the windfall profits tax without delay. It will be money well spent. Unlike the billions of dollars that we ship to foreign countries to pay for foreign oil, these funds will be paid by Americans to Americans. These funds will go to fight, not to increase, inflation and unemployment.

Point four: I'm asking Congress to mandate, to require as a matter of law, that our nation's utility companies cut their massive use of oil by 50 percent within the next decade and switch to other fuels, especially coal, our most abundant energy source.

Point five: To make absolutely certain that nothing stands in the way of achieving these goals, I will urge Congress to create an energy mobilization board which, like the War Production Board in World War II, will have the responsibility and authority to cut through the red tape, the delays, and the endless roadblocks to completing key energy projects.

We will protect our environment. But when this nation critically needs a refinery or a pipeline, we will build it.

Point six: I'm proposing a bold conservation program to involve every state, county, and city and every average American in our energy battle. This effort will permit you to build conservation into your homes and your lives at a cost you can afford.

I ask Congress to give me authority for mandatory conservation and for standby gasoline rationing. To further conserve energy, I'm proposing tonight an extra $10 billion over the next decade to strengthen our public transportation systems. And I'm asking you for your good and for your nation's security to take no unnecessary trips, to use carpools or public transportation whenever you can, to park your car one extra day per week, to obey the speed limit, and to set your thermostats to save fuel. Every act of energy conservation like this is more than just common sense—I tell you it is an act of patriotism.

Our nation must be fair to the poorest among us, so we will increase aid to needy Americans to cope with rising energy prices. We often think of conservation only in terms of sacrifice. In fact, it is the most painless and immediate way of rebuilding our nation's strength. Every gallon of oil each one of us saves is a new form of production. It gives us more freedom, more confidence, that much more control over our own lives.

So, the solution of our energy crisis can also help us to conquer the crisis of the spirit in our country. It can rekindle our sense of unity, our confidence in the future, and give our nation and all of us individually a new sense of purpose.

You know we can do it. We have the natural resources. We have more oil in our shale alone than several Saudi Arabias. We have more coal than any nation on earth. We have the world's highest level of technology. We have the most skilled work force, with innovative genius, and I firmly believe that we have the national will to win this war.

I do not promise you that this struggle for freedom will be easy. I do not promise a quick way out of our nation's problems, when the truth is that the only way out is an all-out effort. What I do promise you is that I will lead our fight, and I will enforce fairness in our struggle, and I will ensure honesty. And above all, I will act.

We can manage the short-term shortages more effectively and we will, but there are no short-term solutions to our long-range problems. There is simply no way to avoid sacrifice.

Twelve hours from now I will speak again in Kansas City, to expand and to explain further our energy program. Just as the search for solutions to our energy shortages has now led us to a new awareness of our nation's deeper problems, so our willingness to work for those solutions in energy can strengthen us to attack those deeper problems.

I will continue to travel this country, to hear the people of America. You can help me to develop a national agenda for the 1980s. I will listen and I will act. We will act together. These were the promises I made three years ago, and I intend to keep them.

Little by little we can and we must rebuild our confidence. We can spend until we empty our treasuries, and we may summon all the wonders of science. But we can succeed only if we tap our greatest resources—America's people, America's values, and America's confidence.

I have seen the strength of America in the inexhaustible resources of our people. In the days to come, let us renew that strength in the struggle for an energy secure nation.

In closing, let me say this: I will do my best, but I will not do it alone. Let your voice be heard. Whenever you have a chance, say something good about our country. With God's help and for the sake of our nation, it is time for us to join hands in America. Let us commit ourselves together to a rebirth of the American spirit. Working together with our common faith we cannot fail.

Above and below: President Carter and Prime Minister Pierre Trudeau in Venice, Italy at the G7 Summit in 23 June 1980. *Photos courtesy of the Jimmy Carter Library.*

Farewell Address to the Nation

14 January 1981

Good evening.

In a few days I will lay down my official responsibilities in this office, to take up once more the only title in our democracy superior to that of president, the title of citizen.

Of Vice President Mondale, my cabinet, and the hundreds of others who have served with me during the last four years, I wish to say now publicly what I have said in private: I thank them for the dedication and competence they've brought to the service of our country. But I owe my deepest thanks to you, to the American people, because you gave me this extraordinary opportunity to serve.

We've faced great challenges together, and we know that future problems will also be difficult. But I'm now more convinced than ever that the United States, better than any other country, can meet successfully whatever the future might bring. These last four years have made me more certain than ever of the inner strength of our country, the unchanging value of our principles and ideals, the stability of our political system, the ingenuity and the decency of our people.

Tonight I would like first to say a few words about this most special office, the presidency of the United States. This is at once the most powerful office in the world and among the most severely constrained by law and custom. The president is given a broad responsibility to lead but cannot do so without the support and consent of the people, expressed formally through the Congress and informally in many ways through a whole range of public and private institutions. This is as it should be.

Within our system of government every American has a right and a duty to help shape the future course of the United States. Thoughtful criticism and close scrutiny of all government officials by the press and the public are an important part of our democratic society. Now, as in the past, only the understanding and involvement of the people through full and open debate can help to avoid serious mistakes and assure the continued dignity and safety of the nation.

Today we are asking our political system to do things of which the Founding Fathers never dreamed. The government they designed for a few hundred thousand people now serves a nation of almost two hundred and thirty million people. Their small coastal republic now spans beyond a continent, and we also now have the responsibility to help lead much of the world through difficult times to a secure and prosperous future.

Today, as people have become ever more doubtful of the ability of the government to deal with our problems, we are increasingly drawn to single-issue groups and special interest organizations to ensure that whatever else happens, our own personal views and our own private interests are protected. This is a disturbing factor in American political life. It tends to distort our purposes, because the national interest is not always the sum of all our single or special interests. We are all Americans together, and we must not forget that the common good is our common interest and our individual responsibility.

Because of the fragmented pressures of these special interests, it's very important that the office of the president be a strong one and that its constitutional authority be preserved. The president is the only elected official charged with the primary responsibility of representing all the people. In the moments of decision, after the different and conflicting views have all been aired, it's the president who then must speak to the nation and for the nation.

I understand after four years in this office, as few others can, how formidable is the task the new president-elect is about to undertake, and to the very limits of conscience and conviction, I pledge to support him in that task. I wish him success, and Godspeed.

I know from experience that presidents have to face major issues that are controversial, broad in scope, and which do not arouse the natural support of a political majority. For a few minutes now, I want to lay aside my role as leader of one nation, and speak to you as a fellow citizen of the world about three issues, three difficult issues: the threat of nuclear destruction, our stewardship of the physical resources of our planet, and the preeminence of the basic rights of human beings.

It's now been thirty-five years since the first atomic bomb fell on Hiroshima. The great majority of the world's people cannot remember a time when the nuclear shadow did not hang over the earth. Our minds have adjusted to it, as after a time our eyes adjust to the dark. Yet the risk of a nuclear conflagration has not lessened. It has not happened yet, thank God, but that can give us little comfort, for it only has to happen once.

The danger is becoming greater. As the arsenals of the superpowers grow in size and sophistication and as other governments, perhaps even in the future dozens of governments, acquire these weapons, it may only be a matter of time before madness, desperation, greed, or miscalculation lets loose this terrible force.

In an all-out nuclear war, more destructive power than in all of World War II would be unleashed every second during the long afternoon it would take for all the missiles and bombs to fall. A World War II every second—more people killed in the first few hours than in all the wars of history put together. The survivors, if any, would live in despair amid the poisoned ruins of a civilization that had committed suicide.

National weakness, real or perceived, can tempt aggression and thus cause war. That's why the United States can never neglect its military strength. We must and we will remain strong. But with equal determination, the United States and all countries must find ways to control and to reduce the horrifying danger that is posed by the enormous world stockpiles of nuclear arms.

This has been a concern of every American president since the moment we first saw what these weapons could do. Our leaders will require our understanding and our support as they grapple with this difficult but crucial challenge. There is no disagreement on the goals or the basic approach to controlling this enormous destructive force. The answer lies not just in the attitudes or the actions of world leaders but in the concern and the demands of all of us as we continue our struggle to preserve the peace.

Nuclear weapons are an expression of one side of our human character. But there's another side. The same rocket technology that delivers nuclear warheads has also taken us peacefully into space. From that perspective, we see our earth as it really is—a small and fragile and beautiful blue globe, the only home we have. We see no barriers of race or religion or country. We see the essential unity of our species and our planet. And with faith and common sense, that bright vision will ultimately prevail.

Another major challenge, therefore, is to protect the quality of this world within which we live. The shadows that fall across the future are cast not only by the kinds of weapons we've built, but by the kind of world we will either nourish or neglect. There are real and growing dangers to our simple and our most precious possessions: the air we breathe, the water we drink, and the land which sustains us. The rapid depletion of irreplaceable minerals, the erosion of topsoil, the destruction of beauty, the blight of pollution, the demands of increasing billions of people, all combine to create problems which are easy to observe and predict, but difficult to resolve. If we do not act, the world of the year 2000 will be much less able to sustain life than it is now.

But there is no reason for despair. Acknowledging the physical realities of our planet does not mean a dismal future of endless sacrifice. In fact, acknowledging these realities is the first step in dealing with them. We can meet the resource problems of the world—water, food, minerals, farmlands, forests, overpopulation, pollution if we tackle them with courage and foresight.

I've just been talking about forces of potential destruction that mankind has developed and how we might control them. It's equally important that we remember the beneficial forces that we have evolved over the ages and how to hold fast to them. One of those constructive forces is the enhancement of individual human freedoms through the strengthening of democracy and the fight against deprivation, torture, terrorism, and the persecution of people throughout the world. The struggle for human rights overrides all differences of colour or nation or language. Those who hunger for freedom, who thirst for human dignity, and who suffer for the sake of justice, they are the patriots of this cause.

I believe with all my heart that America must always stand for these basic human rights at home and abroad. That is both our history and our destiny.

America did not invent human rights. In a very real sense, it's the other way around. Human rights invented America. Ours was the first nation in the history of the world to be founded explicitly on such an idea. Our social and political progress has been based on one fundamental principle: the value and importance of the individual. The fundamental force that unites us is not kinship or place of origin or religious preference. The love of liberty is the common blood that flows in our American veins.

The battle for human rights, at home and abroad, is far from over. We should never be surprised nor discouraged, because the impact of our efforts has had and will always have varied results. Rather, we should take pride that the ideals which gave birth to our nation still inspire the hopes of oppressed people around the world. We have no cause for self-righteousness or complacency, but we have every reason to persevere, both within our own country and beyond our borders.

If we are to serve as a beacon for human rights, we must continue to perfect, here at home, the rights and the values which we espouse around the world: a decent education for our children, adequate medical care for all Americans, an end to discrimination against minorities and women, a job for all those able to work, and freedom from injustice and religious intolerance.

We live in a time of transition, an uneasy era which is likely to endure for the rest of this century. It will be a period of tensions, both within nations and between nations, of competition for scarce resources, of social, political, and economic stresses and strains. During this period we may be tempted to abandon some of the time-honoured principles and commitments which have been proven during the difficult times of past generations. We must never yield to this temptation. Our American values are not luxuries, but necessities—not the salt in our bread, but the bread itself. Our common vision of a free and just society is our greatest source of cohesion at home and strength abroad, greater even than the bounty of our material blessings.

Remember these words: "We hold these truths to be self-evident, that all men are created equal, that they are endowed by their Creator with certain inalienable Rights, that among these are Life, Liberty and the pursuit of Happiness."

This vision still grips the imagination of the world. But we know that democracy is always an unfinished creation. Each generation must renew its foundations. Each generation must rediscover the meaning of this hallowed vision in the light of its own modern challenges. For this generation, ours, life is nuclear survival; liberty is human rights; the pursuit of happiness is a planet whose resources are devoted to the physical and spiritual nourishment of its inhabitants.

During the next few days I will work hard to make sure that the transition from myself to the next president is a good one, that the American people are served well. And I will continue, as I have the last fourteen months, to work hard and to pray for the lives and the well-being of the American hostages held in Iran. I can't predict yet what will happen, but I hope you will join me in my constant prayer for their freedom.

As I return home to the South, where I was born and raised, I look forward to the opportunity to reflect and further to assess, I hope with accuracy, the circumstances of our times. I intend to give our new president my support, and I intend to work as a citizen, as I've worked here in this office as president, for the values this nation was founded to secure.

Again, from the bottom of my heart, I want to express to you the gratitude I feel. Thank you, fellow citizens, and farewell.

Part II

The Man From Plains

The former president and first lady met with a small group of Canadians—Alison Bogle and Arthur Milnes, Beth and Murray Chown and Frances and Peter O'Malley—on a fall day in Plains in 2008. After an hour-long discussion in the auditorium of the Plains High School—now the Visitor's Center for the Jimmy Carter National Historic Site—and a private luncheon, the group travelled to the farm outside Plains, in Archery, where Carter had grown up. There Carter spent close to an hour providing the Canadians with a unique introduction to his own historic site. He also described

President Carter speaks to a small group of Canadians in 2008 at the farm where he grew up in the 1930s. From left: Jimmy Carter, Murray Chown, Peggy Carson (Carter office), Beth Chown, Alison Bogle and Frances and Peter O'Malley. *Photo by Arthur Milnes.*

Lunch with the Carters at the Plains High School, September 2008. From left: Arthur Milnes, President Carter, Frances O'Malley, Alison Bogle, Peter O'Malley, Mrs. Carter, Beth Chown. *Photo by Murray Chown.*

Mrs. Carter in conversation with Canadians David Lockhart and Thomas S. Harrison, Plains Historic Inn, March 2010. *Photo by Steve Paikin.*

racial and economic conditions in rural Georgia of the 1930s. President and Mrs. Carter graciously allowed the group to record the event and what appears below is an edited version of the 2008 conversation. Less than two years later, on 13 March, 2010, the Carters again met with a tiny group of Canadians, this time over dinner at the Plains Historic Inn. This time Milnes was accompanied by Thomas Harrison, David Lockhart and Steve Paikin. In Part II of this section, readers will find essays written afterwards by some members of these groups and a variety of articles the editor had written over the years for Canadian and US newspapers.

Plains High School

20 September 2008

CARTER: We have about six hundred and thirty people that live here in Plains. It has been growing steadily since I was child. It is about 60 percent African American and about 40 percent white and we work very closely together. This was our school—Rose's mother went here—and we both went here for eleven years; that's all we had then. It was an outstanding school, one of the best in Georgia, because we had a superb superintendant, Miss Julia Coleman, who shaped our lives. I quoted her in my Inaugural address and also in my Nobel Peace Prize acceptance speech. The quote I used was "We must adapt to changing times, but cling to unchanging principles."

We were very competitive in all kinds of literary events. I was a Future Farmer so I was also competitive in the growing of cattle and the growing of peanuts and the cutting of rafters for barns and houses and things like that. Miss Julia made us, every week, take part in spelling contests and also in reading; she gave us a list of books to read. I think I was possibly the only one who ever read all the books on her list and I got a prize for it. We competed in one-act play presentations, and in debating as well as what was called ready-writing back then. She would put three or four themes on the board and we would write as quickly as we could, maybe fifteen hundred words extemporaneously. She had phonograph records of fifty of the most famous classical compositions and opera and so forth and we had to compete about who could identify those accurately and the quickest. She had fifty or so of the most famous paintings in the world and she would hold them up and we would have to identify them and the artists who painted them. It was a very advanced little country school.

ROSALYNN: I am writing a book right now about mental health. I wrote one in 1996 and everything has changed since then—everything except stigma. It is beginning to lift a little bit since I first began working on it in 1971. I'm not a very pleasant person to be with when I'm writing a book.

CARTER: (laughing) Right.

ROSALYNN: I'm a night person and he's a day person. It's easy for him. He wrote his whole book about his mother and I hadn't written the first chapter of mine.[1]

I was actually the first spouse, wife, that campaigned for her husband like that and it was very interesting. The first thing I did after we started campaigning was go to Florida with a friend. We had no schedule and we would just stop and walk around the towns and look for a radio station or television station or newspaper. I'd say "I'm here for the interview. I'm Mrs. Carter and my husband is going to be president." And they'd say, "President of what." And I'd say, "Of the United States!" I learned a lot. We were trying to get Jimmy's name out there. It was interesting. I was in one hundred and five communities in Iowa.

CARTER: And I won. Nobody knew who I was. We didn't have any money and then I won in New Hampshire as well.

ROSALYNN: We had different campaigns going. We had our boys and Jimmy's momma, aunt Sissy … It was a great experience.

CARTER: That's how we won the election. We didn't have any money. We didn't have enough money to rent hotel or motel rooms at night. So, all of our families and all of our workers had to find a family who would let them stay in their home. When I was finally elected we had a reception for all of those who opened their homes and seven hundred people came … We had seven campaigns going on at the same time. We would come here to Plains—everybody would come back to Plains on Friday night or very early Saturday morning. We would spend Saturday at our home in Plains. Everybody would report what they had learned that week, people they had met, the questions they were being asked. We had to make sure we were all preaching the same sermon. On a sensitive issue like abortion, Rosalynn had to say the same thing in Iowa as I was saying in Massachusetts. Then we would go to Sunday school and church and kind of have a political rally and we would disperse again … The other candidates who were very famous and had plenty of money and so forth—they didn't know what hit them. By the time the people started voting we had already won it and they didn't know it.

---

1 Jimmy Carter. *A Remarkable Mother*. Simon and Schuster. (New York). 2008.

O'MALLEY: Can you imagine that kind of unorthodox campaign happening today?

CARTER: No. It's all money now and negative advertising, tearing down your opponent. We (President Ford and I) never referred to each other as anything but "my distinguished opponent." It would have been suicidal for me to run a negative campaign against President Ford …

CARTER: Pierre Trudeau was a very great friend of mine. I was the only president to go to his funeral. No I'm not. Castro, Fidel and I, were the only presidents. They took about forty-five minutes to arrange the procession and they arranged it in meticulous order of protocol. If they had two foreign ministers, they had to know which foreign minister had been foreign minister first, had been foreign minister longest. They had a tremendous line; there must have been one hundred and fifty people in it. But Castro and I were the only two presidents so there wasn't any question about us, we were at the front of the line and so we had about thirty-five minutes to talk to each other and we got very acquainted. Because of that, Rosalynn and I later visited Cuba.

ROSALYNN: Jimmy made his speech (in Havana), kind of blasting him—in a nice way. We didn't know what he was going to say and he came over and just said, "Let's go play baseball."

O'MALLEY: Shortest speech he ever gave.

CARTER: There was an all-star game that night and I had promised to go. I didn't criticize him but I criticized his human rights policy and I bragged on his education system. It was a balanced speech.

At the farm where President Carter grew up in the 1930s

CARTER: We have refurbished this to be exactly like it was in 1937 when I was thirteen years old. We didn't have electricity then. Daddy had a farm of about three hundred and fifty acres and the Park Service bought twelve acres. The home hasn't been changed and the store hasn't been changed … This is the way I lived from the time I was four until I went off to college when I was sixteen. I lived out here in a little community called Archery. I didn't have any white neighbours, all my neighbours were black people. So I grew up completely on black culture. I later wrote a book, *An Hour Before Daylight*, that tells about these years. Towards the end of the book I tried to think of the five people who had shaped my life, other than my mother and daddy, and only two of those people were white and the rest of them were black people. So I was trained by black people and taught how to behave by them.

We had a very good life compared to what the rest of the nation had. This was during the Great Depression years and unemployment was about 35 percent. We had hundreds of what we called hobos who came down from the north in the wintertime—their factories had closed, they'd lost their jobs—to stay warm and to find jobs. This was the main highway between Savannah, Georgia on the coast and Columbus, Georgia where it split and went to Montgomery and Birmingham, Alabama. This was the main highway between the Atlantic and the Pacific and there was a railway then. It was a dirt road, so we had a constant flow of traffic, including all of those hobos, and they would stop at our house and ask for a drink of water, maybe something to eat, a sandwich and they would offer to do work—to chop wood—just to earn their sandwich. My mother was a registered nurse and she acted like a doctor here among the poor people and she was always hospitable to them. The average income for a grown man who was very accomplished in farming was a dollar a day. That was a standard income. An able-bodied woman could earn seventy-five cents a day and a teenager that was strong enough to do work got fifty cents a day. That was a good income for them because they lived in a house, they had a garden plot, and they could get wood from the forests around here and they could go hunting for possums and coons and squirrels and rabbits and so forth and fish in the streams ... You could buy a cheap pair of coveralls for a dollar a pair. You could buy shoes for a dollar a pair. Fancy shoes were Wolverines and they cost three dollars a pair. Only rich people could wear Wolverines. I wear Wolverines now.

It was a completely segregated society then. I didn't know anything about segregation while I was a child. I always felt like I was in an alien community when I went to Plains for church or for school and I was always ready to get back home to play with my black playmates. It was not a time for blacks and whites to be treated equally. Blacks didn't have the vote then ... All the churches were segregated ... So this is where I really learned about the ravages of racial segregation, not only on the black people but also on the white people who imposed it. When I ran for governor and was elected in 1970 I gave a very short inaugural speech and I said that I had travelled Georgia and I could say to you quite frankly that the time for racial discrimination is over and that never again should a black child have an unequal chance for an education, or healthcare. That speech put me on the cover of *Time* magazine.

[These were] the roots of my life.

Ex-president still a Plains man;
Jimmy Carter is right at home in the small Georgia town where he was raised

The Globe and Mail and Kingston Whig-Standard
16 May 2008

By Arthur Milnes

People who occupy the White House don't tend to go home again. Bill Clinton traded Arkansas for faraway New York, and New England product George Herbert Walker Bush is now the "Lone Star Yankee" based in Houston, Texas, although he does spend his summers in Maine. Gerald Ford chose Vail, Colorado, and Rancho Mirage, California, over Grand Rapids, Michigan.

In the twenty-seven years since he was in Washington, Jimmy Carter has become a Nobel Laureate and a tireless campaigner for better health care and human rights, all the while based in Plains, the tiny community (population 636) in southwest Georgia where he was raised.

Today he is helping to dedicate a museum that now occupies the gas station once operated by someone a little more typical of the town: his colourful younger brother. Billy Carter died two decades ago, but his ramshackle little building remains a big draw—and has never looked this good.

The building is all spruced up, and more than a few speakers note that it looks better today than at any time in the past. It will now be the home of the Plains Better Hometown Program, and will forever display items related to Billy Carter. They include cans of Billy Beer, pictures of Billy with the many famous folks he met, a plaque honouring the first station owner who made the place famous—in Plains, that is—and items of rare correspondence from when Billy's brother, President Jimmy Carter, lived in the White House.

My favourite item? A letter from Jimmy Carter's private secretary in the West Wing, sent shortly after he moved into the White House, telling Billy and other close family members how to ensure their president-relative received their mail. "President Carter has instructed the mail room staff to deliver your correspondence to him immediately upon its receipt," she wrote. "In order to expedite the mail sorting process it would be best if you use a code on the envelope. The President has suggested '611' since that was Rosalynn's phone number when he was calling on her. Please write '611,' preferably circling it, in the upper left hand corner of the envelope."

While in office, Carter often seemed embarrassed by his brother's antics, but now he can look back and laugh. "As I think all of you know, Billy Carter is the one who put me on the map," he jokes.

"Quite often when I'd have a press conference in the White House, the first question would be, 'Mr. President, how do you respond to what Billy said last night about the belly-busting contest in Canada?'"

In a more serious vein, he recalls a side of his brother that few outside Plains ever saw. "Billy got himself into trouble on occasion, particularly with the irresponsible Yankee newspaper reporters," he says, "but Billy was one of those who inspired, I would say, tens of thousands of people. He was an alcoholic, he knew it, but the last ten years of his life he was completely sober, and he and Sybil both devoted their lives to talking to other people who had an alcohol or drug problem and getting them to follow in Billy's footsteps."

I ask Billy's widow, Sybil, what she and her children and grandchildren hope to take away with them after visiting the museum dedicated to her late husband. "The reason for doing the museum and what the Carter family would like to portray is the whole Billy Carter," she tells me. "So many times all you saw were snippets of conversations in a newspaper and you never knew whether it was true or not. Billy was a devoted father. He was a good businessman. He had problems with alcoholism, but he was a recovering alcoholic for ten years and we are so proud of that. He was a military man, a Marine. He loved this town and he loved the people in this town. He never met a stranger. This place was sort of a gathering place for tourists as well as community people: friends, farmers, politicians—a lot of people walked through these doors."

The Billy Carter Service Station Museum cost $200,000 to establish, and Jimmy Carter and his wife Rosalynn donated $50,000, but government grants have yet to appear. If the pride of Plains is upset, he's not showing it. Later in the evening, still in his jeans, he is all smiles as he mingles with the crowd, white wine in hand, at a fundraising dinner for the new museum at the Plains Historic Inn, a community-owned bed and breakfast. (Tickets to the event cost $2,500, with all proceeds going to the museum, and included a private dinner with President and Mrs. Carter. Organizer Mill Simmons let the lone Canadians in for free; he was happy we'd travelled all this way to see the hometown he's so proud of and to meet the man he calls "Brother Jimmy.")

Jimmy Carter's life seems to be pretty much an open book (he has written more than twenty books on such topics as growing up in rural Georgia and confronting racial segregation and poverty). He cuts the lawn, teaches Sunday school every week at Maranatha Baptist Church with his wife and takes a turn keeping the church tidy.

Not that he's a prude. "My wife and I went to the Canadian side [of Niagara Falls] on our 50th anniversary," he recalls during the fundraiser. It was 1996, and "[former Canadian prime minister] Pierre Trudeau was there with his tiny daughter—and I thought it was his granddaughter!"

A wink and a laugh leave the distinct impression that, at 83, even a strict Southern Baptist doesn't entirely disapprove of Trudeau's belated fatherhood (he was in his 70s when his daughter was born).

Clearly, Carter can reconcile his roots with his more cosmopolitan nature. As journalist and academic Frye Gaillard writes in *Prophet From Plains: Jimmy Carter and his Legacy*, the man "was not simply one of the boys down in Plains. The other boys didn't … jet off now and again to Damascus, Buenos Aires, or Cairo."

And yet "it was more than a matter of sentiment whenever he declared that Plains was home. There was probably no other place where the nuances of his personality, or the subtlety of his values, were sketched with better clarity."

Of course, there was one big change upon Carter's return home from service in the Oval Office in January of 1981. He followed the advice fellow Democrat Harry Truman was given thirty years earlier when he returned, unpopular and alone, to small-town Missouri: Build a fence.

According to Truman, ex-president Herbert Hoover had told him how "souvenir hunters had even taken the doorknobs … and some of the weatherboarding off his house."

But Carter had his personal privacy protected in style. No doubt the home-spun Truman, who once described Richard Nixon as "a shifty-eyed, goddamn liar," would have enjoyed knowing that the fence put up in Plains by the Secret Service around Carter's residence off Main Street once surrounded Nixon's "winter White House" in Key Biscayne, Florida.

Jimmy Carter, The Teacher

16 March 2010

By Steve Paikin

"I'll be teaching, not preaching, in church tomorrow morning," he told our group last Saturday night in Plains, Ga. "Any of you going to come?" Well, of course, we all wanted to be there.

President Carter has been "teaching" since he was eighteen years old. He spends much of his Saturday night preparing, then peeks rarely at his notes and speaks extemporaneously for forty-five minutes on a biblical lesson of the day on Sunday.

The day our group was in Plains, he spoke about the metaphor of Jesus' body as bread, his blood as wine. After a thoroughly riveting talk, he seemed almost wistful that he hadn't explained his views well enough.

"It's a complicated message I'm trying to explain," he offered.

The woman who prepares the parishioners to hear Carter admits, "I hear him every Sunday and I still hear my heart have that extra beat. It's amazing that this man came from this little bitty town."

Plains has a population of fewer than six hundred and fifty souls.

Carter is believed to be the only president to teach a Sunday school lesson while holding that office. He's certainly the only former president to do so.

There are only thirty permanent members of the Carters' church (wife Rosalynn is with him, as she has been for more than six decades). But there were perhaps three times that many people there last Sunday morning, the vast majority of them from out of town, some from as far away as several Latin American countries.

Apparently, it was a relatively small crowd. Frequently there are three hundred people occupying the pews and once eight hundred and seventy-eight, requiring the use of an overflow room. Remarkably, the Carters pose for pictures with everyone who wants one after services are over.

The Carters are also anything but uncommitted to their church, where they've been members since 1981, the year Carter left the presidency. They're both deacons and serve on committees. And President Carter, whose handy-man skills are well known thanks to his work for Habitat for Humanity, made the four collection plates and the wooden cross that grace the sanctuary.

Besides the teacher at the front of the assembly, the other significant difference between this congregation and any other is the presence of secret service agents. Three of them frisk and wand you on the way in. A bomb-sniffing dog met our car seconds after we pulled into the parking lot. That is a new reality of post-9/11 America.

The woman who prepares the congregation before the Carters arrive lectured us on the do's and don'ts. Pictures were allowed for the first few minutes, but then the cameras had to go away during the sermon.

"And you are not to stand when Mr. Carter enters the church. He's not the president anymore. And we do not give him any applause. He's not here to entertain you. He's here to be your Sunday school teacher. The applause is how you use what he's taught you in your daily lives," she admonished us.

Whether you like Jimmy Carter's politics or you don't, this much cannot be denied. He and his wife have returned to their roots, committed themselves to keeping Plains, Ga. alive, and are doing a spectacular job of it. They still live here on a well-guarded compound in the town. They still preside over a working farm.

Quietly, people in Plains are asking what will happen to the Carter property, which has been in the family for almost two hundred years, once they're gone? What will happen to the church?

Jimmy and Rosalynn Carter, ages 85 and 82, put Plains, Ga. on the map, even though he barely carried the county when he ran for president. Rural Georgia is very red-state, politically.

What will happen to Plains in a post-Carter era is, frankly, a bit worrisome.

Special Evening with the Carters in Plains, Ga.

Watertown Daily Times and Kingston Whig-Standard
5 April 2010

By Arthur Milnes

The meal begins with grace at the Plains Historic Inn, a community-owned bed and breakfast in Plains, Ga. The 85-year-old man to my right leads the prayer. He holds out his hands and all of us around the small table link hands as he offers the grace, thanking his God for the food and the safe arrival of the four Canadians from far-off Ontario to this rural Georgia town of about 640 people.

TV Ontario's Steve Paikin and Scarborough's Thomas S. Harrison in Plains, Georgia, March 2010. *Photo by Arthur Milnes.*

Canadian speechwriter David Lockhart with President Carter. *Photo by Thomas S. Harrison.*

I hold his left hand while my friend Steve, on the other side of him, clasps his right hand. While normally one to keep my eyes open during prayers, I keep them firmly shut this time. I consider the man's words as he speaks.

This grace is special. I will never probably experience it again.

Indeed, the man whose hand I am clasping as his grace continues is one I admire more than almost any other in our world. While not normally religious in a church-going sense, I have long viewed him as more of a positive religious and moral force in our world than a politician—great political leader though he was.

My respect and admiration for him and his wife—she is at the other end of the table now—began in the late 1970s when I was just a boy. My parents used to speak about him around the dinner table and my late mother always called him "a good and decent man who deserved better from our American neighbours." Mom had a particular respect and fondness for his wife, someone who had raised the profile of mental health issues in the deep American South in the 1970s, helping battle the stigma those battling depression and other challenges face.

Before dinner, I have the rare opportunity to tell this special lady of my late mother's respect for her. Mom would have wanted me to do that.

Welcome to an evening spent in private with the 39th president of the United States, Jimmy Carter, and former First Lady Rosalynn Carter.

As a journalist, and previous visitor to tiny Plains, I've had the honour of interviewing President Carter in the past. He's spoken to me about the Canadian prime ministers he worked with while in the White House, Joe Clark and Pierre Trudeau, his work as a young naval officer helping to clean up the nuclear accident at Chalk River, Ontario, in the early 1950s, and so much more.

But on this evening, I keep my notebook in my hotel room. I simply want to enjoy this rich and unique experience which I still can't believe has come about.

Our journey to the Carters' dinner table began the weekend before the four of us—myself; Tom Harrison, a friend from my hometown of Scarborough who was my roommate at Queen's during our undergraduate years; David Lockhart, an Ottawa speechwriter; and David's university roommate, Steve Paikin, a friend who is also the host of *The Agenda* on TV Ontario—were set to fly to Atlanta and then make the drive to Plains. Our plan was to attend an auction on March 13 the Carters were holding to benefit their hometown. If we were lucky, I told my friends, we might get the chance to meet the former president briefly.

But then my cell phone went off the Sunday before as I was in my kitchen at home in Kingston.

"Arthur," a voice with a thick southern US accent said when I answered, "it's Jimmy Carter. I have terrible news—we've had to cancel the auction."

The former president went on to tell me that his wife and he had been worried about "the Canadians" as the four of us had probably already bought our plane tickets and couldn't refund them.

Would we like to join he "and Rosalynn" for dinner in lieu of the auction the coming Saturday, he asked?

We drove into Plains the afternoon of the dinner. Acting as tour guide, I stopped in front of the public housing complex in Plains. Still in use, it looks the same as similar units around the world—except for one. It has a large historic plaque on the front.

Yes, I tell my friends, the future president and first lady lived in public housing for a year in the 1950s. And despite the financial and other challenges the young couple faced, they—working in true partnership so evident today, more than sixty years after they were married—made it from Public Housing Apartment 9a in Plains to the White House.

We also visit the Plains High School where the future president's life was changed by a teacher, Miss Julia Coleman. In both his Inaugural address and during his Nobel Peace Prize lecture, Carter shared her words with the world: "We must adapt to changing times, but cling to unchanging principles."

Then it is off to Carter's boyhood home, outside of Plains. Growing up in the racially divided South, most of Carter's friends and mentors were African-Americans. We walk through the grounds of the farm, now a historic site, once owned by Earl and Lillian Carter in times past.

All of Plains is now a historic district and we all agree that it is one of the best presidential sites in all America. Canadians who haven't taken the time to leave the major highways and visit Plains on the way to or from Florida don't know what they are missing.

Over wine and an excellent meal of fish, grits and bacon-wrapped asparagus, the Carters enthusiastically answer any questions we have. The public affairs expert amongst us, Steve Paikin, skilfully asks away while I mostly watch and listen.

After about three hours, the dinner is over. We present the Carters with some gifts we've brought from Canada for them. The bottle of Ontario ice wine is a big hit with the president and his wife. There are two American couples also at the table and the 39th president, having visited a winery with Rosalynn in the Niagara region where ice wine is made, eagerly explains to his fellow countrymen how the product is harvested.

Before leaving, they invite us to the auction that is being rescheduled for the fall. Having left their Secret Service detail in large Suburbans outside, they go down the stairs to rejoin them and return home off Main Street—the only house they have ever owned.

The four of us are left with our thoughts after an evening spent in the company of a man and his wife who changed our world for the better and continue to do so through the Carter Center today. They wage peace, battle for human rights, the environment and public health.

And this work all began here—in Plains, Georgia—where they chose to return to from Washington in 1981.

I am a lucky man.

President Carter and Habitat for Humanity

By Murray Chown

It was with great excitement that Beth and I were looking forward to our luncheon with President and Mrs. Carter in the fall of 2008. That excitement was accompanied with a degree of trepidation. What does one say to the 39th president of the United States? How does one carry on a conversation with him? The typical Canadian discussion about the weather won't last for very long.

It was with some relief that we realized that we might have something in common with the Carters. Something that might keep the conversation alive for more than a few minutes—Habitat for Humanity. Habitat helps to provide simple, decent, affordable housing in partnership with low-income families. Being involved in Habitat projects provides an opportunity for people of all cultures, religions, races and economic well being to work together for a common cause.

I first became involved with Habitat for Humanity in 2002, in what was known as the "Ed Schreyer Work Project" in Ottawa, Canada. This work project built ten homes in six days. The work project gave volunteers from across North America the opportunity to work together and swing a hammer beside Mr. Schreyer, a former premier of the Province of Manitoba, and a former governor general of Canada.

I had the privilege of sitting on the Board of Directors for Habitat for Humanity—National Capital Region (Ottawa, Canada) for several years.

Over those years I experienced the joy of seeing several projects planned and completed in the Ottawa area, providing simple, decent homes for low income families.

President and Mrs. Carter have participated for decades in Habitat projects all around the world. A Carter Work Project has taken place every year, since the mid-1980s. Locations of Carter Work Projects include the United States, Canada, Mexico, Philippines, Korea, India and countries in the Far East. The first Carter Work Projects outside of the United States were in Canada in 1993.

In the summer of 2010, I was in Thunder Bay, Ontario for a meeting with city staff. While waiting for the meeting I noticed a large hardcover volume documenting the 1993 Carter Work Project, building eighteen homes in Winnipeg, Manitoba. There was President Carter, swinging a hammer alongside volunteers from across North America. That same year a Carter Work Project built ten homes in Waterloo, Ontario. Mr. Schreyer was a part of these Carter Work Projects in 1993, leading to his commitment to Habitat for Humanity Work Projects in Canada.

The thousands of people around the world who have volunteered for Habitat projects have a common goal. They all help provide suitable, af-

Ontario Premier Bob Rae joined the Carters on a Habitat for Humanity build in Kitchener-Waterloo, Ontario in July of 1993. *Photo courtesy of the Toronto Star.*

fordable housing for families in need. Some of these volunteers have had the privilege of working beside President and Mrs. Carter.

As it would turn out, there was only limited discussion of Habitat during our luncheon with the Carters. There was no need to worry about making conversation. Instead we enjoyed the warmth and friendliness of this engaging couple. We were enthralled by their stories, many with connections to Canada and in particular the Ottawa valley that we call home.

It was an honour and privilege to meet President and Mrs. Carter. It is a memory that we will cherish forever.

Murray Chown, MCIP, RPP, is a past member of the Board of Directors, Habitat for Humanity, National Capital Region.

Rosalynn Carter: A Tribute

By Thomas S. Harrison

It is sometimes said that behind every successful man is a supportive woman. In a lifetime of service to politics, the United States, and to the world, Rosalynn Carter has been the epitome of a supportive wife. She has also stood beside her husband and shared in his efforts, and pioneered her own path as a person of tremendous accomplishment.

She is a dedicated political campaigner on behalf of her husband. During Carter's campaign for the Georgia State Senate in the early 1960s, she got her first experience with the rough and tumble of politics. One supporter of Carter's opponent expressed his unhappiness about Carter's candidacy, by directly threatening Mrs. Carter. With Rosalynn's aid, Jimmy went on to win that first campaign. Later during the 1975 presidential campaign, she visited forty-one of the fifty states campaigning on her own.

The former First Lady is a charming conversationalist. During the meal, the couple told us about their farm operations that grow several crops including the peanuts that became such a symbol of the Carter presidency in the 1970s.

When asked, Mrs. Carter said she grew "so tired" with the focus on peanuts during the presidential election.

"I got so tired of peanuts on the campaign—but I do eat peanuts now," she told us. "We had peanut pies and peanut cakes and you can imagine why I started to shy away from it. I was campaigning and I went to a country fair in Texas and I was supposed to cut "my" peanut cake and all the TV cameras were there and everybody … I started to cut the cake. It was a cake made like a pancake with a ring in the middle and no icing, with raw peanuts in the middle and I was embarrassed to start with. And I started to cut it and I sawed and I sawed and never cut all the way through. And it was supposed to be my recipe! It was one of my most embarrassing moments."

At all times, Rosalynn Carter was a full participant in her husband's endeavours. In later times, President Bill Clinton famously characterized Hillary Clinton's role in his presidency as a deal in which the American people got "two for the price of one." The Clintons might have learned something from the Carters who undertook their duties as America's First Family as a real partnership.

At a time when many women were still struggling for equal rights, Mrs. Carter advised her husband and sat in on cabinet meetings. She represented him in meetings with officials at home and abroad, including acting as envoy to Latin America in 1977, and leading a special delegation to Thailand in 1979. On the legislative front, Mrs. Carter acted as Honourary Chair of the President's Commission on mental health and testified before the Senate in support of the passage of the Mental Health System Bill in 1980.

She is an accomplished author. She has written or co-written five books, including two that deal with mental health. As a longtime advocate for such issues, Mrs. Carter told us a story at dinner about her collaboration with Margaret Trudeau on a program for mental health. When she called the prime ministerial residence to discuss the details, she spoke to Pierre Trudeau. However, the prime minister only said that his wife was not available and could not come to the phone. Mrs. Carter did not understand what had happened until the next day when she read in the paper that Margaret Trudeau had left the marriage, the first step in a very public separation of Canada's own first family.

Since her time as First Lady, Mrs. Carter has earned seven honourary degrees, has been a distinguished lecturer and Fellow at several colleges and has received numerous awards and recognitions for her ongoing public service. In 1999 she received the Presidential Medal of Freedom, the highest honour a civilian can be awarded in the United States. In 2002, she was only the third former First Lady inducted into the National Women's Hall of Fame.

But for all of her national and international work, Rosalynn Carter still makes herself available to help out at a local level.

While they are advancing in years, Mrs. Carter mentioned that she and President Carter still play an active role in their home town. The evening before our meeting they had been invited to a dance for teenagers in the local community centre in Plains. She smiled broadly as she related how "nice" all the young people looked "all dressed up" and she appeared genuinely delighted to have attended the event.

At the end of the meal, the server offered some liqueur for my coffee. Mrs. Carter's eyes danced as she whispered that she had "never tried that" and asked me what the liqueur tasted like. I told her it was sweet and a nice substitute for coffee cream. She turned to the server and asked to try the liqueur as well. In all of her many experiences, it's hard to believe that the First Lady had never had Bailey's in her coffee. I suspect she was simply making a congenial gesture to make me and all her guests feel comfortable.

Undoubtedly this was one of many such gestures by a well mannered and accomplished woman, throughout a truly remarkable life.

Thomas Harrison is senior adviser to the Chief Justice of Ontario's Superior Court.

Jimmy Carter's Greatest Speech

By David Lockhart

Much can be revealed in an unguarded moment. Such was the case during a conversation I had with President and Mrs. Carter during a visit to Plains in 2010. As a student of presidential speeches and a speechwriter myself, I was intrigued to know what the president felt was the best speech he had ever delivered as well as the best speech he had ever heard. His response to the latter question was not surprising—Martin Luther King Jr.'s magnificent "I have a Dream" speech from August, 1963.

However his choice for "the best speech I ever delivered" did surprise me. Without a moment's hesitation, Carter replied, "the speech I gave on energy and the economy."

"The so-called 'malaise' speech?" I asked, incredulous.

"Yes", he said, "It was a deep and penetrating psychological analysis of America and what was causing our problems [and how] if we could achieve a comprehensive energy policy … it would be a great triumph for us."

Now, if there is one speech which has become infamous from the Carter presidency, it's that one. Ask anyone old enough to remember, and you'll likely get rolling eyes and shaking heads. Here was Carter at his worst—cursing the darkness, seeing the clouds and bemoaning the country's fate. He spoke of a "crisis of confidence" besetting Americans, "a crisis," he said, "that strikes at the very heart and soul and spirit of our national will."

This loss of confidence was, the speech continued, taking the country down "[a] path that leads to fragmentation and self-interest. Down that road lies a mistaken idea of freedom; the right to grasp for ourselves some advantage over others. That path would be one of constant conflict between narrow interests ending in chaos and immobility. It is a certain route to failure."

Not exactly feel-good stuff! And, not surprisingly, an existentialist treatise on their souls that Americans, battered by recession and oil shocks, were unreceptive to hearing.

The speech also outlined the president's plan to wean the United States off foreign oil, pledging that, "this nation will never use more foreign oil than we did in 1977—never. From now on, every new addition to our demand for energy will be met from our own production and our own conservation. ... I am tonight setting the further goal of cutting our dependence on foreign oil by one-half by the end of the next decade..."

President and Mrs. Carter correctly pointed out that the president had never actually used the word "malaise" in the speech; that Senator Kennedy and Ronald Reagan had started describing it that way and it had caught on in the media. The antagonism toward those two men, especially Senator Kennedy, was still fresh, nearly thirty years later.

At the same time, here was Carter's manifest pride in his strong and principled stand at a moment of great crisis. And beyond the pride, vindication—not only on the consequences of addiction to foreign oil, a dependency every succeeding president has also addressed, but also on the direction of the American body politic itself.

How better to describe the current culture of Washington, where gridlock stymies progress and lobbyists shape legislation, than Carter's warning of "constant conflict between narrow interests ending in chaos and immobility"? And how much different would American foreign policy have been, would Americans' quality of life have been, if they had, in fact, ended their dependency on foreign oil?

In identifying the Crisis of Confidence speech as his best, Carter revealed much: old political wounds that had not fully healed and the knowledge that time and events had proven him right. Revealed, too, was his characteristic fighting against the tide of collective opinion. He knows how history has remembered that speech. But he also knows that on two of the most important issues of the past thirty years—energy and the political culture of America—he was more than just prescient; he was right.

Perhaps it was his best speech, after all.

David Lockhart is an Ottawa-based speechwriter and president of Lockhart Communications. He has written for some of Canada's leading public figures.

Trudeau, Clark remembered fondly by Carter in *White House Diary*: review

7 October 2010

By Arthur Milnes, The Canadian Press

When then US President Jimmy Carter struggled with the skyrocketing costs of health care, he and his cabinet looked north to Canada during their first year in office.

When Carter went looking for friends and allies around the summit table in the 1970s, he found one, first, in Pierre Trudeau and then in Joe Clark.

And when desperate US diplomats needed cover and an escape route from revolutionary Iran in 1979 and Canada stepped forward, Carter could barely contain his appreciation.

Carter's fondness for Canada and its leaders was expressed in several entries in private diaries that have just been published. *White House Diary* is considered particularly timely given current US President Barack Obama's struggles in his first term and the comparisons drawn between the 39th and 44th occupants of the White House.

But where Obama has achieved modest success on health-care reform, Carter's administration tried to come to terms with cost disparities between Canada and the United States.

"At the cabinet meeting we discussed a wide range of issues, including the fact that Canada, with its public health program, had 7 percent of its GNP spent on health," President Jimmy Carter noted in his private diary on September 26, 1977; "our figure is 10 percent."[2]

Carter, in a recent annotation to his *White House Diary*, then updates readers to the present-day situation in the United States. "US spending on health care was more than 17 percent of its GNP in 2009."

Carter's respect for, and friendship with, two Canadian prime ministers of opposing parties is obvious.

"Joe Clark had done his homework and protected Canadian interests but was willing to accommodate the ultimate conclusions when necessary," Carter wrote after first encountering Canada's new Progressive Conservative prime minister at the 1979 G7 Summit in Tokyo.[3]

"Later, we invited Mrs. Thatcher and Prime Minister (Joe) Clark to come over (to the US Embassy)," Carter also noted. "He came first, and I

---
2 Jimmy Carter, *White House Diary*, Farrar, Straus and Giroux. (New York). 2010. p. 108.
3 Ibid. p. 337.

Joe Clark takes a minute to view the roster of candidates during the elections in the Democratic Republic of Congo. After he left office, Prime Minister Clark was co-leader of a Carter Center election monitoring team for the DRC's July 2006 elections—the first in that nation in forty years. *Photo courtesy of the Carter Center.*

liked him immediately."[4]

Carter had earlier invited Trudeau to be one of his first foreign visitors soon after he took office in 1977. Trudeau gave a speech to the US Congress during the visit and Carter was obviously impressed by his Canadian counterpart's interventions at that year's G7 Summit in England later that year.

"I was surprised at the strength of Pierre Trudeau who seems to be at ease with all the others, quite uninhibited in his expressions of opinion, and they seemed to listen to him quite closely," Carter confided to his diary.[5]

"There was a general feeling put forward by (Helmut) Schmidt (of West Germany) and me and Trudeau that the major outcome of our meeting ought to be a genuine expression of confidence in the future without misleading the people about the problems we face."[6]

Both Clark and Trudeau remained active with the Carter Center in Atlanta long into their political retirements. Carter was an honourary pall bearer at Trudeau's Montreal funeral ten years ago. Clark continues to work

---

4   Ibid. p. 335.
5   Ibid. p. 47.
6   Ibid. p. 48,

with Carter on election monitoring and other Carter Center projects.

Now 86, Carter has taken the time to annotate his diaries. These fresh perspectives on some of the entries he made in private more than thirty years ago become important for Canadian readers. Carter revives memories of the waves of goodwill and appreciation that washed across the border when word came out that Canada's ambassador and staff in Iran had sheltered six Americans during the Iranian crisis.

Carter described this as one of the greatest moments of his presidency during a private dinner in his hometown of Plains, Ga. earlier this year.

"Six of our diplomats evaded capture by militants in the compound and made their way to the Canadian embassy," Carter writes in a present-day reflection in the book. "Ambassador Ken Taylor decided to smuggle the Americans out of Iran, disguised by the CIA, and using Canadian passports.

"As meticulous plans were made, we maintained the fiction that all American diplomats were being held hostage. On January 27 (1980), after we received indications that their concealment was known, the six diplomats left the embassy, boarded a Swissair flight, and flew to safety. The Canadian embassy was then closed, and Ken Taylor and his staff returned to Canada."

"Ambassador Taylor was subsequently awarded the Congressional Gold Medal, and Americans responded to the liberation of these hostages with a tremendous expression of appreciation for the Canadians."[7]

With these glimpses of Canada–US cooperation and notes from a US president about our own leaders, this impressive volume contains lessons that politicians of all stripes in Ottawa today could learn from.

In a bitter era in Canadian national politics—one that brings no credit to any of our parties—readers of Carter's diaries will note the respect this president afforded his one-time opponent, Republican Gerald Ford, and the willingness by both men and other members of their parties to put partisanship aside and work for the common good wherever possible.

In one case, on March 24, 1977, only two months after Carter was sworn in, Ford visits his former office.

"President Ford came, and our scheduled thirty-minute meeting lasted for about an hour and fifteen minutes. He's extremely interested in what is going on in our diplomatic relationships and in my dealings with the Congress. He was quite complimentary about what we had done so far, except he was concerned about spending getting out of hand and the budget becoming even more deeply unbalanced. I have the same concerns, and I

---
7 Ibid. p. 396.

think our meeting was productive."[8]

Sadly, it is hard to imagine any of our political leaders of recent memory having the same sort of bi-partisan conversation with their predecessors.

White House Diary is a must-read for any student of the US presidency. It is also part of a refreshing re-examination of the Carter presidency that has been going on for many years now. Considered a failed president by many in the past, Carter in fact has much to be proud of as this book reminds us. On energy conservation, human rights promotion, the Panama Canal Treaty, SALT II, Camp David, his call for a more inclusive US medical system and so much more, Carter was a man ahead of his time.

Walter Mondale remembers

Kingston Whig-Standard
17 April 2008

By Arthur Milnes

Both the United States and Canada took part in the boycott of the 1980 Moscow Olympics at the height of the Cold War. While everyone is sympathetic to the plight of the athletes who lost their dreams that year—as today's Olympians would if the games in China this summer are boycotted as some are demanding—what about the politicians who devised and implemented the plan in 1980?

Do they think their own generation's boycott worked? So far, current leaders like Prime Minister Stephen Harper of Canada and US President George W. Bush, are holding firm and resisting calls to boycott the games this summer, despite the recent bloody crackdown by Chinese authorities in Tibet. There have also been violence and protests as the Olympic Flame makes its way around the world ahead of its arrival in the land of Tiananmen Square.

"The boycott (of 1980) may perhaps be summarized as a success with reservations," Mark MacGuigan, Canada's foreign minister at the time of the 1980 boycott, concluded in his memoirs "but the alternative would have been in my opinion much worse: to let what the Soviets hoped would be a vast endorsement of the legitimacy of their system and policy go ahead as if nothing had happened in Afghanistan."[9]

And today, if you replace the word "Afghanistan" with "Tibet," and

---

8 Ibid. p. 36-37.
9 P. Whitney Lackenbauer (ed). *An Inside Look at External Affairs during the Trudeau Years: The Memoirs of Mark MacGuigan*. University of Calgary Press. (Calgary). 2002. p. 39.

"USSR" with "China" in what MacGuigan had to say, you realize Canadians—and the world—are in many ways back to the future again.

In Minnesota, former Vice President Walter Mondale says he has no regrets about assisting President Jimmy Carter in the West's boycott of Moscow that year. For him, there is no looking back and he remembers well why he and the administration wanted America's Canadian neighbours on their boycott team.

"We needed international support because most of what we wanted to do would not work unless we had a lot of friends around the world," Mondale said in an interview from his home, " ...Did we do an easy thing? No. It had a lot of cost to it. Above all, the athletes who lost their chance to show their stuff at the height of their careers had to forgo their moment in order to let us put pressure on the Soviet Union for their atrocious act of invading Afghanistan, a violation of a fundamental principle.

"We had to find ways, short of war, to make them pay a big price. And there is no question in my mind there are parallels between the 36th Olympics where Hitler used the Berlin Olympics to justify himself to his folks at home and in the world as being acceptable and normal...and to try to characterize his Germany as sort of Grecian in its stature...I think we ruined that Moscow Olympics and you helped us do it. I think it helped bring down the Soviet system."

Recently de-classified documents from the Jimmy Carter Library in Atlanta provide a rare glimpse into this issue and the internal workings of the American White House at the height of such a crisis. Contrary to much of Canadian opinion, it is obvious that what happens in Canada is very much of interest to decision-makers in Washington, especially in such a high-pressure issue as the boycott was in 1980.

"Embassy Ottawa reports that former Prime Minister (Joe) Clark vigorously attacked the Liberal (Prime Minister Pierre) Trudeau government for reluctance to display leadership or commitment on the Olympic boycott or in responding to the president's request for stronger measures against Iran," a formerly classified report from the White House Situation Room to Carter's National Security adviser, Zbigniew Brzezinski dated 16 April 1980. "Clark added that this was not the time for nations like Canada to be flirting with soft-headed notions of neutrality. He added that the US was Canada's principal ally and asserted that real friends don't hide in the crowd until it's safe to stick their heads out."[10]

---

10 Arthur Milnes Fonds, Queen's University Archives. Staff at the Jimmy Carter Library provided me with copies of a great many documents from their collections relating to the Carter Presidency and Canada. Unfortunately, many of the call numbers were lost in fax transmission. All these copies have been placed in my own Fonds at Queen's Archives and are open to researchers.

In response to the invasion of Afghanistan by the Soviet Union in 1979, Carter had called for a boycott of the Olympic Summer Games in Moscow. Carter was also in the early days of dealing with the kidnapping of American diplomats from the US Embassy in Iran by extremists.

Then in the midst of a Canadian election campaign, Progressive Conservative Prime Minister Clark announced in January of 1980 that Canada would boycott the Moscow Olympics if the Soviets didn't withdraw as Carter was asking.

"Recent international developments, particularly in Iran and Afghanistan, have made foreign policy an issue in this election," a confidential US intelligence memorandum, forwarded to President Carter states. "… But the major advantage foreign policy holds for Clark is that it gives him a forum for demonstrating leadership abilities. He has held weekly press conferences devoted largely to announcements on decisive Canadian actions in response to the Soviet invasion of Afghanistan or in support of US initiatives on Iran. The Canadian rescue of American officials from Tehran was especially opportune, and Clark has been making the most of it."

The anonymous American intelligence officer offered a dispassionate view of both Clark and Liberal leader Pierre Trudeau in conclusion.

"Should Joe Clark win re-election, he will continue his present policies with a strongly pro-US, pro-NATO stance," the document states. "For example, Canada will maintain support for US initiatives related to Iran and Afghanistan, such as a boycott of the Olympic Games in Moscow. In the likelier event of a Liberal victory, Trudeau will also support US initiatives in Iran and Afghanistan. He has even attacked Clark for not doing enough in support of the United States. He, too, advocates an Olympic boycott as long as other Western allies go along. Trudeau's support for Western solidarity reflects his desire to be identified with an issue with strong popular support in Canada."

On March 17, 1980, US Secretary of State Cyrus Vance sent a four page secret memo to Carter that the president reviewed and commented on in his own hand. "I plan to make a one-day visit to Ottawa to meet with the new (Trudeau's Liberals having by then defeated Clark's Progressive Conservatives in the election of February 18, 1980) Secretary of State for External Affairs, Mark MacGuigan. This will provide a useful review of a number of difficult bilateral questions. Also, the visit should be helpful in keeping the Canadians with us on important global issues. Trudeau is expected to be making his decision on whether to boycott the Moscow Olympics at about the same time."

MacGuigan, who is now deceased, wrote about that meeting in his memoirs as well. The Trudeau cabinet decided to support the Olympic boycott and announced this on April 21, 1980 "...doing so before the arrival ... of Vance so that its issuance could not be attributed to American pressure," he wrote.[11]

"Vance arrived in Ottawa," MacQuigan continued, "just after the abortive American attempt to forcibly rescue the besieged American diplomats at their embassy in Teheran, and in time for a full morning of meetings with me before a luncheon at the prime minister's residence ... At lunch, Trudeau harangued him at length about the dangers implicit in further US attempts to rescue the American diplomats confined in Teheran by the revolutionary Iranian mob."[12]

Unbeknownst to Canada's prime minister, Vance was shortly to resign because he too disagreed with Carter's rescue mission. Out of loyalty and respect for his president, however, Vance had agreed not to announce it until after the mission was over.[13]

But back to Mondale today. Does he believe the United States and Canada, based on his own experience in high office, should follow his and Carter's lead and boycott this summer's games over human rights concerns today?

"I think the price could be much greater than what we'd be accomplishing," Mondale said firmly, agreeing that in 1980 the USSR was a creaky empire—unlike China which is now on the rise in the world—beginning its final slide to oblivion. "And we were dealing with an act (by the Soviets in 1980) that was unequivocal—invading across an international border is the most basic violations of international law—to have this go unpunished was out the question I thought."

"I think it would be helpful if Canada (for example) through its embassy in Beijing went to the Chinese government and said, "We have to have this thing resolved somewhere. China needs to give these Tibetans some room, some autonomy. We're not talking about independence; we're just talking about some dignity here. We have to cool it or otherwise this thing is going to get out of hand ... Surely something can be done too, in that little part of your country, to allow them to survive as people. If you don't resolve it some way we might be pressed to do something else. We don't want to."

---

11 P. Whitney Lackenbauer (ed). *An Inside Look at External Affairs during the Trudeau Years: The Memoirs of Mark MacGuigan.* University of Calgary Press. (Calgary). p. 38.
12 Ibid. p. 38-39.
13 Ibid. p. 39.

An idealist in an age of hollow men
Jimmy Carter's a giant of our time

The Hill Times, 21 October 2002

By Arthur Milnes

Jimmy Carter won the Nobel Peace Prize two weeks ago, but I still have to a few things to say: he is truly a citizen of the world and has more than earned this year's Nobel Peace Prize.

Defeated by Republican Ronald Reagan in 1980, Carter left office and returned home to Plains, Georgia, as Citizen Carter. Most pundits and opponents thought he would go quietly into the night.

They thought wrong.

Since then, Carter has been an unfailing and tireless champion for peace and human rights around the world. Just ask the citizens of Ethiopia, Sudan, Somalia, North Korea, Haiti, Palestine and Bosnia—nations he's offered his services to as a mediator of national and international disputes in his post-presidential life.

He's acted positively un-American along the way. "We select a favourite side in a dispute and [the other] side becomes satanic," Carter once said in a critique of his nation's usual foreign policy.

"This all-white or all-black orientation is usually not true. In most cases, both sides are guilty of atrocities."

In Africa, Carter has helped eradicate disease and famines few dared tackle before. He monitors elections in nations most North Americans would have trouble locating on a map and shows few signs of slowing down.

Carter has shown the world that human rights are much more than a phrase. "My concept of human rights has grown to include not only the right to live in peace, but also to adequate health care, shelter, food and to economic opportunity," he said upon news he was receiving this year's prize.

There are estimates he's made personal interventions that have led to the release of as many as fifty thousand prisoners worldwide. Who can ever forget pictures of Carter the carpenter helping to build homes each year for the working poor—freeing them from a different kind of imprisonment—through Habitat for Humanity?

In awarding Carter his medal, the committee made special mention of the fact that he brokered the Camp David Accords between Israel and Egypt in 1978. Where there was war and death, Carter brought hope and the chance for peace.

The committee also said Carter's example stands in contrast to that shown by the Texas unilateralist who became president. George W. Bush seems intent on war with Iraq regardless of either the consequences or world opinion. Jimmy Carter's official citation makes this point clear.

"In a situation currently marked by threats of the use of power, Carter has stood by the principles that conflicts must as far as possible be resolved through mediation and international cooperation based on international law, respect for human rights, and economic development," it states.

In fairness to Bush, it should be noted that he gave his predecessor a gracious call of congratulations after Carter's award was announced.

With the passage of time, Carter's presidency glows much brighter, too. From Panama, to SALT II, Camp David and beyond, Carter as president was also a faithful force for peace and an example to the world.

An idealist in an age of hollow men, Carter is a giant of our time.

"We'll never know whether something new and wonderful is possible unless we try," he once told a bible class. "Let's scratch our heads, stretch our minds, be adventurous! Serve God with boldness, and who knows what wonders the Lord may work?"

Luckily for the world, President Carter, now 78, is still trying.

As more of us should.

You have our congratulations, Mr. President. Now accept our thanks.

Afghan mission worth cost to Canada

Columbus (Ohio) Dispatch
22 March 2008

By Arthur Milnes

Like millions of Canadians, I've been agnostic about Canada's participation in the military mission to Afghanistan. I have been neither among the 30 percent who strongly support it, nor part of the 20 percent strongly opposed.

"The rest are churning back and forth from soft support to soft opposition," said Frank Graves of EKOS, a Canadian research company.

My soft opposition to the mission, however, has increased whenever we've lost another soldier. Since we joined our American friends in the mission, eighty-two Canadians—eighty-one soldiers and one diplomat—have made the supreme sacrifice in Afghanistan. While this number may seem small compared with the nearly five hundred Americans killed, a look at our relative populations (thirty-three million for Canada, three hundred million for America) shows what a massive contribution Canada has made.

Recently one of the hearses carrying a slain Canadian serviceman passed by me on the highway, and I pulled off respectfully. I thought of the many students at my wife's primary school, whose military parents leave for deployments in Afghanistan regularly, leaving their children behind, and how these mothers and fathers put themselves at risk in a way I never fully will comprehend.

For many Canadians and Americans, it has been difficult to differentiate between the Afghanistan mission and the seemingly endless stalemate that has become Iraq. While we didn't participate in the Iraq war this time—unlike 1990-91—the two are often linked, though wrongly, in our minds.

And as a result I was sure that day as the hearse and escort went by that I was against my country continuing in Afghanistan. No child should lose a parent in war, especially so far from home. I moved then to the 20 percent strongly opposed.

But that was on the outside. Inside, if truth be known, I was still confused. In my name my government had agreed to participate in the mission from Day One. How could I, from a family that left blood in Europe in World War II, and who is proud that we, as Canadians and founding members of NATO, held firm in Europe through the Cold War—and from a land that has taken part in peace-keeping missions around the globe since then-Prime Minister Lester Pearson invented the concept in the 1950s—countenance Canada's backing out of our international obligations while Afghanistan was still in flames?

And then along came Jimmy Carter. Because of him in large part, I found myself approving as Canada's parliamentarians voted last week last to extend our mission in Afghanistan to 2011.

Why did the views of a man from rural Georgia, so far from us, touch me so? Carter is the man who, as president, brought Israelis and Egyptians together at Camp David. In the 1990s he put his life in danger to prevent an invasion of Haiti, and who, rightly or wrongly for a former commander in chief, spoke out against his country's military plans before the first Iraq war. And lastly, there's Carter, the Nobel Peace Prize winner—an earned medal if there ever was in considering his demonstrated worldwide crusade for peace, justice and health.

He granted a televised interview to Canadian journalist Evan Soloman that I happened to see on the Internet a few weeks ago. With Parliament's vote getting closer, I listened to Carter carefully. Until then, I had been leaning toward wanting our MPs to vote no.

"If you were to give advice to the prime minister of Canada right now, we're in the middle of a mission in Afghanistan right now...what would (you) say to that mission to the Canadian prime minister?" Soloman asked.

"I've ordinarily been against approximately one hundred adventures that have been launched by the US since I've left office, many of which resulted in military action," Carter answered. "I think the one in Afghanistan was necessary. I think our invasion of Afghanistan after 9/11 in order to root out al-Qaida and capture Osama bin Laden was necessary... So, I think now to rebuild Afghanistan and to try to persist and to bring a good life and democracy and freedom to the Afghan people is a worthy cause."

While I will still worry about the parents of my wife's students, and pray they'll return safely, a former American president has provided me, as a Canadian, with a certain assurance about Afghanistan none of my own leaders could.

If our mission is right and just, by America's greatest peacemaker, that is good enough for me.

When Jimmy Carter faced radioactivity head-on

Ottawa Citizen, 28 January 2009

By Arthur Milnes

Editor's note: Just over a year ago, technical troubles at Chalk River's NRX reactor touched off a controversy for the government of Prime Minister Stephen Harper.

The head of the Nuclear Safety Commission shut the aging reactor due to safety concerns. But when this led to a dangerous scarcity of isotopes for medical purposes, the government passed special legislation to reopen the reactor and shortly after fired Linda Keen, president of the nuclear watchdog.

The issue continues to simmer, with Ms. Keen requesting a judicial review of her dismissal. Just this past December, the 51-year-old reactor was shut down for five days to fix a leak, leading to short-term shortages of isotopes.

On Jan. 8, a leading US scientist called on president-elect Barack Obama to abandon the "unreliable and unsafe" supply of medical isotopes and start a US-based manufacture. This week, it was revealed a small amount of radioactive water escaped from the reactor in December.

A political headache, yes, but at least Mr. Harper has never had to climb into the belly of the reactor, which is exactly what happened in 1952 to Jimmy Carter, then a young US naval officer. Mr. Carter became the 39th president of the United States.

Last fall, journalist and academic Arthur Milnes was part of a small group of Canadians who attended a luncheon hosted by the Carters (one of the prizes in a charity auction). They discovered that Mr. Carter's memories of Chalk River were still fresh in his mind and had influenced his actions as president.

"It was a very exciting time for me when the Chalk River plant melted down," Jimmy Carter, now 83, said in a recent interview in his hometown of Plains, Georgia.

"I was one of the few people in the world who had clearance to go into a nuclear power plant."

On Dec. 12, 1952, the NRX reactor at Atomic Energy of Canada's Chalk River Laboratories suffered a partial meltdown. There was an explosion and millions of litres of radioactive water ended up in the reactor building's basement. The crucial reactor's core was no longer usable.

With the Cold War then in full swing, and considering this was one of the first nuclear accidents in the West, the Americans took a great interest in the cleanup.

Mr. Carter was a young US Navy officer based in Schenectady, New York, who was working closely with Admiral Hyman Rickover on the nuclear propulsion system for the Sea Wolf submarine. He was quickly ordered to Chalk River, joining other Canadian and American service personnel.

"I was in charge of building the second atomic submarine ... and that is why I went up there," said Mr. Carter. "There were twenty-three of us and I was in charge. I took my crew up there on the train."

Once his turn came, Mr. Carter, wearing white protective clothes that probably, by today's standards, provided little, if any, protection from the surging radiation levels, was lowered into the reactor core for less than ninety seconds.

When he was running for president in 1975-76, Carter briefly described this Canadian experience in his campaign book, *Why Not the Best?*

"It was the early 1950s ... I had only seconds that I could be in the reactor myself. We all went out on the tennis court, and they had an exact duplicate of the reactor on the tennis court. We would run out there with our wrenches and we'd check off so many bolts and nuts and they'd put them back on ... And finally when we went down into the reactor itself, which was extremely radioactive, then we would dash in there as quickly as we could and take off as many bolts as we could, the same bolts we had just been practicing on.

"Each time our men managed to remove a bolt or fitting from the core, the equivalent piece was removed on the mock-up," he wrote.

Years later, he was asked if he was terrified going into the reactor. He paused, growing quiet, before answering.

"We were fairly well instructed then on what nuclear power was, but for about six months after that I had radioactivity in my urine," Mr. Carter said. "They let us get probably a thousand times more radiation than they would now. It was in the early stages and they didn't know."

Carter biographer Dr. Peter Bourne, who also served as the president's "drug czar" and who later became assistant secretary general of the United Nations, believes the Chalk River experience had a lasting impact on the man from Georgia, influencing him when he had to confront nuclear issues as the leader of the western alliance from 1977 to 1981.

"My sense is that up until that point in his career, (Mr. Carter) had approached nuclear energy and nuclear physics in a very scientific and dispassionate way," he said. "The Chalk River experience made him realize the awesome and potentially very destructive power he was dealing with. It gave him a true respect for both the benefits but also the devastatingly destructive effect nuclear energy could have. I believe this emotional recognition of the true nature of the power mankind had unleashed informed his decisions as president, not just in terms of having his finger on the nuclear button, but in his decision not to pursue the development of the neutron bomb as a weapon."

Mr. Carter agreed." It was one of the few times I was actually inside a nuclear reactor when it was radioactive, so I learned the dangers," he said.

At the recent lunch, Mr. Carter grew animated when Beth Chown of Arnprior asked him about his work at Chalk River.

One can only conclude that at the height of the Cold War, when the nuclear threat was highest, the man with the power to unleash those weapons knew exactly their dangers for humanity.

And this is thanks, in large part, to his experiences with the dangers of radioactivity as a young man at Chalk River more than five decades ago.

US President Carter was 'visionary leader,' despite 1979 'Malaise speech'

The Hill Times and Watertown Daily Times
17 August 2009

By Arthur Milnes

The most exciting facet of American political history is the fact the subject area never remains static. Unlike as is often the case in Canada, common assumptions about past presidents and other leaders are constantly challenged by younger generations of historians and journalists as time goes on.

I was reminded of this only recently while on a trip through upper New York State on my way to our annual camping trip to Vermont. As always, I made sure I picked up a copy of the *Watertown Daily Times*—the best small town daily newspaper in America. I was lucky as I happened to be near Ogdensburg on a Sunday, meaning the edition of the paper I picked up was larger than usual.

Turning to the Sunday supplement, my eyes were immediately drawn to an article about Professor Kevin Mattson of Ohio University's new book examining President Jimmy Carter's so-called "Malaise" speech that the 39th president gave thirty years ago this summer. *What the Heck are you Up to Mr. President? Jimmy Carter, America's 'Malaise,' and the Speech that Should Have Changed the Country*, was yet another example—and a very well researched and written one at that—of what has often been missing from Canadian political historiography in recent decades: reappraisal and the brave willingness to challenge prevailing views of a past leader rendered by fellow historians.[14]

(It took more than fifty years after the publication of historian Donald Creighton's two-volume study of our founding Prime Minister, Sir John A. Macdonald, for a journalist, not a historian, Richard Gwyn, to re-examine Macdonald. The last full-length study of Sir Wilfrid Laurier was published in the 1960s and a nine-year majority prime minister, Louis St. Laurent, has never, in fact, had a full-length academic biography produced! Canadian historians have much to learn from their American colleagues.)

When Carter's Malaise speech is considered from 2009's vantage point—when global warming, environmental degradation and concerns about energy—are at the top of the western world's agenda, it is hard not to

---

[14] Kevin Mattson. *What the Heck are you Up to Mr. President?* Bloomsbury. (New York).

conclude that Carter, who was defeated after one term in office, was in fact a visionary leader. North Americans didn't follow his plea to turn down thermostats, choose conservation over consumption and opt for public transit over gas-guzzlers.

And look where we are today.

"I ask Congress to give me authority for mandatory conservation and for standby gasoline rationing," Carter said from the Oval Office on July 15, 1979. "To further conserve energy, I'm proposing tonight an extra $10-billion over the next decade to strengthen our public transportation systems. And I'm asking you for your good and for your nation's security to take no unnecessary trips, to use carpools or public transportation whenever you can, to park your car one extra day per week, to obey the speed limit, and to set your thermostats to save fuel. Every act of energy conservation like this is more than just common sense—I tell you it is an act of patriotism," Carter said. "Just as a similar synthetic rubber corporation helped us win World War II, so will we mobilize American determination and ability to win the energy war. Moreover, I will soon submit legislation to Congress calling for the creation of the nation's first solar bank, which will help us achieve the crucial goal of 20 percent of our energy coming from solar power by the year 2000." [15]

According to one source consulted via Google, the United States now produces 0.1 percent of its electricity generation from solar power.

Professor Mattson, who was only thirteen years old when Carter gave the speech so maligned by the politicos and experts before him, concludes: "Looking back at the speech helps us understand what we became after we turned the corner in 1979, and it reminds us of what we forgot when we put Carter's words of warning behind us."[16]

It is often said today that Jimmy Carter is the "best ex-president" the United States has ever had. Mattson's book, however, following in the footsteps of others (see Douglas Brinkley's *The Unfinished Presidency*) is part of a growing body of literature making an excellent case that the Carter presidency looks better and better as the years go on. His post White House leadership of the Carter Center (with Rosalynn Carter) and his constant quest for peace and justice in the world is but a continuation of the work he began as president.

Contrary to popular belief, there is a good chance that Carter returned home to tiny Plains, Georgia in January of 1981—like Harry Truman did to Independence in his own time—quietly confident of history's verdict.

---

15 Ibid. p. 216.
16 Ibid. p. 12.

James Earl Carter was not interviewed for Mattson's book and the author doesn't tell us if he tried to secure a discussion with the former president.

Regardless, Mattson didn't need to have one. The 39th president's actions in office—and ever since—speak for themselves. That's what history will say. Jimmy Carter the loser in 1980? Think again.

At a dinner with Canadians at the Plains Historic Inn, March 2010, President Carter was given an out-of-print copy of *Between Friends*, a tribute to the friendship between Canada and the United States for America's Bicentennail in 1976. *Photo by Steve Paikin.*

Part III
After the White House

Queen Charlotte Steelheads

By Jimmy Carter[1]

One of the best things that ever happened to our state was that Jack Crockford came to Georgia from Michigan about thirty years ago to work in game and fish management. Jack is a small, quiet woodsman who moves swiftly and silently through the forests or along a stream, noticing everything around him and recognizing most of the plants, rocks, insects, and small animals by name. One of his earliest assignments was to try to restore the deer population in the southeastern states which had been almost completely decimated in our area.

Although I spent most of my early life in the fields and woods, I saw only two deer during the eighteen years before I went off to college. Wild turkey were more plentiful; we even came across a black bear every now and then, but to see a white-tailed deer was a momentous event. There were a few within the protected areas on the coastal islands of Georgia, and a lot of dedicated biologists joined in the concerted and expensive attempt to trap some of them and release them in the wilder areas on the mainland—mostly without success.

Eventually, Crockford developed the now widely used tranquilizer projectile, utilizing almost pure nicotine as a fast-acting narcotic. This device made it possible to capture large numbers of wild deer and to transfer them without harm to hundreds of new homes. The restocking program has been so successful that now there are substantially more deer in the southeast than there were before white men came to this continent. In many of the small rural counties of our state several thousand bucks are harvested each season by hunters, and still the deer population continues to grow.

Recently retired as director of Georgia's Game and Fish Department, Crockford supplements his income as a craftsman and artist, producing for necessarily patient customers and friends a few muzzle-loading rifles and knives of great beauty, ornamented with engraving or scrimshaw figures of

---

1 Jimmy Carter. Queen Charlotte Steelheads. From *An Outdoor Journal*. Copyright 1988 by Jimmy Carter. Reprinted with the permission of the University of Arkansas Press. www.uapress.com.

birds, fish, and animals. He is one of my favorite hunting and fishing companions, having been the first person to introduce me to fly-fishing and to the pursuit of woodcock—both along the Chattahoochee River.

One damp and chilly night near the end of May 1983, Jack, Wayne Harpster, and I were sitting around a table in the Spruce Creek cottage after a relatively disappointing day of fishing. We were bent over a disassembled tranquilizer bullet, as Jack described his experiments with the projectile and how the final patented design evolved. Wayne asked if we wanted to ride around the farm and see if there were any deer feeding in the woods and fields. Soon we were bouncing along wildly in his pickup truck. Wayne had planted the grain, corn, and alfalfa as much for the deer as for his dairy cows, and was as proud of their size and number as of his state record in milk production. At each place we stopped, we would enter the field as rapidly and as quietly as possible, and then dash across the open area, swinging the truck lights and a strong spotlight around to examine the startled deer. They were in all the fields, sometimes as many as fifteen or twenty grazing together. Most of them were does, fawns, or young bucks; among almost two hundred we saw that night, less than half a dozen were mature males. Jack and Wayne explained that the males tended to stay alone except during rutting season and could seldom be found grazing in open places with other deer.

After we returned to the warm fireplace and the murmur of Spruce Creek, our thoughts and conversation turned back to fishing. Jack and I had come up to Pennsylvania for the annual Green Drake hatch, but it was late this year because of the unseasonably cold weather. As we had to leave the next morning, we were naturally making plans for our next excursion. Both my friends were extolling the excitement and challenge of fishing for the steelhead. I listened with growing interest as they described their experiences in the Michigan and Oregon rivers, mostly fishing from boats using light bait-casting or spinning equipment, with spoons and salmon eggs as bait.

I wanted to try fly-fishing in streams small enough for wading. Jack's eyes lit up as he began to tell us about his recent visit to the Queen Charlotte Islands of British Columbia, off the west coast of Canada just a short distance south of Alaska. Before the night was over we had commissioned Jack to make arrangements for the following spring.

Now, almost a year later, we were on our way. Wayne was to meet us in Canada, and Rosalynn would come a day or so later after she finished the first week of publicizing her new autobiography. All of us were equipped with chest waders, #8 fly rods and sinking tip lines. I had swapped George Harvey a package of quail feathers for some of his beautiful steelhead flies and had also brought a dozen or so of my own. To supplement my already bulging library, Wayne had sent me his favorite books about steelhead. After studying it I got another copy and sent it to Jack; on the flight from Atlanta to Vancouver we shared what we had learned.

Anyone who reads or listens a lot to fishermen will soon discover that there is one never-ending argument: What is America's greatest fighting fish? Bass, tarpon, bonefish, trout, and other types all have their champions, but the sharpest debates are between the Atlantic salmon (*Salmo salar*) and the steelhead (*Salmo gairdneri*), the anadromous or migratory rainbow trout. The steelhead spend a good portion of their lives in the Pacific Ocean or in the Great Lakes, returning to the streams of their birth to spawn. A mature fish will repeat this cycle several times over a period of six or seven years. In most rivers the average size of a steelhead is about seven or eight pounds, with the world record being a forty-two pounder taken off the coast of Alaska.

A steelhead or Atlantic salmon of half these maximum weights is considered a trophy catch. Since I had caught my large Atlantic salmon on my same tackle, I was sure it would handle the steelhead we would meet. However, I was worried about my right arm. I had recently injured it cutting heavy brush with a brush hook, and it was badly swollen and painful. X-rays had not revealed a serious fracture, but I thought I could feel one of the bones move on occasion. I'd wrapped the arm tightly in an Ace bandage and tested it at home in my backyard. I thought—I hoped—I could still crank the single action fly reel as long as the weight of the rod and fish would be on my left side. A normal person would never have taken the trip under these circumstances, but fly-fisherman aren't always normal.

There was only one flight each day to Sandspit, our destination on the east coast of the Queen Charlotte Islands, and so we had to spend an afternoon and night in Vancouver. We decided to visit a local sporting-goods store for advice and a few supplies, and then go to the anthropology museum to learn as much as possible about the history and indigenous people of the area we were to visit.

At Bob's Tackle Shop we got our most fervent comments and advice: "Fly-fishing? Don't waste your time trying to catch steelhead on flies." One customer said he had been fishing for steelhead for five years with all kinds of bait and had not yet caught his first fish. After I bought a fly line for Rosalynn, the proprietor gave me a small book, How to Catch Steelhead. Illustrated with amusing cartoons, the book advised that heavy spinning tackle and salmon roe (spawn) be offered on or near the bottom of the stream, kept deep in the currents by heavy lead weights. The store's owner also reported that on the twenty thousand British Columbian steelhead fishermen who stalked their prey every year, fewer than five thousand were successful.

Maintaining both our composure and our resolve, we left for the museum to enjoy learning about Queen Charlotte's Haida Indians, whose ancient and regionally dominant civilization is now survived only by some impressive totem poles from the previous century and by two small villages still occupied in the islands. The totem carvings were very similar to those of the Maoris, a Polynesian group who Rosalynn and I had visited in New Zealand. I was particularly impressed by the beautifully sculptured canoes, each carved with hand adzes from a single large cedar tree.

The next morning we took the daily commercial flight about four hundred and fifty miles northwest to Sandspit. I walked down the aisle of the plane and talked to the other passengers: a few Indians and a number of loggers returning to their island work after a brief vacation with friends and families in the more-populated areas of British Columbia. For the final few miles I rode in the cockpit, watching the pilot evade some of the prevalent rainstorms along the east coast of the Queen Charlotte Islands. Suddenly the pilot said, "That's Copper Bay, where you'll be staying, over to the left." I could see one small cottage and another building that appeared to be a garage or storehouse, perched on a bluff overlooking a wave-torn beach. He also gestured at the rain squalls all around, commenting that the "misty isles" really earned their name.

Sandspit turned out to be about the size of Plains, inhabited by fewer than eight hundred souls, and so it did not take us long to drive through it on the way to the cottage.

Our host and guide was Walter Ernst, an Austrian who had been an outfitter in the Yukon and then moved to the Queen Charlotte Islands thirteen years ago. His wife, Maria, was a nurse, originally from East Germany, whom we would come to know as a fine cook and gracious hostess.

Walter told us that because of the steady rain the two closest streams, the Copper and Pallant, were too high to wade or fish, but that we might travel to a more distant creek on the northern coast of the island. Although it was already midafternoon, we changed into our fishing clothes and began the one-hour drive to Deena Creek, whose flooded condition always receded more quickly because it drained a smaller geographical region, and no large lakes were in its headwaters. Parts of the area were being heavily logged, and the large clear-cut zones left terrible scars on the mountainsides. At best, they would not be healed even within the next forty years.

The bald eagles along the coastal road were either sitting on rocks near the sea or in the tops of the few Sitka spruce, hemlock, or cedar trees that had been left standing. We also saw hundreds of ... Canada geese and ducks of many species flying and swimming in the bays and inlets, and a few seals around the rocks.

The dirt roads in the region were quite narrow, reserved for the enormous trucks that rushed from the cutting areas on the mountains down to the sheltered basin on the coast. There the twenty or more logs in each load were dumped into the sea for water transport to the distant paper mills and sawmills. Then the empty trailer was unhooked and lifted onto the main truck bed by a huge crane, to provide needed traction for the rear wheels on the steep and muddy roads and to permit the shortened truck to turn around in the forest before its trailer was reattached and more logs were loaded.

It would have been a disaster to meet one of the empty or loaded trucks head-on, because the drivers assumed there would be no oncoming traffic, and the roads, only wide enough for one vehicle, had no shoulders. The truck drivers all used radios to monitor each other's movements, and we had to wait each time at the unloading point or creek until we could follow one of these behemoths from the coast to and from our fishing place. During the week it became routine for us to wait our turn patiently, trusting our lives to these drivers. On one or two occasions we had to detour because of delays in the logging operation; a detour could be as long as thirty miles—at least an hour's extra travel time. It was clear that this territory was primarily for loggers, not tourists or fishermen. This pleased me; the last thing I wanted was to be surrounded by a crowd of other seekers of the same fish in the relatively tiny stream.

We found the Deena a little higher than normal and slightly stained with tannin, like the streams in our southeastern states. This was better, Walter said, than having the stream crystal-clear, when the fish could be spooked even with long leaders and light tippets.

Jack and Wayne had fished here last October for coho salmon and were familiar with the creek, so they moved confidently downstream. I went upstream with Walter for my first experience with steelhead. We were thankful that the remaining virgin timber in this narrow valley area was not being cut, destroying the beauty of the area and filling the creek with debris from the logging operation. The banks of the stream were quite steep and often overgrown. On occasion we had to circumvent enormous logjams; the tops of the intertwined logs were often twice as high as my head. The surrounding woods were like rain forests, with moss-covered ground and fallen trees surrounding the enormous stumps that had been left from the harvest of a few of the virgin trees many years earlier. Some of the huge logs, after being felled by the sawyers, simply could not be moved to a nearby ocean without the jumbo trucks and roads to accommodate them. They were still lying there intact, some spanning the stream, so large that dozens of second-growth saplings as much as eight inches in diameter had spouted and were growing out of the ancient bark and moss. Having been raised in the Georgia woods, I was most startled that there were no briers or thorns of any kind. None of us understood why, and no one has ever explained it.

We fished hard, using mostly a Skyomish Sunrise fly or other patterns similar to it, but with no takers. It was not easy fishing with a fly rod, wading in the rough stream without being upended or spooking any fish, placing the fly as far as possible up under the overhanging logs and accumulated debris and having it drift naturally, while trying at the same time to prevent the swift currents from fouling the line or embedding the hook on the myriad underwater snags. Furthermore, it was bitterly cold and steady rain was falling.

Needless to say, after a couple of hours without a strike I was discouraged. Walter had been fishing downstream from me, and now he drew near. I said to him: "I guess there just aren't any steelhead running now." He came over, removed my artificial fly, tied on a plain #6 hook, and applied a few salmon eggs from a bunch in his raincoat pocket, which was full of water. Before we had to leave because of darkness, I had caught three silvery steelhead, one five-pounder and two eight-pounders. We released two of them and kept one of the larger ones to eat during the week.

The next morning, April 14, was clear and cold. I got up early, before the others, to walk down to the sea in Copper Bay. There were twenty-seven-foot tides and vast expanses of exposed rocks between the water and the cliff on which the Ernst cottage was built. The entire shore was lined with hundreds of large logs, either lost or abandoned by the Queen Charlotte logging crews. One mystery that I couldn't resolve was that of the numerous blacktail-deer tracks going down to the surf, with none coming back up that I could find anywhere along the beach for a mile or more. I could only presume that the deer had swum or waded farther down the shore than I had walked.

I was impatient to go fishing, even when the cold rain resumed, but it was after 10:00 a.m. before we had any lines in the water. When Rosalynn arrived, we advised her to try salmon roe for a while instead of artificial flies—at least until she had caught one fish. On her first cast, she landed a six-pound steelhead, almost more than she could handle because she had underestimated the power of the fish. She was upended in the icy water before the contest was over, but she didn't seem to mind. After putting on a dry woolen shirt, she continued fishing, with Walter staying in sight of her to help if she needed his advice.

Having already caught several the previous day on natural bait, I decided to stick with flies for today. On the creek bank that morning we'd met a young man named Bob Long, who, hearing I was there, had brought us three dozen of his special files, small patterns made of a multicolored woolen blend—red, pink, green, and yellow—which he exchanged for our promise to join the Steelhead Society.

Late that afternoon, having had two strikes but no fish, I was floating one of the small woolen flies under a great log lying diagonally across the Deena. We had lost many of the flies to the swift current, rocks, and snags. Now I was hung up again, about ready to give up on the fly altogether as a lost cause. Just then, the "snag" began to move. I had a fish on my line, large enough that for a few minutes he was uncontrollable. I could only try to conserve as much line on my reel as possible while that steelhead did as he wished.

I tried to remember what I had learned about handling big fish on relatively light tackle. After getting the slack out of my line and on my reel, I maintained steady but firm pressure, moving down the shallow side of the creek whenever possible until I was downstream of the steelhead. Nevertheless, I almost lost him as he made two hard runs, one up a small tributary stream for a short distance. I applied as much restraint as the tackle would bear, although at other times I tried to moderate the tension to prevent the frantic runs.

Time dragged on. The fish and I moved slowly but inexorably down the stream. Fortunately, I was able to follow him, using the bank when possible and wading at other times. At this point the other fishermen came together to watch our pas de deux. On occasion they gave me some quiet encouragement—or laughed rather impolitely when I stumbled or fell. The steelhead jumped several times, and we could see from its bright colors that this one had been out of the sea for a number of days. I was mostly worried about the line getting fouled on one of the many snags in the stream, but each time the fish swam into an old treetop or among some roots the line later came clear. Because of the difficult footing and cluttered bank, I was engaged in a more sustained and difficult contest that I'd had with the much larger Atlantic salmon, but after half an hour the fish was obviously tiring. Finally, Walter was able to slip his net under the big male. We let him rest for a few minutes heading upstream and then watched him swim away, estimating his weight at fourteen pounds.

Clearly, it was the climax of this day's fishing. For a while, I had forgotten about the rain and cold. Now, trembling with excitements and fatigue, I decided to rest on my laurels and watch Rosalynn and the others fish for a while.

On the way back home we talked about the different fish that spawned in these Queen Charlotte streams. The biologists who monitored their movements estimated that each year there were about thirty thousand chum salmon and eight thousand coho, but fewer than one thousand steelhead. Since the rivers are relatively small and have a short run between their sources in the high mountains and the sea, without careful conservation practices the steelhead population could quite easily be decimated.

The next morning it was storming, with a gale blowing from the southeast. Rosalynn was hesitant, but we decided to go fishing despite the weather and found that in the river valley the big trees blocked the wind enough for us to manage our tackle well—although at one point a large tree did fall within twenty feet of us. Rosalynn and I each caught a couple of steelhead. For one of mine, a six-pounder, its mate (or, probably, schoolmate) circled and followed my hooked fish around in its evasive manoeuvres and right up to the net. After release, they swam off together.

So far, in a day's fishing I usually had a half-dozen steelhead on, landing one or two. When I fished with the fly rod but used salmon roe instead of flies, I could catch two or three times as many, but it was not nearly as much of a challenge. Also, because the fish was more likely to swallow natural bait, the artificial fly was safer for the fish.

The weather stayed cold and wet, with hail substituting for rain every now and then. Our spirits were high, however, because of the good fishing and the wildlife that was so prevalent. Sometimes we could see a pair of bald eagles circling overhead, building their nests and giving the high-pitched cries of love, excitement, or warning. On the way to the river one morning, we stopped to watch a gray whale moving slowly along the coast, only a few yards offshore, spouting regularly. Large otter were in the river, and we saw uncounted numbers of blacktail deer. We also saw the tracks and scat of black bear often, sighting three of them during the week.

One morning we received word that a logging company had offered to let us use one of its helicopters to visit the southern part of the Queen Charlottes. The next day we loaded our tackle and took off for a flight down the east coast. It was obvious from the air that the Copper and Pallant rivers were still too high from the constant rain for wading or convenient fishing. On small Skedans Island, just a rocky cliff jutting out of the waves a mile or so off the coast, we saw a large colony of sea lions. Keeping far enough away not to disturb them, we watched as they dived into the sea from a height of fifteen or twenty feet, moving over the rocky ledges with ease for creatures of such a cumbersome appearance.

We then landed on Lyell Island to observe the logging operation. There were sixty men and forty women and children at the camp, located on the shore of a small and protected bay. They were busy clear-cutting the sometimes virgin stands of spruce, hemlock, and red and white cedar. Earlier loggers had been able to harvest the trees conveniently near the sea, close enough to drag them down to the water with long cable rigs known as skidders. Now, with modern equipment, even the most remote trees could be cut and moved down for loading on barges and ships. A crew of "fallers" could cut down an average of thirty trees a day, but some of the trees were so large that it took a full day of work to cut one tree. The logs were loaded on the huge trucks and hauled down and dumped into the bay, where they were kept confined until the barges arrived to haul the timber to sawmills on the mainland. While we toured the recently completed recreation lodge we realized how enormous some of the trees were: The centre table had been made from a single slab of spruce burl—nine feet in diameter.

It was really disturbing to see this virgin stand of timber harvested. The denuded areas were to be replanted as soon as possible, but several decades would pass before the slow-growing trees would be large enough to provide full cover again. It was an unforgettable reminder of how wasteful we are in our use of paper, containers, and other wood products, and what a responsibility we have to prevent timber harvests altogether in some of the most beautiful sites.

After lunch we flew down to the southern tip of the islands, to Ninstints, an ancient village of the Kunghit tribe of Haida Indians. Along the shore enormous totem poles were lined up, each carved from a single cedar tree.

Some were still erect; others had fallen over and were in various stages of decay. Stone foundations of old buildings outlined the pattern of the village. The site had long been abandoned, most of the native population having succumbed to European diseases. They had been fierce warriors with an advanced civilization in their day. An 1840 census showed 308 people living here in twenty houses, with eleven other Kunghit villages in the islands. Now there were only two small settlements left.

Coming back up the west coast of the Charlottes, we decided to head east and stop on Louise Island to try the fishing. Jack and Wayne went to Mathers Creek, while Rosalynn, Walter, and I tried nearby Skedans Creek. The current was dangerously strong, and many of the large round rocks on the bottom were covered with slime. After falling in twice, I decided to confine my wading to places near the shore where I could maintain a relatively firm footing.

Within a few minutes I had a heavy strike on the small multicolored fly. I quickly realized that this fish was by far the largest one yet. I could see his bright-silver colour as he leaped three times far downstream. Because of the deep water and dangerous currents I could not move far from where I was, and yet in spite of maximum pressure on my tackle, the steelhead continued to head toward the sea at a steady pace. Even with my most vigorous efforts, when all the backing was gone from my reel the leader broke and the fish was free. This was a fish so strong that there was never a real contest, and I could only stand there and admire one who had conquered me so easily. We had been in the stream for a long time; I was too cold and exhausted to fish anymore, and soon we were on our way back to a fisherman's cherished destination: a fire, hot shower, and some dry clothes.

That evening we decided to go into town and accept an invitation to be guests at the Sandspit Inn for supper. The seafood platter we ordered included shrimp, octopus, razor clams, spring salmon, oysters, scallops, and Alaska crab legs, along with all the necessary trimmings. While we were enjoying it, a group of men from the 442nd Rescue Squadron sent us over a bottle of white wine and their business card, which read:

> ALWAYS READY—QUICK RESPONSE—GOOD ENDURANCE—HARD WORKING—ANYTIME, ANY PLACE—BUSH JUMPS—EXTRA PUMPS—
> BIG BUNDLES INTO TIGHT PLACES—CELESTIAL POSITIONING—AURAL HOMING—ILLUMINATING PATTERNS—THE SEARCH AND RESCUE SPECIALISTS THAT SMART PEOPLE IN DISTRESS CONTACT IN B.C. AND THE YUKON.

After reading this (and laughing) I felt much safer about the dangers of stormy weather, falling trees, swift currents, wild animals, enormous log trucks, and being lost in the forests.

Our last day, when we fished inland on the Pallant River, was the best day of all. It was blustery again, with winds reported in excess of sixty knots, but we caught and released eleven large and heavy steelhead. It had been a stormy week. Although we'd never felt at risk, when we arrived back in Vancouver we learned that two fishing trawlers and one sailing sloop had been lost at sea off the Queen Charlotte Islands. None of the crews was ever found.

Later, when I thought back to the trip, remembering the beauty and fragility of the wilderness, the denuded hills stuck in my mind. As a timber grower myself, I knew that all harvesting could not be prohibited, but I felt strongly that some of the more precious places, especially lovely or retaining the ancient history of the indigenous people, had to be preserved. I joined many other interested citizens who wrote to the prime minister of Canada, urging the government to protect the river valleys and especially scenic sites from logging operations.

Two years later, it was announced that special legislation had been passed by the Canadian Parliament, restricting logging operations throughout the southern part of the Queen Charlotte Islands, including the Haida Indian village and its carved totems.

The Promise and Peril of Democracy

Inaugural Lecture Series of the Americas at the Organization of American States, Washington, D.C.
25 January 2005

I have long been interested in this organization. Thirty years ago, as governor of Georgia, I invited the OAS General Assembly to meet in Atlanta—the first meeting in the US outside of Washington. Later, as president, I attended and addressed every General Assembly in Washington.

Back then, I realized that most of this hemisphere was ruled by military regimes or personal dictatorships. Senate hearings had just confirmed US involvement in destabilizing the government of Salvador Allende in Chile, and a dirty war was being conducted in Argentina. I decided to stop embracing dictators and to make the protection of human rights a cornerstone of US foreign policy, not only in this hemisphere, but with all nations.

When we signed the Panama Canal treaties in this same august hall in 1977, many non-elected or military leaders were on the dais. Key Caribbean states were absent, not yet part of the inter-American system. Then in 1979, Ecuador started a pattern of returning governments to civilian rule. The inter-American convention on human rights soon came into force, and our hemisphere developed one of the strongest human rights standards in the world.

These commitments have brought tremendous progress to Latin America and the Caribbean. Citizens have become involved in every aspect of governance: more women are running for political office and being appointed to high positions; indigenous groups are forming social movements and political parties; civic organizations are demanding transparency and accountability from their governments; freedom of expression is flourishing in an independent and vibrant press; ombudsmen and human rights defenders are active; and many countries are approving and implementing legislation to guarantee that citizens have access to information.

The English-speaking Caribbean has sustained vibrant democracies. A democratic Chile is removing military prerogatives from the Pinochet-era constitution and the military has acknowledged its institutional responsibility for the torture and disappearances of the 1970s. Central America has ended its civil wars and democracy has survived. The Guatemalan government offered a public apology for the murder of Myrna Mack, and a Salvadoran responsible for the assassination of Archbishop Romero was tried and convicted last year, although *in absentia*.

Venezuelans have avoided civil violence while enduring a deep political rift in the last three years. Mexico developed an electoral institution that has become the envy of the world. Argentine democracy weathered the deepest financial crisis since the 1920s depression and its economy is on the rebound.

Four years ago, Canada and Peru took the lead in developing a new, more explicit commitment to democracy for the hemisphere. On the tragic day of September 11, 2001, the Inter-American Democratic Charter was signed.

I am proud to have witnessed these demonstrations of the courage, persistence and creativity of the people of this hemisphere.

But I am also worried. I am concerned that the lofty ideas espoused in the Democratic Charter are not all being honoured. I am concerned that poverty and inequality continue unabated. And I am concerned that we in this room, representing governments and, in some cases, privileged societies, are not demonstrating the political will to shore up our fragile democracies, protect and defend our human rights system, and tackle the problems of desperation and destitution.

Since our years in the White House, my wife Rosalynn and I have striven to promote peace, freedom, health, and human rights, especially in this hemisphere and in Africa. Our dedicated staff at The Carter Center have worked in fifty-four elections to ensure they are honest and competitive. Civil strife has become rare, and every country but Cuba has had at least one truly competitive national election.

Yet, tiny Guyana, where we have been involved for more than a decade, remains wracked with racial tension and political stalemate. Haiti, where we monitored the first free election in its history and where the world contributed many tens of millions of dollars in aid, has been unable to escape the tragedy of violence and extreme poverty. In Nicaragua, I was privileged to witness the statesmanship of Daniel Ortega transferring power to Violeta Chamorro; yet today that country continues enmeshed in political deadlock and poverty that is second only to Haiti.

Across the hemisphere, UNDP and Latin barometer polls reveal that many citizens are dissatisfied with the performance of their elected governments. They still believe in the promise and the principles of democracy, but they do not believe their governments have delivered the promised improvements in living standards, freedom from corruption, and equal access to justice. We run the very real risk that dissatisfaction with the performance of elected governments will transform into disillusionment with democracy itself.

How can we protect the advances made and avoid the dangerous conclusion that democracy may not be worthwhile after all? The greatest challenge of our time is the growing gap between the rich and poor, both within countries and between the rich north and the poor south. About 45 percent (225 million) people of Latin America and the Caribbean live under the poverty line. The mathematical coefficient that measures income inequality reveals that Latin America has the most unequal income distribution in the world, and the income gap has continued to increase in the past fifteen years.

When people live in grinding poverty, see no hope for improvement for their children, and are not receiving the rights and benefits of citizenship, they will eventually make their grievances known, and it may be in radical and destructive ways.

Governments and the privileged in each country must make the decision and demonstrate the will to include all citizens in the benefits of society.

Democratic elections have improved, but we have also witnessed a dangerous pattern of ruling parties naming election authorities that are partisan and biased, governments misusing state resources for campaigns, and election results that are not trusted by the populace. I include my own country in saying that we all need to create fair election procedures, to regulate campaign finance, and to ensure that every eligible citizen is properly registered and has the opportunity to cast votes that will be counted honestly.

But democracy is much more than elections. It is accountable governments; it is the end of impunity for the powerful. It is giving judiciaries independence from political pressures so they can dispense justice with impartiality. It is protecting the rights of minorities, including those who do not vote for the majority party. It is protecting the vulnerable—such as those afflicted with HIV/AIDS, street children, those with mental illnesses, women abused with domestic violence, migrants, and indigenous peoples.

Governments of this hemisphere have carried out enormous economic reform efforts in the last two decades, but these efforts have not yet brought the needed reduction in poverty and inequality. Too many governments still rely on regressive sales taxes because the privileged classes can manipulate governments and avoid paying taxes on their incomes or wealth.

Military spending has been significantly reduced, but additional reductions are advisable now that the region is democratic and most border issues have been resolved. Health and education are more important than expensive weapons systems.

Access to land, small loans, and easier permits for small businesses can harness the potential dynamism of each nation's economy. Brazil has initiated a zero hunger program to address poverty, and Venezuela is using oil wealth to bring adult education, literacy, health and dental services directly to the poor. These and other creative social programs should be studied to see which might be appropriate in other areas.

When political leaders do make the right choices to address the needs of all citizens, those citizens have a responsibility as well—to comply with the established rules of the political process. Political honeymoons are short, and sometimes a frustrated people are tempted to unseat an unsatisfactory government, by violence or unconstitutional means. Elected leaders deserve a chance to make the tough decisions, or to be removed at ballot boxes.

News media play an especially important role in a free society. Press freedom is vibrant in the hemisphere, and must be kept that way. "Insult" (desacato) laws and harassment of journalists should be eliminated. The media also have a responsibility to investigate carefully and to corroborate their stories before publication.

Those of us in the richer nations have additional obligations. We must recognize that we live in an ever-closer hemisphere, with mutual responsibilities. Trade and tourism of the US and Canada are increasingly connected with all of Latin America and the Caribbean, as the sub-regions of the hemisphere are forging closer economic ties.

We are also connected by the scourge of crime, which is a two-way street. Drug demand in the US fuels drug production among our neighbours, undermining the ability of democratic institutions to enforce the rule of law, and the easy availability of small arms from the US has made crime a serious problem for governments in the Caribbean and Central America.

Globally, Americans give just fifteen cents per $100 of national income in official development assistance. As a share of our economy, we rank dead last among industrialized countries. The recently announced millennium challenge account is designed to provide additional help for governments pursuing transparency and accountability, but in this hemisphere only Bolivia, Honduras and Nicaragua are being considered for this aid.

The United States has another role to play as well: of setting an example of protecting civil liberties and improving democratic practices at home, and by its unwavering support of democracy and human rights abroad.

The international lending agencies also have important roles to play: by being more flexible and responsive to political pressures and social constraints when deciding conditionality; by involving local citizens and governments in developing consensus for poverty-reduction strategies; and by helping the hemisphere carry out the mandates adopted by presidents at the periodic summits of the Americas.

Finally, I call on all governments of the hemisphere to make the Democratic Charter more than empty pieces of paper, to make it a living document. The charter commits us to help one another when our democratic institutions are threatened. The charter can be a punitive instrument, providing for sanctions when a serious challenge to the democratic order occurs, but it is also an instrument for providing technical assistance and moral encouragement to prevent democratic erosion early in the game.

Let us strengthen the charter and not be afraid to use it. Right now the charter is weak because it is vague in defining conditions that would constitute a violation of the charter—the "unconstitutional alteration or interruption" of the democratic order noted in Article 19. The charter also requires the consent of the affected government even to evaluate a threat to democracy. If the government itself is threatening the minimum conditions of democracy, the hemisphere is not prepared to act, since there would certainly not be an invitation.

Two simple actions would help to remedy this problem and allow the governments of this hemisphere to act when needed. First, a clear definition of "unconstitutional alteration or interruption" would help guide us. These conditions should include:

1. Violation of the integrity of central institutions, including constitutional checks and balances providing for the separation of powers.
2. Holding of elections that do not meet minimal international standards.
3. Failure to hold periodic elections or to respect electoral outcomes.
4. Systematic violation of basic freedoms, including freedom of expression, freedom of association, or respect for minority rights.
5. Unconstitutional termination of the tenure in office of any legally elected official.
6. Arbitrary or illegal, removal or interference in the appointment or deliberations of members of the judiciary or electoral bodies.
7. Interference by non-elected officials, such as military officers, in the jurisdiction of elected officials.
8. Systematic use of public office to silence, harass, or disrupt the normal and legal activities of members of the political opposition, the press, or civil society.

We also need a set of graduated, automatic responses to help us overcome the inertia and paralysis of political will that result from uncertain standards and the need to reach a consensus *de novo* on each alleged violation. When a democratic threat is identified, the alleged offenders would be requested to explain their actions before the permanent council. A full evaluation would follow, and possible responses could be chosen from a prescribed menu of appropriate options, involving not only the OAS, but incentives and disincentives from multilateral institutions and the private sector.

There is also a role for nongovernmental leaders. We at The Carter Center have convened a group of former hemispheric leaders to aid in raising the visibility of the charter, to engage the OAS, and to help it provide appropriate responses when democracy is challenged.

Let me close by congratulating the OAS, which has come a long way from my first association with it thirty years ago. As a promoter of freedom, democracy, and human rights, the OAS is one of the foremost regional organizations in the world. This hemisphere adopted the world's first anti-corruption convention and has developed a multilateral evaluation mechanism on drugs. The OAS has worked on de-mining, peacemaking, and providing scholarships to students. It exemplifies the notion that our best hope for the world is for sovereign states to work together.

The OAS is going through a difficult transition at the moment, but it will emerge even stronger. A new secretary-general will be chosen this year, and important discussions will be forthcoming at the General Assembly in Florida and the Fourth Summit of the Americas in Argentina.

We need each other. Let us work together to make our hemisphere the beacon of hope, human dignity, and cooperation for the twenty-first century.

Remarks by Jimmy Carter at the conference

Human Rights Defenders on the Frontlines of Freedom

Atlanta, Ga.
11 November 2003

We are delighted to have this assembly here. It is a great honour for The Carter Center, and I want to welcome all of you. We have the largest committee on human rights represented here. We have America's Watch represented here and other groups. We don't have any governments represented here, right? Nobody directly representing any government is here, so we can speak very freely about governments without fear of having too much competition or contradiction here in this meeting.

It is a pleasure to reminisce with you for a few moments at the beginning of this program, and then to cover a few issues. Twenty-seven years ago or so, I became president of the United States, a nation that was founded on the principle of human rights. One of the comments I made in my inaugural address was that the United States did not invent human rights; human rights invented the United States. We decided even before I was inaugurated, to escalate human rights to the top position on the agenda of our foreign policy. Never did I meet with a foreign leader that human rights was not on the official agenda. Every American ambassador in the world was my direct human rights representative. Every embassy was designated by me personally, as a president, as a haven for those who were persecuted in foreign countries. This policy was looked on by some as naive or weak or a violation of commitments we had made to dictators and others who were very close allies with us in some of the global issues that we had to face. But it was a great challenge for the United States, and a great honour, to be recognized as the champion of human rights that never failed to raise high the banner of freedom and liberty and the absence of persecution.

Ten years ago, I and my wife, Rosalynn, went to Geneva. I made one of the keynote speeches in the World Conference on Human Rights. We had some very clear items on our own Carter Center agenda. One of which was the creation of the Office of High Commissioner for Human Rights of the United Nations. I spoke about this in my address, and immediately thereafter, the secretary-general of the United Nations, Boutros-Boutros Ghali, invited me and Rosalynn to have breakfast with him and his wife the next morning, where he told me that he was very strongly opposed to having a high commissioner for human rights. He thought it would be an interference with the function of his own office and that his assistants and his deputies could adequately take care of the problem of human rights. But The Carter Center persisted, along with many of you, and eventually this office was created, and I think it has had substantial success. Not adequate yet, of course, because many governments who controlled the operations of the United Nations, as you know, are themselves persecutors of defenders like you. But this has been one of the challenges that we face.

We thought we had made good progress ten years ago in Vienna with our declaration, but shortly afterwards we were faced, as you know, with Bosnia and then with the horrible massacre of innocent people in Rwanda.

The Carter Center worked five years in Rwanda and Burundi in the Great Lakes area (of Africa), and eventually we saw the need of an international criminal court. The Carter Center was the host in the United States for more than one conference to promote the concept of the international criminal court. We were never able to get our own government to participate in a positive way. Most of them, the US representatives, raised objections to the key points that would have been crucial to the international criminal court. But in the last few days of President Clinton's administration, he did agree, somewhat reluctantly, to sign this authorization for the international criminal court. With the advent of the Bush administration however, as you know, there's been a literal crusade against the implementation of the international criminal court.

So there have been struggles for a long time over this inherent and all pervasive concept of governments being abusive to their own citizens, which is a key factor that precipitates human rights violations. It breeds disrespect for the government. It results in a few courageous people like the defenders represented here being willing to speak out and explain, within their own countries and to the world, this is happening in my county. It's a direct violation of the principles of human rights that have been established, even shortly after the United Nations itself was established. Those defenders, quite often, are persecuted by their governments. This creates additional animosity, hatred, and violence, within the countries affected. That is one of the breeding places for terrorism.

We have continued our efforts, along with many of you, in trying to promote human rights. It has not been always successful. There are gross human rights violations still throughout the world, as many of you can testify directly.

I read some of the testimony that you've given here already, with the advent of the attack on the United States known as 9/11, our country began to make, in my opinion, some very serious mistakes. It was natural for a nation with approximately three thousand people killed in the worst terrorist attack perhaps in history to react in a way to defend our own people. But we have begun, in our country, and in our foreign policy, to work against the spirit of human rights.

As all of you know by now, without any public discussion, our government ordered about twelve hundred United States citizens to be arrested secretly and held incommunicado in prison—sometimes with leg chains on them, refused the right of accusations to be presented about their alleged crimes, deprived of the right to counsel, deprived of the right to communicate with their own families. And they were kept that way for sometimes many months. Although most of them have now been released, the United States government has still refused to release the list of those who were persecuted. Almost of all them were found completely innocent. But this was an unprecedented thing in our country in after more than two hundred years of protecting civil rights. We went to war, as you know, in Afghanistan, maybe for justifiable causes, and captured some people there who were on the opposite side in the war, from different countries in the world—some from Great Britain, some from Australia, some from Kuwait—our allies. We brought six hundred of those to Guantanamo. It's a small enclave of, in effect, United States territory on the island of Cuba, and they are still being held there without official charge. They don't know what their crimes, or alleged crimes, were. They have still been deprived of a right to counsel or to basic standards that have always applied to those captured in war.

We've been to war many times in our country—Vietnam, the First World War, the Second World War and others that I need not name, the Gulf war, so-called, the first war against Iraq. We've never done that before or since—captured people and held them in cages afterward. I say these things, which you all know, to point out that this is a violation of the basic character of my country, and it's very disturbing to me. As we have done these things, which are known throughout the entire world, it has lowered the standard of what is the definition of human rights. It is giving, in effect, a blank cheque to governments that were inherently inclined to violate human rights already. We have in addition encouraged governments to tighten up on state control over freedom of speech and other human rights, which we all cherish.

This is bad. But I think it's very important at this meeting that we're having here at The Carter Center not to single out the United States, because there are much worse violations in many countries in the world. We need to make sure that our voice is one of moderation and one of courageous but positive advice and counsel that others can look upon and not just an attack on my own country, which still preserves the right of defenders. We're not in any case in our country controlling the right of defenders.

I made a major address at Georgia Tech, a great university here in Atlanta, and condemned these policies just as I'm doing this morning. This week former Vice President Al Gore made a superb speech in which he outlined these and other violations of human rights in a very open and provocative way. So our country still protects the right of people like me and Al Gore and others to defend the principles that we all espouse, so we shouldn't just single out the United States as the worst violator. It is not. It has departed radically from previous policies, which is very disturbing to us, but we should make sure that we don't just single out the United States for condemnation.

I understand that the group has already begun to work on a so-called Atlanta Declaration, which may hopefully encapsulate the recommendations for us to promulgate. I have already communicated with the secretary of state and with others in Washington to make an appointment for a representative number of this group, a small group, to meet with some of the leaders in Washington. So I think that our main purpose is not just to talk to each other, because we all agree on basic principles. There won't be very much debate among us, but the main thing is for us to have a stronger concerted voice.

My co-chairman for this meeting was originally going to be Sergio Vieira de Mello. I talked to him several times about this conference. He was very enthusiastic about it. In fact even when he went to Iraq to represent the secretary-general directly, I talked to him on the phone. He said his first love was human rights, and although he was there to serve the Iraqi people for just a few months, he would be back here before the time for this conference. He is one of the heroes who has given his life for this purpose, and I think we should remember him as we proceed with our deliberations. After his death, the secretary-general appointed Bertrand Ramcharan to be the acting high commissioner on human rights. Berti has in the past been the deputy high commissioner for human rights. He has been assistant secretary-general of the United Nations, and he has served in the United Nations for thirty years. He's taught as an adjunct professor of international human rights law at Columbia University, and he's been a prolific author. I see he's written some twenty books. I've only written eighteen books, so I'm still behind him in that respect. He holds a doctorate in international law from the London School of Economics, and we are honoured to have him here with us this morning. I'd like to now introduce Berti Ramcharan to make some remarks.

Camp David Accords
Jimmy Carter Reflects 25 Years Later

Washington, D.C.
17 September 2003

I just came back a few days ago from Japan and China. The Carter Center has had programs in sixty-five nations in the world. In Sub-Sahara Africa, we have had about one million test plots in agriculture financed by a Japanese partner, and we are involved—The Carter Center is—in monitoring elections in almost eight hundred thousand small villages in China. They are very honest and democratic elections.

While I was in Japan, I remembered going through China and Japan in 1981, soon after I left the White House. At that time I was asked to make a speech at a small college near Osaka. When I got to this little college, everybody was so nervous, it made me nervous. So, I got up to make a speech, and I thought I would put the Japanese at ease—the students and professors and their parents—by telling a joke. It takes so long to translate English into Japanese that I didn't choose my funniest joke—I just chose my shortest joke. So I told my joke, and then the interpreter gave it and the audience collapsed in laughter. It was the best response I have ever had to a joke in my life.

I couldn't wait for the speech to be over to get to the green room and ask the interpreter, "How did you tell my joke?" He was very evasive. But I persisted, and finally he ducked his head and said, "I told the audience, 'President Carter told a funny story. Everyone must laugh.'" So there are some advantages in having been president. That is one of the advantages in my life.

Today, I'm not sure I have an advantage in trying to summarize what we've done this morning. I had some notes made out beforehand, but almost everything I wanted to say has already been said. I will just take a few moments to encapsulate what has been done involving the Middle East, at least during my time in public life.

I remember the earliest stages of my involvement in the Middle East. I took a trip over there with Jody Powell and Rosalynn in 1972 when I was governor, and we had a chance to travel around Israel and to try to understand the problems there. We spent about half the time looking at biblical places and half the time learning about what was going on between Israel and her neighbours after the wars that had attacked the existence of that nation.

I formed an alliance there that came to the forefront when I was president. After the election, even before I was inaugurated as president, I had decided that I would make every possible effort to get away from a step-by-step process, which was very effective in the past in some cases, and try to deal with the entire gamut of Mideast problems. That was really what precipitated my meeting during the first few months of my administration with the leaders of the Middle East.

All of them came to the United States except Assad [president of Syria]. He refused to come to the United States throughout his entire life, so I did go to Geneva, Switzerland to meet with him. But that started a process, at least in my own administration, for the Camp David effort.

Looking back on all of the issues or events that took place, including the Camp David accords, there is a continuity that is both discouraging and also offers some modicum of hope. United Nations resolution 242 was passed unanimously, including a positive vote by the United States and Israel, at the conclusion of the 1967 war. Its basic premises call for withdrawal of Israel from the occupied territories and for the acknowledgement of Israel's existence and sovereignty—and its right to exist in peace—by all the nations of the world. And a third thing that it calls for is a just settlement of the refugee problem.

Those were the three basic elements for peace, but obviously peace was not achieved. Additional wars took place—the latest one was in 1973. When we went to Camp David, it was with an effort to continue the process that had been begun a long time before.

I'm not going to try to repeat what we have talked about this morning, but I would like to just outline a few things, because, in reading my voluminous notes that I took at the time, it's obvious that some issues were in the forefront.

First was Arab recognition of Israel's right to exist in peace. Second was Israel's withdrawal from the occupied territories, with exceptions that had to be negotiated for Israel's security. A contiguous, or Palestinian, state was assumed with—to use Prime Minister Begin's phrase, "full autonomy for the Palestinians," or to use his more precise phrase "Palestinian Arabs"—because he maintained to me that Israeli Jews were also Palestinians.

And third was an undivided Jerusalem. As a matter of fact, while we were at Camp David, we negotiated a paragraph that for a number of days was completely acceptable to both Begin and Sadat. But toward the end of the session, the last few hours, both of them urged me to delete that paragraph from the final document because it was so sensitive on both sides. They thought they had enough sensitive stuff in it to begin with.

The other issue that has been persistent throughout all these years has been the United States playing a very strong role. I personally used what was called a single document—I have been involved in a lot of negotiations since then, and I've always used a single document—getting my superb assistants, who were all on the program this morning, to ultimately prepare a proposal that was presented precisely word by word to the Israelis, primarily to Prime Minister Begin, and to Sadat and to the Egyptians on the other side. We didn't have one document for one and one for the other.

This was a very long and torturous effort to get everybody to agree on exactly the same document. It has been pointed out this morning that some of the things were put in with an element of ambiguity because we could not decide on precise definitions, and we could not decide on precise schedules.

We had alternatives. One was for me to prepare a document that was patently fair, at least in our opinion, and that would be acceptable by one side. Then to use the threat against the other side of being isolated when the document was made public, and it became obvious that one side had rejected it.

I'll give you a quick example that may not necessarily be the only one involved. If everything else had been accepted that we had in the entire Camp David accords, including full diplomatic recognition for Israel, the right to traverse the Suez Canal, all of those elements and the only issue that remained was Israel's insistence on maintaining a few Israeli settlements in the Sinai, and that was the only thing, then Israel would have been in a very difficult position to put their whole premise on that point. In my opinion the Israeli people would have been disappointed had the entire process been voided because of a few settlements.

That was a technique of negotiation that, luckily, didn't have to be implemented because at the last minute Prime Minister Begin did permit the settlements to be dismantled. One was at Yamit, which I believe had about three thousand settlers, it was a fairly large settlement, and there were thirteen other very small ones.

What Sadat wanted was very clear. He wanted good relations with the United States, which Begin also wanted. He wanted his sovereign territory returned. That was something on which he would not deviate at all. He wanted peace with Israel for many reasons so that he could deal with other challenges to his own regime. There were some very important and serious challenges, for instance, from Libya against Egypt at that time, and Sadat wanted to be looked upon at the end of the whole discussion as making a strong attempt to protect the rights of the Palestinians.

Begin, as I said, wanted good relations with the United States, and he wanted Israel to be accepted in the world community by the major Arab nation that had been a threat militarily and politically to Israel above all others. The fact that Sadat was finally willing during the Camp David accords to give full diplomatic relations with Israel was important to him. He wanted peace, and he wanted to demilitarize the Sinai if he gave up control of it.

The worst disagreement that we had at the end of the Camp David accords, as we've discussed quite thoroughly this morning, was concerning the Israeli settlements: whether Israel would continue to build the settlements in the West Bank and Gaza or whether they would be frozen during the time that we were negotiating to conclude all of the elements of autonomy for the Palestinians. I misunderstood what Prime Minister Begin said. I have no reflection on his integrity or his honesty.

A couple of days ago I got the "Road Map to Peace" text that has been prepared under the leadership of President George W. Bush and I read it very carefully. It was very interesting to me how almost completely compatible it is with what was done at Camp David and what was confirmed later on in the Oslo negotiations performed by the Norwegians in 1993, almost exactly ten years ago.

I will quote one paragraph from it, and this is a key paragraph. This was issued on the 30th of April this year.

"A settlement ... will result in ... an independent, democratic, and viable Palestinian state living side by side in peace and security with Israel and its other neighbours. The settlement will resolve the Israel-Palestinian conflict, and end the occupation that began in 1967, based on the foundations of the Madrid Conference, the principle of land for peace, United Nations resolutions 242, 338, and 1397, agreements previously reached by the parties, and," it went on to say, "the initiative of Saudi Crown Prince Abdullah—endorsed by the Beirut Arab League Summit—calling for acceptance of Israel as a neighbour living in peace and security, in the context of a comprehensive settlement."

"This initiative," it concludes by saying, "is a vital element of international efforts to promote a comprehensive peace on all tracks, including the Syrian-Israeli and the Lebanese-Israeli tracks."

You can see that this description of what the so-called "Road Map to Peace" now encompasses is almost identical to the basic premises of the Camp David accords combined with the Oslo agreement.

Unfortunately, at this time, the most difficult decisions in the "Road Map to Peace," which is what we are talking about now and what we will be talking about this afternoon, were avoided or postponed to some uncertain time. I say that not in criticism, because there were some elements of the Camp David accords that we delayed to be implemented within three years or five years. Some of the most difficult decisions were delayed.

Its key early provisions, however, a good number of them, have been rejected by the Israeli cabinet. There are fourteen caveats that have been promulgated by the present Israeli cabinet that subvert some of the major portions of the "Road Map to Peace."

Terrorist attacks, as you know, have been launched and continue to be launched by Hamas and other violent Palestinians.

There are four partners in the "Road Map to Peace," hopefully combining enough international strength to implement and to convince doubtful parties. But the European Union, Great Britain, and Russia have been put aside, and the United States plays the same role that we did twenty-five years ago, almost a unilateral one. The entire effort seems to be languishing. Again, let me point out that I'm not saying that in a critical way, because I understand, having been president, that President Bush and his administration are deeply involved with other issues of international importance affecting the security of the United States. One is obviously the Iraqi war, another is Afghanistan, another one is the challenge of nuclear capabilities from Iran, and some statements have come out in the last few hours concerning Syria and North Korea. I need not go on any more. There is enough there to show that it would be impossible now even if he wanted to, for President Bush to go up in isolation for thirteen days to try to deal exclusively with the Mideast peace process.

In the meantime, as you all know, a wall or a fence is being constructed, which can be of great concern. I don't know the exact delineation of it, although I've seen a map of it. It follows, in some ways, the pre-1967 border or the so-called "green line." In other places, it is departing from the pre-1967 line and encroaching substantially on Palestinian land in the occupied territories.

I've outlined very briefly a parallel series of challenges and problems that have been disturbingly persistent for the last half-century. I, and many others, have attempted to resolve these issues. Well-meaning and courageous and deeply committed leaders of the opposing parties have participated as well.

Do we face a hopeless prospect for peace? No, I don't think so because I think there is a tremendous focusing of global attention and deep concern on this existing or remaining problem.

Let me point out that United Nations resolution 242, the Camp David accords in 1978, the Oslo agreement in 1993, and the "Road Map to Peace" in this current year all agree that peace will come to the Mideast only if two things happen.

One is that Israel refrains from retaining in the occupied Palestinian territories or the West Bank and Gaza, the multiple settlements that have to be defended militarily and connected with a web of relatively uncrossable highways. That's important and extremely difficult.

The other one is that the Palestinian national authority and all Arab nations must acknowledge the sovereignty and the territorial integrity of Israel and its right to live in peace, and must exert their combined effort to control and to prevent any further acts of terrorism or violence by any Palestinian group against the people in Israel.

Those are the two basic issues that must be addressed. There are others with which I am very familiar. One is Jerusalem and the other is the right of return. The right of return is required to be resolved fairly in United Nations resolution 242 and, also as you notice, in the current "Road Map to Peace." But, in my own opinion, that can be handled. I think a tiny number of Palestinians could ever hope to return to Israel proper, and the number that would come to even the West Bank and Gaza would be limited. There is something of an escape valve there and that is the generally accepted principle that Palestinians who can put forward a legitimate claim for the right to return can be compensated for property they've lost, not as determined by Israel or the Palestinians in another altercation, but through some international claims tribunal.

When I resolved the hostage crisis with Iran, during the last few hours of my administration, I also agreed to a process for determining what would happen to $12 billion in Iranian assets that had been frozen by the United States. There was a multitude of claims against Iran filed by a wide range of Americans, and Iranians also had claims against the US. An Iran–US Claims Tribunal was established in The Hague to resolve these disputes through binding third-party arbitration. Essentially all of the claims involving private claimants were resolved successfully. A similar process could be established for resolving the Palestinian claims.

So I think the refugee question and the Jerusalem question are not the burning issues. I think the issues are full acceptance of Israel's right to live in peace—to stamp out any hope that terrorists can prevail and to prevent further acts of terrorism against Israel—and the relinquishing of a substantial portion of the settlements that now permeate the West Bank and Gaza. Those are the two basic issues, and I don't see them as impossible to resolve.

With strong leadership, determined mediation that is trusted, a balanced role between Israel and the Palestinians, and good faith, I believe we can still see peace in the Middle East in our lifetime. That is my prayer. And that is my expectation.

2002 Nobel Peace Prize Lecture

10 December 2002

It is with a deep sense of gratitude that I accept this prize. I am grateful to my wife Rosalynn, to my colleagues at The Carter Center, and to many others who continue to seek an end to violence and suffering throughout the world. The scope and character of our Center's activities are perhaps unique, but in many other ways they are typical of the work being done by many hundreds of nongovernmental organizations that strive for human rights and peace.

Most Nobel laureates have carried out our work in safety, but there are others who have acted with great personal courage. None has provided more vivid reminders of the dangers of peacemaking than two of my friends, Anwar Sadat and Yitzhak Rabin, who gave their lives for the cause of peace in the Middle East.

Like these two heroes, my first chosen career was in the military, as a submarine officer. My shipmates and I realized that we had to be ready to fight if combat was forced upon us, and we were prepared to give our lives to defend our nation and its principles. At the same time, we always prayed fervently that our readiness would ensure that there would be no war.

Later, as president and as commander-in-chief of our armed forces, I was one of those who bore the sobering responsibility of maintaining global stability during the height of the Cold War, as the world's two superpowers confronted each other. Both sides understood that an unresolved political altercation or a serious misjudgment could lead to a nuclear holocaust. In Washington and in Moscow, we knew that we would have less than a half hour to respond after we learned that intercontinental missiles had been launched against us. There had to be a constant and delicate balancing of our great military strength with aggressive diplomacy, always seeking to build friendships with other nations, large and small, that shared a common cause.

In those days, the nuclear and conventional armaments of the United States and the Soviet Union were almost equal, but democracy ultimately prevailed because of commitments to freedom and human rights, not only by people in my country and those of our allies, but in the former Soviet empire as well. As president, I extended my public support and encouragement to Andrei Sakharov, who, although denied the right to attend the ceremony, was honoured here for his personal commitments to these same ideals.

The world has changed greatly since I left the White House. Now there is only one superpower, with unprecedented military and economic strength. The coming budget for American armaments will be greater than those of the next fifteen nations combined, and there are troops from the United States in many countries throughout the world. Our gross national economy exceeds that of the three countries that follow us, and our nation's voice most often prevails as decisions are made concerning trade, humanitarian assistance, and the allocation of global wealth. This dominant status is unlikely to change in our lifetimes.

Great American power and responsibility are not unprecedented, and have been used with restraint and great benefit in the past. We have not assumed that super strength guarantees super wisdom, and we have consistently reached out to the international community to ensure that our own power and influence are tempered by the best common judgment.

Within our country, ultimate decisions are made through democratic means, which tend to moderate radical or ill-advised proposals. Constrained and inspired by historic constitutional principles, our nation has endeavoured for more than two hundred years to follow the now almost universal ideals of freedom, human rights, and justice for all.

Our president, Woodrow Wilson, was honoured here for promoting the League of Nations, whose two basic concepts were profoundly important: "collective security" and "self-determination." Now they are embedded in international law. Violations of these premises during the last half-century have been tragic failures, as was vividly demonstrated when the Soviet Union attempted to conquer Afghanistan and when Iraq invaded Kuwait.

After the Second World War, American Secretary of State Cordell Hull received this prize for his role in founding the United Nations. His successor, General George C. Marshall, was recognized because of his efforts to help rebuild Europe, without excluding the vanquished nations of Italy and Germany. This was a historic example of respecting human rights at the international level.

Ladies and gentlemen:

Twelve years ago, President Mikhail Gorbachev received your recognition for his pre-eminent role in ending the Cold War that had lasted fifty years.

But instead of entering a millennium of peace, the world is now, in many ways, a more dangerous place. The greater ease of travel and communication has not been matched by equal understanding and mutual respect. There is a plethora of civil wars, unrestrained by rules of the Geneva

Convention, within which an overwhelming portion of the casualties are unarmed civilians who have no ability to defend themselves. And recent appalling acts of terrorism have reminded us that no nations, even superpowers, are invulnerable.

It is clear that global challenges must be met with an emphasis on peace, in harmony with others, with strong alliances and international consensus. Imperfect as it may be, there is no doubt that this can best be done through the United Nations, which Ralph Bunche described here in this same forum as exhibiting a "fortunate flexibility"—not merely to preserve peace but also to make change, even radical change, without violence.

He went on to say: "To suggest that war can prevent war is a base play on words and a despicable form of warmongering. The objective of any who sincerely believe in peace clearly must be to exhaust every honourable recourse in the effort to save the peace. The world has had ample evidence that war begets only conditions that beget further war."

We must remember that today there are at least eight nuclear powers on earth, and three of them are threatening to their neighbours in areas of great international tension. For powerful countries to adopt a principle of preventive war may well set an example that can have catastrophic consequences.

If we accept the premise that the United Nations is the best avenue for the maintenance of peace, then the carefully considered decisions of the United Nations Security Council must be enforced. All too often, the alternative has proven to be uncontrollable violence and expanding spheres of hostility.

For more than half a century, following the founding of the State of Israel in 1948, the Middle East conflict has been a source of worldwide tension. At Camp David in 1978 and in Oslo in 1993, Israelis, Egyptians, and Palestinians have endorsed the only reasonable prescription for peace: United Nations Resolution 242. It condemns the acquisition of territory by force, calls for withdrawal of Israel from the occupied territories, and provides for Israelis to live securely and in harmony with their neighbours. There is no other mandate whose implementation could more profoundly improve international relationships.

Perhaps of more immediate concern is the necessity for Iraq to comply fully with the unanimous decision of the Security Council that it eliminate all weapons of mass destruction and permit unimpeded access by inspectors to confirm that this commitment has been honoured. The world insists that this be done.

I thought often during my years in the White House of an admonition that we received in our small school in Plains, Georgia, from a beloved teacher, Miss Julia Coleman. She often said: "We must adjust to changing times and still hold to unchanging principles."

When I was a young boy, this same teacher also introduced me to Leo Tolstoy's novel, *War and Peace*. She interpreted that powerful narrative as a reminder that the simple human attributes of goodness and truth can overcome great power. She also taught us that an individual is not swept along on a tide of inevitability but can influence even the greatest human events.

These premises have been proven by the lives of many heroes, some of whose names were little known outside their own regions until they became Nobel laureates: Albert John Lutuli, Norman Borlaug, Desmond Tutu, Elie Wiesel, Aung San Suu Kyi, Jody Williams, and even Albert Schweitzer and Mother Teresa. All of these and others have proven that even without government power—and often in opposition to it—individuals can enhance human rights and wage peace, actively and effectively.

The Nobel prize also profoundly magnified the inspiring global influence of Martin Luther King, Jr., the greatest leader that my native state has ever produced. On a personal note, it is unlikely that my political career beyond Georgia would have been possible without the changes brought about by the civil rights movement in the American south and throughout our nation.

On the steps of our memorial to Abraham Lincoln, Dr. King said: "I have a dream that on the red hills of Georgia the sons of former slaves and the sons of former slave owners will be able to sit down together at a table of brotherhood."

The scourge of racism has not been vanquished, either in the red hills of our state or around the world. And yet we see ever more frequent manifestations of his dream of racial healing. In a symbolic but very genuine way, at least involving two Georgians, it is coming true in Oslo today.

I am not here as a public official, but as a citizen of a troubled world who finds hope in a growing consensus that the generally accepted goals of society are peace, freedom, human rights, environmental quality, the alleviation of suffering, and the rule of law.

During the past decades, the international community, usually under the auspices of the United Nations, has struggled to negotiate global standards that can help us achieve these essential goals. They include: the abolition of land mines and chemical weapons; an end to the testing, proliferation, and further deployment of nuclear warheads; constraints on global warming; prohibition of the death penalty, at least for children; and an international criminal court to deter and to punish war crimes and genocide. Those agreements already adopted must be fully implemented, and others should be pursued aggressively.

We must also strive to correct the injustice of economic sanctions that seek to penalize abusive leaders but all too often inflict punishment on those who are already suffering from the abuse.

The unchanging principles of life predate modern times. I worship Jesus Christ, whom we Christians consider to be the Prince of Peace. As a Jew, he taught us to cross religious boundaries, in service and in love. He repeatedly reached out and embraced Roman conquerors, other Gentiles, and even the more despised Samaritans.

Despite theological differences, all great religions share common commitments that define our ideal secular relationships. I am convinced that Christians, Muslims, Buddhists, Hindus, Jews, and others can embrace each other in a common effort to alleviate human suffering and to espouse peace.

But the present era is a challenging and disturbing time for those whose lives are shaped by religious faith based on kindness toward each other. We have been reminded that cruel and inhuman acts can be derived from distorted theological beliefs, as suicide bombers take the lives of innocent human beings, draped falsely in the cloak of God's will. With horrible brutality, neighbours have massacred neighbours in Europe, Asia, and Africa.

In order for us human beings to commit ourselves personally to the inhumanity of war, we find it necessary first to dehumanize our opponents, which is in itself a violation of the beliefs of all religions. Once we characterize our adversaries as beyond the scope of God's mercy and grace, their lives lose all value. We deny personal responsibility when we plant landmines and, days or years later, a stranger to us—often a child—is crippled or killed. From a great distance, we launch bombs or missiles with almost total impunity, and never want to know the number or identity of the victims.

At the beginning of this new millennium I was asked to discuss, here in Oslo, the greatest challenge that the world faces. Among all the possible choices, I decided that the most serious and universal problem is the growing chasm between the richest and poorest people on earth. Citizens of the ten wealthiest countries are now seventy-five times richer than those who live in the ten poorest ones, and the separation is increasing every year, not only between nations but also within them. The results of this disparity are root causes of most of the world's unresolved problems, including starvation, illiteracy, environmental degradation, violent conflict, and unnecessary illnesses that range from Guinea worm to HIV/AIDS.

Most work of The Carter Center is in remote villages in the poorest nations of Africa, and there I have witnessed the capacity of destitute people to persevere under heartbreaking conditions. I have come to admire their judgment and wisdom, their courage and faith, and their awesome accomplishments when given a chance to use their innate abilities.

But tragically, in the industrialized world there is a terrible absence of understanding or concern about those who are enduring lives of despair and hopelessness. We have not yet made the commitment to share with others an appreciable part of our excessive wealth. This is a potentially rewarding burden that we should all be willing to assume.

Ladies and gentlemen:

War may sometimes be a necessary evil. But no matter how necessary, it is always an evil, never a good. We will not learn how to live together in peace by killing each other's children.

The bond of our common humanity is stronger than the divisiveness of our fears and prejudices. God gives us the capacity for choice. We can choose to alleviate suffering. We can choose to work together for peace. We can make these changes—and we must.

The United States and Cuba: A Vision for the 21st Century

University of Havana, Cuba
14 May 2002

I appreciate President Castro's invitation for us to visit Cuba, and have been delighted with the hospitality we have received since arriving here. It is a great honour to address the Cuban people.

After a long and agonizing struggle, Cuba achieved its independence a century ago, and a complex relationship soon developed between our two countries. The great powers in Europe and Asia viewed "imperialism" as the natural order of the time and they expected the United States to colonize Cuba as the Europeans had done in Africa. The United States chose instead to help Cuba become independent, but not completely. The Platt Amendment gave my country the right to intervene in Cuba's internal affairs until President Franklin Roosevelt had the wisdom to repeal this claim in May 1934.

The dictator Fulgencio Batista was overthrown more than forty-three years ago, and a few years later the Cuban revolution aligned with the Soviet Union in the Cold War. Since then, our nations have followed different philosophical and political paths.

The hard truth is that neither the United States nor Cuba has managed to define a positive and beneficial relationship. Will this new century find our neighbouring people living in harmony and friendship? I have come here in search of an answer to that question.

There are some in Cuba who think the simple answer is for the United States to lift the embargo, and there are some in my country who believe the answer is for your president to step down from power and allow free elections. There is no doubt that the question deserves a more comprehensive assessment.

I have restudied the complicated history (in preparation for my conversations with President Castro), and realize that there are no simple answers.

I did not come here to interfere in Cuba's internal affairs, but to extend a hand of friendship to the Cuban people and to offer a vision of the future for our two countries and for all the Americas.

That vision includes a Cuba fully integrated into a democratic hemisphere, participating in a Free Trade Area of the Americas and with our citizens travelling without restraint to visit each other. I want a massive student exchange between our universities. I want the people of the United States and Cuba to share more than a love of baseball and wonderful music. I want us to be friends, and to respect each other.

Our two nations have been trapped in a destructive state of belligerence for forty-two years, and it is time for us to change our relationship and the way we think and talk about each other. Because the United States is the most powerful nation, we should take the first step.

First, my hope is that the Congress will soon act to permit unrestricted travel between the United States and Cuba, establish open trading relationships, and repeal the embargo. I should add that these restraints are not the source of Cuba's economic problems. Cuba can trade with more than one hundred countries, and buy medicines, for example, more cheaply in Mexico than in the United States. But the embargo freezes the existing impasse, induces anger and resentment, restricts the freedoms of US citizens, and makes it difficult for us to exchange ideas and respect.

Second, I hope that Cuba and the United States can resolve the forty-year-old property disputes with some creativity. In many cases, we are debating ancient claims about decrepit sugar mills, an antique telephone company, and many other obsolete holdings. Most US companies have already absorbed the losses, but some others want to be paid, and many Cubans who fled the revolution retain a sentimental attachment for their homes. We resolved similar problems when I normalized relations with China in 1979. I propose that our two countries establish a blue-ribbon commission to address the legitimate concerns of all sides in a positive and constructive manner.

Third, some of those who left this beautiful island have demonstrated vividly that the key to a flourishing economy is to use individual entrepreneurial skills. But many Cubans in South Florida remain angry over their departure and their divided families. We need to define a future so they can serve as a bridge of reconciliation between Cuba and the United States.

Are such normal relationships possible? I believe they are.

Except for the stagnant relations between the United States and Cuba, the world has been changing greatly, and especially in Latin America and the Caribbean. As late as 1977, when I became president, there were only two democracies in South America, and one in Central America. Today, almost every country in the Americas is a democracy.

I am not using a US definition of "democracy." The term is embedded in the Universal Declaration of Human Rights, which Cuba signed in 1948, and it was defined very precisely by all the other countries of the Americas in the Inter-American Democratic Charter last September. It is based on some simple premises: all citizens are born with the right to choose their own leaders, to define their own destiny, to speak freely, to organize political parties, trade unions and non-governmental groups, and to have fair and open trials.

Only such governments can be members of the OAS, join a Free Trade Area of the Americas, or participate in the Summits of the Americas. Today, any regime that takes power by unconstitutional means will be ostracized, as was shown in the rejection of the Venezuelan coup last month.

Democracy is a framework that permits a people to accommodate changing times and correct past mistakes. Since our independence, the United States has rid itself of slavery, granted women the right to vote, ended almost a century of legal racial discrimination, and just this year reformed its election laws to correct problems we faced in Florida eighteen months ago.

Cuba has adopted a socialist government where one political party dominates, and people are not permitted to organize any opposition movements. Your Constitution recognizes freedom of speech and association, but other laws deny these freedoms to those who disagree with the government.

My nation is hardly perfect in human rights. A very large number of our citizens are incarcerated in prison, and there is little doubt that the death penalty is imposed most harshly on those who are poor, black, or mentally ill. For more than a quarter century, we have struggled unsuccessfully to guarantee the basic right of universal health care for our people. Still, guaranteed civil liberties offer every citizen an opportunity to change these laws.

That fundamental right is also guaranteed to Cubans. It is gratifying to note that Articles 63 and 88 of your constitution allows citizens to petition the National Assembly to permit a referendum to change laws if ten thousand or more citizens sign it. I am informed that such an effort, called the Varela Project, has gathered sufficient signatures and has presented such a petition to the National Assembly. When Cubans exercise this freedom to change laws peacefully by a direct vote, the world will see that Cubans, and not foreigners, will decide the future of this country.

Cuba has superb systems of health care and universal education, but last month, most Latin American governments joined a majority in the United Nations Human Rights Commission in calling on Cuba to meet universally accepted standards in civil liberties. I would ask that you permit the International Committee of the Red Cross to visit prisons and that you would receive the UN Human Rights Commissioner to address such issues as prisoners of conscience and the treatment of inmates. These visits could help refute any unwarranted criticisms.

Public opinion surveys show that a majority of people in the United States would like to see the economic embargo ended, normal travel between our two countries, friendship between our people, and Cuba to be welcomed into the community of democracies in the Americas. At the same time, most of my fellow citizens believe that the issues of economic and political freedom need to be addressed by the Cuban people.

After forty-three years of animosity, we hope that someday soon, you can reach across the great divide that separates our two countries and say, "We are ready to join the community of democracies," and I hope that Americans will soon open our arms to you and say, "We welcome you as our friends."

President Carter's Cuba Trip Report

21 May 2002

Having received several verbal invitations from President Fidel Castro to visit Cuba, I accepted an official one in January, and we made arrangements for the trip through the Cuban Interest Section in Washington. Our key request was for me to speak directly to the Cuban people, preferably in the evening and with live television coverage, and this was granted.

Prior to the trip, we had a number of briefings from interested groups, including the conservative Cuban American National Foundation, moderate and relatively unbiased experts, international agencies, and the US State Department and intelligence agencies. One key question that we asked American officials was if there was any indication that Cuba had been involved with any foreign government in promoting terrorist activities, directly or indirectly. We were assured that no such evidence existed.

Our goals were to establish a dialog with Castro, to reach out to the Cuban people, and to pursue ways to improve US–Cuban relations. I wanted to explore with the president and other Cuban leaders any indication of flexibility in economic or political policy that might help to ease tensions between our two countries. For instance, having been quite familiar with Deng Xiaoping's transformation of China's economy by gradually permitting small family businesses to expand, I thought this might be one possibility. Also, foreign investors would be more inclined toward Cuba if they could hire and pay their own employees directly instead of through state agencies.

The Varela Project was a subject of great publicity, and a petition from more than eleven thousand citizens was presented to the National Assembly a few days before our arrival. As apparently permitted under Cuba's constitution, the petition called for a referendum on: a) freedom of expression and association; b) amnesty for political prisoners not accused of attempted murder; c) rights of private enterprise; d) direct election of public officials; and e) elections to be held within one year. In my speech to the nation, I called for some of these rights, for the establishment of a blue-ribbon commission to resolve property claims, an extensive exchange of university students, and for the utilization of responsible Cuban Americans as a possible bridge between Cuba and the United States.

We were received at the Havana airport by the president with full honours and a warm welcoming address. We considered it significant that he

Jimmy Carter and Cuban President Fidel Castro leave the church following funeral services for former prime minister Pierre Trudeau, 3 October 2000, in Montreal. *Canadian Press photo by Jacques Boissinot.*

wore a business suit rather than his normal military uniform, and this was his custom throughout our visit until he said goodbye at the airport the day we left. I responded in Spanish, giving the time and place of my major speech and expressing hope that it could be broadcast both through television and radio. I wanted to be sure that there would be some public awareness of the university address. Subsequently it was advertised in advance in the government newspaper *Granma*.

During our ride in to the hotel, President Castro and I had a friendly chat about growing peanuts, the total freedom we would have while in Cuba, and his hope that I would attend the All-Star baseball game and perhaps throw out the first ball. He was thoroughly familiar with our plans for the visit, and assured me that there would be no restraints, that all my activities and statements would be covered by the large media contingent, and that my Tuesday speech would be on TV and radio and rebroadcast at later times.

When we arrived at the small Santa Isabel Hotel in colonial Havana, President Castro introduced us to Eusebio Leal, the historian and curator who has been responsible for the renovation of the old city. After lunch and a tour of the historic area, we met with Foreign Minister Felipe Perez Roque. I decided to cover the major items I wanted to discuss later with President Castro, so that he would be forewarned and we might be more likely to focus on the specific matters. We then visited with the US Interest Section for a briefing and to greet the families.

That evening President Castro and I had a general discussion of issues and then enjoyed an ornate banquet, attended by our group and by President Castro, Vice President Carlos Lage, National Assembly President Ricardo Alarcon, Foreign Minister Felipe Perez Roque, and a few other officials. President Castro had apparently been urged to abbreviate our meeting, but he was inclined to recite detailed information about Cuban achievements in health, education, and other matters. I gave him a collection of recently declassified documents from my administration and tried to concentrate on a few key suggestions.

Among the items I discussed were the themes that would be included in my speech, such as the Varela Project, the right of families to have small businesses and hire neighbours, Cuba's inviting the International Red Cross and the UN High Commissioner on Human Rights to visit the country and ascertain the status of prisons and human rights, and student exchanges. President Castro took notes, said he would consider all the issues, and that he would explore assisting with African health problems.

Monday morning we met with Oswaldo Payá, leader of the Varela Project and Elizardo Sanchez, Cuba's best-known human rights leader. Paya explained the process of securing more than eleven thousand signatures on the petition, assured us that the US government had not given assistance in the effort and stated that he would refuse such help. I described to them the responses I had received during the previous evening's banquet, which were technical in nature, and attempted to distinguish between changes in laws vs. constitutional amendments. Our hotel was staked out by some of the one hundred and fifty or so foreign reporters who are covering our visit, and they talked to Payá and Sanchez afterward.

We then went to the Centre for Genetic Engineering, where we received a detailed report on some of Cuba's extraordinary commitments to research and production of advanced medicines needed in the Third World, including Hepatitis B and C, some forms of cancer, and meningitis. They have shared technology with several nations and a number of international pharmaceutical companies, under tight constraints against use for illicit purposes. They have agreed to a recent arrangement with Iran that is not yet implemented, but none with Iraq or Libya. I informed the research scientists that I had been briefed by state and intelligence agencies and discussed my trip with the White House, but no one had mentioned any concern about Cuba's involvement with bio-terrorism or any other terrorism. In fact, when we had asked pointedly if there was evidence of any kind about Cuba's contributing to terrorist activities in any foreign country, the answer was "No." If there is evidence, I'm sure the US will reveal it, or take advantage of President Castro's public offer to welcome any international investigative team to biomedical laboratories.

We had lunch with Vice President Carlos Lage and the Director of the Central Bank, and talked mostly about economic matters. They were proud of Cuba's relatively stable currency (twenty-seven pesos per dollar), and Lage seemed adamant against any liberalizing of Cuba's policy concerning self-employment. We then visited a school for social workers, where high school graduates who do not pass the high standards for the university are given two years of college level education in subjects that train them to serve the needy, distribute books, become assistant teachers and health workers, etc.

Our next visit was to a remarkable medical school for students from African countries, twenty-three Latin American nations, plus the United States. Here, with all expenses paid, more than six thousand young people receive six years of education and are then prepared to pass the international examination to practice medicine. The thirty-one American students have completed their first year, including Spanish language training, and told us that their only cost is the airplane ticket when they return home for a visit. After enjoying a brief outdoor musical presentation to the entire student body, I made a few remarks about health projects of The Carter Center, and then Fidel spoke to them for more than an hour.

We were late for our private supper with the ambassadors of Canada, Spain, Mexico, and the UNDP representative, each of whom gave us a detailed analysis of Cuba's internal and foreign relations.

Tuesday we visited the Los Cocos AIDS sanatorium, where each patient is given three to six months of treatment and counselling. Any pregnant woman found to be HIV positive receives a complete course of AZT treatment (produced in Cuba). The people are then free to return to their home communities. WHO statistics show that the incidence of AIDS in Cuba is the lowest in this hemisphere, and there are now more than eight hundred Cuban doctors in Haiti alone working to control the AIDS epidemic. President Castro has offered an almost unlimited number to be sent to Africa, to be paid by the Cuban government with only a small stipend from the host countries.

Our next visit was to an agricultural cooperative, where one hundred and fifty-one farm families work about seven hundred acres of land, producing a wide variety of grain, vegetables, fruits, and flowers. The elected leader of the co-op made a very large salary, the equivalent of $1,200 annually. They pointed out that there is a high degree of private enterprise in the marketing of agricultural products and that city families have recently been encouraged to plant small plots around their homes and sell their excess produce. This is one of the few opportunities for self-employment permitted in Cuba, except for motor transport, the renting of rooms in one's home, and doing home repair work for others.

That evening at the University of Havana I made a speech and then answered questions that, as promised, was carried live on television and radio. It was later rebroadcast, and the entire transcript was published in the two Cuban newspapers. Subsequently, we could not find anyone on the streets or in the markets who had not heard it. All analysts said it was the first time in forty-three years that citizens had heard any public criticism of the Cuban government, much less direct condemnation of human rights violations, a call for international inspectors, and promotion of the Varela project. I anticipated President Castro would be upset, but he greeted me after the session, and we attended the Cuban All-Star baseball game, where I threw out the first pitch.

The next morning we visited centres for the treatment of mentally retarded and physically handicapped children, who gave amazing musical and dance performances. Later, Rosalynn and Dr. Hardman met with psychiatrists who described the treatment of patients with mental illnesses. We visited Las Guasimas, a housing development similar to a Habitat for Humanity project, with families obtaining title to their homes and making monthly payments of 40 pesos, equivalent to US$1.50. Not even President Castro's enemies questioned the fact that 85 percent of Cubans own their own homes, or that practically 100 percent of the people are literate, immunized against thirteen diseases, and have family physician care.

After this we had an alfresco lunch with National Assembly President Alarcon, and spent most of the time talking about how he will handle the Varela petition. He replied in circuitous language that the government had not yet made a decision, but he saw both a technical issue based on interpretation of the law and also a political issue. Legally, the petition could be peremptorily rejected, and many arguments could be made against it. Politically, it would be necessary to justify a decision to the people, with those already knowing or caring about it, he said, already realizing that it was a "North American" project. We tried to convince him that the petitioners deserved a full and open hearing even if their effort was rejected.

That afternoon we went to the Martin Luther King Center for an assembly of Jews and Protestant Christians. After songs and the main sermon, mostly concerning suffering caused by the US embargo, I gave an impromptu Christian message in Spanish. This group seemed fervent in their faith but almost totally aligned with Cuba and when questioned could think of no criticisms or prospective changes in government policies. They did ask for more access to mass media, publishing materials, and new church buildings, and realized that they had to be more united.

That evening Rosalynn and I met privately for almost two hours with President Castro, where I pressed him unsuccessfully on some suggestions for opening up his closed political and economic system. We assessed his motivations to be a genuine belief in maintaining equity of treatment and an absence of class distinctions for Cubans and determination to retain the tightest possible control over all aspects of life in the nation. Also, he fears that any conciliatory action would be seen as a sign of weakness against a country "that is still attacking us." After an exchange of gifts, we attended a large, ornate, and delightful official banquet, to which my son Chip and his entire Friendship Force exchange group were invited. The courses of food were interspersed with delightful musical entertainment, and afterward we lingered to greet all the performers and the guests. After our party left for the hotel, President Castro stayed for another hour to have individual photos and to sign autographs for the twenty-three Friendship Force members.

Thursday morning we drove to the Pinar del Rio province for bird watching, followed by unscheduled visits to villages and public markets that were arranged by Luis Gomez Echeverria, the UNDP representative who has been in Cuba for three years. In one typical small city of about twenty-five thousand there were three health clinics and one hospital, with a doctor for each one hundred and seventy people. Doctors at the poorest clinic saw about eighty patients daily, had some shortages of medicine, and an EKG machine with the wrong kind of paper; but they said they could act to prevent illnesses, give routine family care and emergency treatment, and that the EKG in the hospital worked properly.

At a large farmers' market we visited some of the seven hundred booths that are rented to private entrepreneurs for 5 percent of their sales. There was a wide assortment of prepared foods, vegetables, fruits, and meats. The shopkeepers said they bought their produce directly from campesinos, and their businesses were thriving. The place was packed with hundreds of customers, and the prices were astonishingly low, about one-twentieth of those in US stores. There was a small section devoted to sales by the government, with very few customers in the area.

We then had extensive meetings with a wide range of the most notable dissidents, each the leader of an organization and many having completed prison sentences for their demands for change in the socialist regime. They were unanimous in expressing appreciation for my speech, willingness to risk punishment rather than be silent, hope that American visitation could be expanded, and opposition to any elevation of harsh rhetoric from the United States toward Cuba and to any funding of their efforts from the US government. Any knowledge or report of such financial support would just give credibility to the long-standing claims of President Castro that they were "paid lackeys" of Washington. Although some doubted the efficacy of the Varela project, all except one of the twenty-seven agreed that their organizations should support it.

We then met with Catholic Church leaders, who deplored their lack of freedom, were grateful for permission to have services and not be outlawed completely, and extremely cautious about any public challenge to the government on any controversial issue.

After a tour through Ernest Hemingway's home, we attended a concert of classical music and dance, modern Cuban music, and folklore. At the end, all of us joined the performers on the outdoor stage and continued dancing. Alarcon was at the performance and gave me a summary of comments derived from a public opinion poll after my speech. There was a broad range of opinion, in general much more negative than the reaction of people who lined the streets, cheered us at every stop, and greeted us profusely in the market places.

Friday morning I summarized my thoughts about issues and our experiences in Cuba during a press conference before our departure.

Remarks At Korea University

A Nuclear North Korea and Peace in the Korean Peninsula?

Seoul, Korea
23 March 2010

My speech will cover three main subjects, and I hope to stimulate some questions from the audience.

I have had a longtime interest in this peninsula, since serving as a submarine officer in the Pacific during the Korean War. Later, as president, I was able to establish diplomatic relations with the Peoples' Republic of China after thirty years of estrangement—and to encourage China to develop similar relationships with South Korea. I interceded strongly in your nation's domestic affairs when the life of Kim Dae Jung was endangered, and developed a personal friendship with him.

My most interesting involvement in the peninsula occurred in 1994, when the United States and other nations were attempting to implement a UN Security Council resolution to condemn North Korea and impose more punitive sanctions because of Kim Il Sung's apparent plans to purify spent nuclear fuel rods into weapons-grade plutonium.

I had a series of urgent messages from President Kim, followed by personal visits to my home from his emissaries, urging me to come to Pyongyang to consult with him on how he might alleviate the international tension. Leaders in Washington refused to have any direct communication with North Korea. I was also reluctant to do so, until some Chinese friends came to tell me that, to save face, North Koreans would launch a military strike against Seoul if the DPRK was condemned as an outlaw nation and their "great leader" branded as a criminal. The US Commander in Korea,

General Gary Luck, told me that the conflict would probably not last ninety days and much of North Korea would be destroyed, but more than a million people in and around Seoul would die from such an attack.

I finally told Kim Il Sung that I would accept his invitation if my wife and I could come to South Korea, cross the DMZ, and go directly to his capital city. This had not been permitted since the Korean War. He finally agreed, and we first went to Seoul, where we had talks with president Kim Young Sam and his top advisers. Then my wife and I were welcomed at the Panmunjom crossing in June, 1994, and proceeded to Pyongyang. We were the first people to make this direct trip in forty-three years.

Over the next few days we had very frank, substantive, and pleasant discussions with president Kim Il Sung and his experts on the nuclear issue. I was trained as a nuclear engineer and able to discuss the issues in detail. Rosalynn and I were surprised at how knowledgeable president Kim was on every matter. He had already expelled the international inspectors and disconnected surveillance equipment within their old graphite-moderated atomic power plant at Yongbyon, but he listened carefully to my proposals. Here are some of my personal notes:

> President Kim Il Sung is 82 years old, but we found him to be vigorous, alert, intelligent, and remarkably familiar with the issues. He consulted frequently with his advisers, each of whom bounced up and stood erect while speaking to their "great leader."
>
> Finally, in effect, he accepted all my suggestions, with two major requests:
>
> That the US support their acquisition of modern light water reactor technology, realizing that the funding and equipment could not come directly from America. He was willing to freeze their nuclear program, but needed alternative sources of power, including fuel oil.
>
> That the US guarantee there would be no military attack against his country. He agreed with me that the entire Korean peninsula should be nuclear-free.

We talked for many hours, and we were invited the next morning to go on a long ride with the president and his wife on Kim Jong Il's yacht—from Pyongyang down the river to the "barricade," a remarkable five-mile dam that controlled the tides.

Kim Il Sung expressed pleasure that South Korean president Kim Young Sam had suggested a summit meeting, and said it should be done without preconditions or extended preparatory talks. He proposed reciprocal military site inspections and a step-by-step reduction of Korean armed forces to one hundred thousand men on each side, with US forces to be reduced in the same proportion. He offered to remove all weapons from within the

DMZ, jointly to pull back military forces from near the zone, and to permit unrestricted cross border visitation.

Kim Il Sung died soon after my visit, but I received a letter from his son pledging to honour the commitments. All the nuclear agreements were later adopted by Kim Jong Il and president Bill Clinton and put into effect.

South Korean president Kim Dae Jung began a "sunshine policy" to lessen tensions and build reconciliation between North and South Korea, and in June 2000 the postponed summit talks were held in Pyongyang, the first such contact in fifty years. The leaders agreed to work toward reunification, for which Kim Dae Jung was awarded the Nobel Peace Prize that year.

However, two years later president George W. Bush condemned North-South reconciliation, branded North Korea as an "axis of evil," and threatened military action.

The North reacted by expelling IAEA inspectors, disconnecting surveillance cameras, and withdrawing as a signatory of the non-proliferation treaty. They began reprocessing spent fuel rods into plutonium, and now it is assumed that North Korea has atomic material enough for approximately ten weapons. Production capability at Yongbyon is enough for two explosive charges per year, and they may also have a facility to enrich uranium.

Let's review later developments: in September 2005 after North Korea had tested a nuclear weapon, Pyongyang and the other members of the six power talks signed a joint commitment to work for the denuclearization of the peninsula, to improve bilateral ties with North Korea, and to support North Korea's economic development.

In February 2007, to implement the September 2005 statement, the six powers agreed to provide North Korea with ample supplies of heavy fuel oil if Pyongyang provided a "complete and correct" declaration of its nuclear facilities. The IAEA monitors returned to North Korea and work began to dismantle some of the plutonium-based operations, but this cooperation stalled during the last months of the Bush administration.

Early in president Obama's term, North Korea launched a multi-stage rocket using ballistic missile technology in violation of UN Security Council resolution 1718, conducted another test of a nuclear weapon, and also tested a series of shorter-range missiles.

US Special envoy, Stephen Bosworth, went to Pyongyang in March 2009 and returned in December. He continues to consult with the other six party partners.

Let's look for a few moments at the overall nuclear situation. All nations are signatories of the non-proliferation treaty except North Korea, Pakistan, India, and Israel. There are more than forty nations that have the capability of developing a nuclear arsenal, and it is encouraging and somewhat remarkable that there are now only nine nuclear states, sixty-five years after the only nuclear attack on Japan in 1945.

At this time there are three major threats: from Iran's potential plans, from some of Pakistan's weapons being taken by militants, and from North Korea.

Your neighbour's arsenal causes serious re-examinations of the non-nuclear policy in Japan and South Korea. It is well known that Japan has a large stockpile of highly enriched uranium, and could have an arsenal almost overnight.

To be technical for a moment: the explosive u-235 is about 0.7 percent of the natural metal, which can be enriched in a stage of centrifuges to about 4 percent, then from 4 percent to approximately 20 percent, then from 20 percent to about 90 percent, adequate for a bomb. Volume drops with enrichment, so fewer centrifuges are needed at each stage. Iran probably has about ten thousand centrifuges, with a capability of producing twelve pounds of enriched uranium per day, or enough low-enriched atoms every four months, if further enriched, to make a bomb. Saudi Arabia, Egypt, and Turkey might follow in the footsteps of an Iranian nuclear weapons test.

The greatest threat is from Pakistan, which has been rapidly expanding its arsenal (now to about one hundred bombs) and dispersing weapons to minimize the damage from a potential Indian pre-emptive strike. Al Qaeda has moved from Afghanistan into Pakistan, and poses a danger of weapons falling into the hands of terrorists. Also, it is known that Pakistani nuclear scientist A. Q. Khan sold nuclear fuel and technology to several eager buyers, including North Korea and Iran.

There are now three groups pushing for legitimate nuclear states to fulfill their long-violated promises as signatories of the NPT, in order to move toward a nuclear-free world. Global Zero has just released a film, produced by the same filmmaker as Al Gore's *An Inconvenient Truth*. I play a small role in the film, and am also supporting two other efforts: one sponsored by leaders of Australia and Japan, and the other originated by Americans Henry Kissinger, George Schultz, Sam Nunn, and Bill Perry. President Obama has endorsed all these efforts and is seeking nuclear arms agreements with Russia.

Unfortunately, in recent years American leaders have reneged on our previous "no first use" pledge, the anti-ballistic missile treaty, and promises to forgo development of new nuclear weapons. The US has not ratified the comprehensive test ban agreement or approved the IAEA proposals for "enhanced safeguards" and a multinational fuel bank. Of special concern was the decision by George W. Bush to provide India with both nuclear fuel and technology despite its refusal to sign the NPT or accept international safeguards.

What can we expect concerning future relationships in the Korean peninsula? A few years ago I wrote a book called *Our Endangered Values*, and I included my thoughts about this important issue.

First of all—and difficult for South Korea and the United States—is the need for more direct negotiations with North Korea. The perpetuation of their regime is paramount in Pyongyang, and the leaders and people have suffered from economic sanctions and diplomatic exclusion for more than fifty years. With their ingrained "su-che" philosophy, they are relatively immune to further deprivation from embargoes.

I don't deny that some of this punishment has been merited, but it was obvious to me when I was in North Korea that there is deep resentment of the past and genuine fear of pre-emptive military attacks in the future. Experience indicates that it is unlikely that the North Koreans will back down unless the United States meets the basic demands that I received from president Kim Il Sung:

- Direct talks with the United States leading to a simple framework of an agreement, with all promised actions to be confirmed, step by step.
- The United States gives a firm statement of "no hostile intent" and moves toward normal diplomatic relations if North Korea remains at peace with its neighbours and foregoes any nuclear weapons program, with compliance to be confirmed by unimpeded international inspections.
- Basic premises of the agreements of 1994 are to be honoured, with Japan, South Korea, the United States, Russia, and China cooperating to provide a replacement for lost energy supplies, with modern nuclear plants and interim fuel oil supplies.

Along with political assurances and economic help for North Korea, the February 2007 agreement should be honoured and denuclearization should be an important part of bilateral and multilateral talks.

No one can predict the final answers from Pyongyang, but there is no harm in making a major effort, including unrestrained direct talks. The initiative must be from America and South Korea.

The alternative is a continuation of the present path of estrangement, isolation, additional suffering of innocent North Korean private citizens, and ever-expanding conventional and nuclear arsenals, perhaps leading to a catastrophic war. This must be avoided, by political courage and wise diplomacy.

Queen's Policy Studies
Recent Publications

The Queen's Policy Studies Series is dedicated to the exploration of major public policy issues that confront governments and society in Canada and other nations.

Manuscript submission. We are pleased to consider new book proposals and manuscripts. Preliminary enquiries are welcome. A subvention is normally required for the publication of an academic book. Please direct questions or proposals to the Publications Unit by email at spspress@queensu.ca, or visit our website at: www.queensu.ca/sps/books, or contact us by phone at (613) 533-2192.

Our books are available from good bookstores everywhere, including the Queen's University bookstore (http://www.campusbookstore.com/). McGill-Queen's University Press is the exclusive world representative and distributor of books in the series. A full catalogue and ordering information may be found on its website (http://mqup.mcgill.ca/).

School of Policy Studies

Making the Case: Using Case Studies for Teaching and Knowledge Management in Public Administration, Andrew Graham, 2011. Paper ISBN 978-1-55339-302-3.

Canada's Isotope Crisis: What Next? Jatin Nathwani and Donald Wallace (eds.), 2010. Paper ISBN 978-1-55339-283-5. Cloth ISBN 978-1-55339-284-2.

Pursuing Higher Education in Canada: Economic, Social, and Policy Dimensions, Ross Finnie, Marc Frenette, Richard E. Mueller, and Arthur Sweetman (eds.), 2010. Paper ISBN 978-1-55339-277-4. Cloth ISBN 978-1-55339-278-1.

Canadian Immigration: Economic Evidence for a Dynamic Policy Environment, Ted McDonald, Elizabeth Ruddick, Arthur Sweetman, and Christopher Worswick (eds.), 2010. Paper ISBN 978-1-55339-281-1. Cloth ISBN 978-1-55339-282-8.

Taking Stock: Research on Teaching and Learning in Higher Education, Julia Christensen Hughes and Joy Mighty (eds.), 2010. Paper ISBN 978-1-55339-271-2. Cloth ISBN 978-1-55339-272-9.

Architects and Innovators: Building the Department of Foreign Affairs and International Trade, 1909–2009 / Architectes et innovateurs : le développement du ministère des Affaires étrangères et du Commerce international, de 1909 à 2009, Greg Donaghy and Kim Richard Nossal (eds.), 2009. Paper ISBN 978-1-55339-269-9. Cloth ISBN 978-1-55339-270-5.

Academic Transformation: The Forces Reshaping Higher Education in Ontario, Ian D. Clark, Greg Moran, Michael L. Skolnik, and David Trick, 2009. Paper ISBN 978-1-55339-238-5. Cloth ISBN 978-1-55339-265-1.

The New Federal Policy Agenda and the Voluntary Sector: On the Cutting Edge, Rachel Laforest (ed.), 2009. Paper ISBN 978-1-55339-132-6.

Measuring What Matters in Peace Operations and Crisis Management, Sarah Jane Meharg, 2009. Paper ISBN 978-1-55339-228-6. Cloth ISBN 978-1-55339-229-3.

International Migration and the Governance of Religious Diversity, Paul Bramadat and Matthias Koenig (eds.), 2009. Paper ISBN 978-1-55339-266-8. Cloth ISBN 978-1-55339-267-5.

Who Goes? Who Stays? What Matters? Accessing and Persisting in Post-Secondary Education in Canada, Ross Finnie, Richard E. Mueller, Arthur Sweetman, and Alex Usher (eds.), 2008. Paper ISBN 978-1-55339-221-7. Cloth ISBN 978-1-55339-222-4.

Economic Transitions with Chinese Characteristics: Thirty Years of Reform and Opening Up, Arthur Sweetman and Jun Zhang (eds.), 2009. Paper ISBN 978-1-55339-225-5. Cloth ISBN 978-1-55339-226-2.

Economic Transitions with Chinese Characteristics: Social Change During Thirty Years of Reform, Arthur Sweetman and Jun Zhang (eds.), 2009. Paper ISBN 978-1-55339-234-7. Cloth ISBN 978-1-55339-235-4.

Dear Gladys: Letters from Over There, Gladys Osmond (Gilbert Penney ed.), 2009. Paper ISBN 978-1-55339-223-1.

Immigration and Integration in Canada in the Twenty-first Century, John Biles, Meyer Burstein, and James Frideres (eds.), 2008. Paper ISBN 978-1-55339-216-3. Cloth ISBN 978-1-55339-217-0.

Robert Stanfield's Canada, Richard Clippingdale, 2008. ISBN 978-1-55339-218-7.

Exploring Social Insurance: Can a Dose of Europe Cure Canadian Health Care Finance? Colleen Flood, Mark Stabile, and Carolyn Tuohy (eds.), 2008. Paper ISBN 978-1-55339-136-4. Cloth ISBN 978-1-55339-213-2.

Canada in NORAD, 1957–2007: A History, Joseph T. Jockel, 2007. Paper ISBN 978-1-55339-134-0. Cloth ISBN 978-1-55339-135-7.

Canadian Public-Sector Financial Management, Andrew Graham, 2007. Paper ISBN 978-1-55339-120-3. Cloth ISBN 978-1-55339-121-0.

Emerging Approaches to Chronic Disease Management in Primary Health Care, John Dorland and Mary Ann McColl (eds.), 2007. Paper ISBN 978-1-55339-130-2. Cloth ISBN 978-1-55339-131-9.

Fulfilling Potential, Creating Success: Perspectives on Human Capital Development, Garnett Picot, Ron Saunders and Arthur Sweetman (eds.), 2007. Paper ISBN 978-1-55339-127-2. Cloth ISBN 978-1-55339-128-9.

Reinventing Canadian Defence Procurement: A View from the Inside, Alan S. Williams, 2006. Paper ISBN 0-9781693-0-1 (Published in association with Breakout Educational Network).

SARS in Context: Memory, History, Policy, Jacalyn Duffin and Arthur Sweetman (eds.), 2006. Paper ISBN 978-0-7735-3194-9. Cloth ISBN 978-0-7735-3193-2. (Published in association with McGill-Queen's University Press).

Dreamland: How Canada's Pretend Foreign Policy has Undermined Sovereignty, Roy Rempel, 2006. Paper ISBN 1-55339-118-7. Cloth ISBN 1-55339-119-5 (Published in association with Breakout Educational Network).

Canadian and Mexican Security in the New North America: Challenges and Prospects, Jordi Díez (ed.), 2006. Paper ISBN 978-1-55339-123-4. Cloth ISBN 978-1-55339-122-7.

Global Networks and Local Linkages: The Paradox of Cluster Development in an Open Economy, David A. Wolfe and Matthew Lucas (eds.), 2005. Paper ISBN 1-55339-047-4. Cloth ISBN 1-55339-048-2.

Choice of Force: Special Operations for Canada, David Last and Bernd Horn (eds.), 2005. Paper ISBN 1-55339-044-X. Cloth ISBN 1-55339-045-8.

Centre for the Study of Democracy

Unrevised and Unrepented II: Debating Speeches and Others, The Right Honourable Arthur Meighen. Foreword by Prime Minister Stephen Harper; Afterword by Senator Michael A. Meighen; edited by Arthur Milnes, 2011. Paper ISBN 978-1-55339-296-5. Cloth ISBN 978-1-55339-297-2.

The Authentic Voice of Canada: R. B. Bennett's Speeches in the House of Lords, 1941-1947, Christopher McCreery and Arthur Milnes (eds.), 2009. Paper ISBN 978-1-55339-275-0. Cloth ISBN 978-1-55339-276-7.

Age of the Offered Hand: The Cross-Border Partnership Between President George H. W. Bush and Prime Minister Brian Mulroney, A Documentary History, James McGrath and Arthur Milnes (eds.), 2009. Paper ISBN 978-1-55339-232-3. Cloth ISBN 978-1-55339-233-0.

In Roosevelt's Bright Shadow: Presidential Addresses About Canada from Taft to Obama in Honour of FDR's 1938 Speech at Queen's University, Christopher McCreery and Arthur Milnes (eds.), 2009. Paper ISBN 978-1-55339-230-9. Cloth ISBN 978-1-55339-231-6.

Politics of Purpose, 40th Anniversary Edition, The Right Honourable John N. Turner 17th Prime Minister of Canada, Elizabeth McIninch and Arthur Milnes (eds.), 2009. Paper ISBN 978-1-55339-227-9. Cloth ISBN 978-1-55339-224-8.

Bridging the Divide: Religious Dialogue and Universal Ethics, Papers for The InterAction Council, Thomas S. Axworthy (ed.), 2008. Paper ISBN 978-1-55339-219-4. Cloth ISBN 978-1-55339-220-0.

Institute of Intergovernmental Relations

Canada: The State of the Federation 2009, vol. 22, Carbon Pricing and Environmental Federalism, Thomas J. Courchene and John R. Allan (eds.), 2010. Paper ISBN 978-1-55339-196-8. Cloth ISBN 978-1-55339-197-5.

Canada: The State of the Federation 2008, vol. 21, Open Federalism and the Spending Power, Thomas J. Courchene, John R. Allan, and Hoi Kong (eds.), forthcoming. Paper ISBN 978-1-55339-194-4.

The Democratic Dilemma: Reforming the Canadian Senate, Jennifer Smith (ed.), 2009. Paper ISBN 978-1-55339-190-6.

Canada: The State of the Federation 2006/07, vol. 20, Transitions—Fiscal and Political Federalism in an Era of Change, John R. Allan, Thomas J. Courchene, and Christian Leuprecht (eds.), 2009. Paper ISBN 978-1-55339-189-0. Cloth ISBN 978-1-55339-191-3.

Comparing Federal Systems, Third Edition, Ronald L. Watts, 2008. Paper ISBN 978-1-55339-188-3.

Canada: The State of the Federation 2005, vol. 19, Quebec and Canada in the New Century—New Dynamics, New Opportunities, Michael Murphy (ed.), 2007. Paper ISBN 978-1-55339-018-3. Cloth ISBN 978-1-55339-017-6.

Spheres of Governance: Comparative Studies of Cities in Multilevel Governance Systems, Harvey Lazar and Christian Leuprecht (eds.), 2007. Paper ISBN 978-1-55339-019-0. Cloth ISBN 978-1-55339-129-6.

Canada: The State of the Federation 2004, vol. 18, Municipal-Federal-Provincial Relations in Canada, Robert Young and Christian Leuprecht (eds.), 2006. Paper ISBN 1-55339-015-6. Cloth ISBN 1-55339-016-4.

Canadian Fiscal Arrangements: What Works, What Might Work Better, Harvey Lazar (ed.), 2005. Paper ISBN 1-55339-012-1. Cloth ISBN 1-55339-013-X.

Canada: The State of the Federation 2003, vol. 17, Reconfiguring Aboriginal-State Relations, Michael Murphy (ed.), 2005. Paper ISBN 1-55339-010-5. Cloth ISBN 1-55339-011-3.

Queen's Centre for International Relations

Europe Without Soldiers? Recruitment and Retention across the Armed Forces of Europe, Tibor Szvircsev Tresch and Christian Leuprecht (eds.), 2010. Paper ISBN 978-1-55339-246-0. Cloth ISBN 978-1-55339-247-7.

Mission Critical: Smaller Democracies' Role in Global Stability Operations, Christian Leuprecht, Jodok Troy, and David Last (eds.), 2010. Paper ISBN 978-1-55339-244-6.

The Afghanistan Challenge: Hard Realities and Strategic Choices, Hans-Georg Ehrhart and Charles Pentland (eds.), 2009. Paper ISBN 978-1-55339-241-5.

John Deutsch Institute for the Study of Economic Policy

The 2009 Federal Budget: Challenge, Response and Retrospect, Charles M. Beach, Bev Dahlby and Paul A. R. Hobson (eds.), 2010. Paper ISBN 978-1-55339-165-4. Cloth ISBN 978-1-55339-166-1.

Discount Rates for the Evaluation of Public Private Partnerships, David F. Burgess and Glenn P. Jenkins (eds.), 2010. Paper ISBN 978-1-55339-163-0. Cloth ISBN 978-1-55339-164-7.

Retirement Policy Issues in Canada, Michael G. Abbott, Charles M. Beach, Robin W. Boadway, and James G. MacKinnon (eds.), 2009. Paper ISBN 978-1-55339-161-6. Cloth ISBN 978-1-55339-162-3.

The 2006 Federal Budget: Rethinking Fiscal Priorities, Charles M. Beach, Michael Smart, and Thomas A. Wilson (eds.), 2007. Paper ISBN 978-1-55339-125-8. Cloth ISBN 978-1-55339-126-6.

Health Services Restructuring in Canada: New Evidence and New Directions, Charles M. Beach, Richard P. Chaykowksi, Sam Shortt, France St-Hilaire, and Arthur Sweetman (eds.), 2006. Paper ISBN 978-1-55339-076-3. Cloth ISBN 978-1-55339-075-6.

A Challenge for Higher Education in Ontario, Charles M. Beach (ed.), 2005. Paper ISBN 1-55339-074-1. Cloth ISBN 1-55339-073-3.

Current Directions in Financial Regulation, Frank Milne and Edwin H. Neave (eds.), Policy Forum Series no. 40, 2005. Paper ISBN 1-55339-072-5. Cloth ISBN 1-55339-071-7.

Higher Education in Canada, **Charles M. Beach, Robin W. Boadway, and R. Marvin McInnis (eds.), 2005. Paper ISBN 1-55339-070-9. Cloth ISBN 1-55339-069-5.**

Our publications may be purchased at leading bookstores, including the Queen's University Bookstore (http://www.campusbookstore.com/) or can be ordered online from McGill-Queen's University Press, at **http://mqup.mcgill.ca/ordering.php**

For more information about new and backlist titles from Queen's Policy Studies, visit http://www.queensu.ca/sps/books or visit the McGill-Queen's University Press website at: **http://mqup.mcgill.ca/**